THE HALL OF FAME

OF WESTERN

FILM STARS

THE HALL OF FAME
OF
WESTERN FILM STARS

ERNEST N. CORNEAU

ERNEST CORNEAU

THE CHRISTOPHER PUBLISHING HOUSE
NORTH QUINCY, MASSACHUSETTS
02171

Library of Congress Catalog Card Number 70-91805
SBN: 8158-0124-6

PRINTED IN
THE UNITED STATES OF AMERICA

This book is dedicated to the memory
of *Charles "Buck" Jones*

ACKNOWLEDGEMENTS

I wish to take this moment to express my sympathy over the loss of the three people who were responsible for my writing this book: the late Franklyn Farnum, Bud Osborne and George "Gabby" Hayes, a trio of fine performers who took time to inspire me.

I would also like to thank the many patient and understanding people who found time to help me with my research. Among these are Kermit Maynard, Andy Devine, Dr. S. Harrison Thomson, Walter Evert, Jr., Charles S. Aaronson, Tom Tyler, George Gobel, Rex Allen, Dave O'Brien, Harry Carey, Jr., Miss Joan Bennett, Dick Jones, Mrs. L. Randall Myers and Mrs. Odille Jones. I would also like to include a special note of gratitude to my devoted wife, Shirley, without whose assistance this volume would never have been completed.

FOREWORD

When you read a book about the history of motion pictures you can be certain that names like Charlie Chaplin, Mary Pickford, Douglas Fairbanks and Rudolph Valentino will occupy a large share of the limelight. Usually, the list will continue to include the dozens of lesser known stars and supporting players but, oddly enough, only two or three very selective Western stars. Quite intentionally, most authors have chosen to let these few represent the entire field of Westerns, a genre that has been accepted the world over as one of America's most original forms of screen folk-art. Therefore, one must naturally conclude that these authors believe that only two or three personalities are deserving of attention in a field which completely dominates any other in the movie industry. For various reasons, the "sagebrush heroes" have been sadly neglected. A principal reason for this neglect is that film-makers refused to accept the Western as a truly artistic form of screen entertainment. The majority held the opinion that, because of the simplicity of their characters and plots, cowboy stories lacked the lustre and glamour of heavy drama. Yet, these same producers were the first to fall back on the Western when a guaranteed profit was required at the box-office. It remained for men like Thomas Ince, D. W. Griffith, William S. Hart, James Cruze and John Ford to prove that a carefully directed Western could hold its own in any competition.

As far as the players were concerned, they all had a certain degree of pride and interest in what they were doing. Some were truly dedicated to the Western, others became only sufficiently involved, and yet they all did not pretend to be artistic thespians. They promised only adventurous entertainment, not super-spectacles of artistic merit. Their main purposes were to entertain and to make a reasonable profit. *There is no doubt that they achieved both goals.*

It is my intention in writing this book that these unsung heroes be recorded for posterity. They drew forth our admiration when we were in our youth and gave us fond memories of adventure to carry into our old age. To the present generation, the thrill of attending a weekend matinee at a local theatre to see a new Western along with the latest episode of an exciting serial seems to be lost forever. To those of us old enough to remember, the names in this book will recall happy times.

Since this project was so vast, I will admit the possibility of having overlooked a few personalities. I do believe, however, that each reader will find at least one favorite among this roster of Western stars. Some of them gained worldwide fame, while others barely seemed to cast a shadow. Many of the lesser known players outlasted the bigger names but, regardless of stature, each and every one of them contributed a share toward the advancement of the Western genre. I have already been asked why certain stars were not included in this book. The answer is simply that, although these players made many excellent Westerns, they were essentially noted for other types of roles. I trust this will explain the absence of performers such as Henry Fonda, Burt Lancaster, Glenn Ford, Robert Mitchum, William Holden, Fred Mac-Murray, James Cagney, Clark Gable, Spencer Tracy, Tyrone Power, Wallace Beery, Brian Donlevy, Charles Bickford, Robert Taylor, Kirk Douglas, Richard Widmark, Dana Andrews, Scott Brady, Forrest Tucker, Jeff Chandler, Walter Brennan, John Payne, Broderick Crawford, Preston Foster, Robert Preston and Rory Calhoun, all of whom were involved occasionally in major Westerns. For the purpose of definition, the persons in this book are, on the one hand, those whose careers were more consistently identified with the Western and, on the other, those who gained a noticeable degree of fame from their cowboy roles. It should also be noted that the list of films following each biography is not meant to be a complete roster of the individual's career.

The photographs and drawings were taken from my private collection. I believe this book has achieved my ambition of recalling to memory the personalities that made the Western a most enjoyable experience, and I hope it will prove to be satisfying reading for those who revere the role of the Western film star in movie history.

Ernest N. Corneau

TABLE OF CONTENTS

14

THE HALL OF FAME

OF WESTERN

FILM STARS

THE WESTERN FILM

Ever since the early American pioneers first migrated to the West and extended the boundaries of our civilization, stories of the frontier have held a deep fascination for people all over the world. Men like Daniel Boone, Jim Bridger, Davy Crockett, Kit Carson, "Buffalo Bill" Cody and "Wild Bill" Hickock helped to form the idealistic image of America's favorite type of hero—the Westerner. Down through the years, these frontiersmen grew in stature until fact and fiction had elevated them into almost superhuman idols. Their adventures were preserved in literature, music, art and motion pictures for millions to admire and they emerged as symbols of honesty, strength and courage. Throughout the pages of American history, no chapter can compare with that of our Western frontier for sheer excitement. It was inevitable, therefore, that the cowboy would become the most suitable type of hero for adventure films.

Although the early silent movies were crude, one has to allow for the fact that the film-makers were experimenting with a new form of art. They soon had skeptical audiences flocking to the Nickelodeon theatres to share the marvelous adventures on the screen. The first important American motion picture was *The Great Train Robbery*. Directed by Edwin S. Porter, in 1903, it had a Western theme and it was the first film to tell a story. Before then, film-makers had merely experimented by photographing simple gestures and actions for the sole purpose of giving the illusion that pictures could move. Because it had a plot, *The Great Train Robbery* brought a new dimension to the film industry and, in fact, opened a whole new world of entertainment to the public.

As the movies grew in stature, so did the Western. Unfortunately, the majority of early film-makers unanimously adopted the policy of using only the barest essentials for making Westerns and this attitude led to a basic pattern for all Westerns. The main ingredient was action, while the theme was simply a conflict of good overpowering evil. The hero represented virtue, honesty and courage while the outlaws stood for the exact opposite. Until recent years, romance always occupied a minor part in Westerns and heroines contributed little to the story. Most important was the fact that the audience was able to take part in the adventures of a bygone era. For the price of a ticket, one could help

17

1. *Alan Ladd and Van Heflin in "Shane"*

2. *Mary Brian, Gary Cooper and Richard Arlen in "The Virginian" (1929)*

3. *Bob Steele, Wally Wales (Hal Taliaferro), "Big Boy" Williams, Hoot Gibson, Buzz Barton, Harry Carey and Tom Tyler in "Powdersmoke Range" (1935)*

4. *Claire Trevor and John Wayne in "Stagecoach" (1939)*

5. *Gary Cooper in "High Noon"*

6. *Richard Dix and Irene Dunne in "Cimarron" (1931)*

1.

2.

4.

5.

6.

the hero overcome the badmen, save the heroine, foil an Indian attack on a wagon train, ride with the Pony Express or make a daring charge with the Cavalry. In addition, Westerns always had the magnificent splendor of the great outdoors for a background. What did it matter if the hero chased the outlaw past the same boulder a few times before catching him? Who cared if he often fired at least ten bullets from his six-shooter without reloading? To the youthful audience, these little details mattered nothing.

In 1908, G. M. Anderson began his famous "Broncho Billy" series and became the first "King of the Cowboys," a title he held undisputed until 1915. Since the "star system" had not yet been established, actors were appearing in films either under assumed names or without billing. By 1912, the serials had entered the scene and when they finally adopted the Western theme four years later, the cowboy adventures really gained momentum. Meanwhile, Dustin Farnum made a hit in the first of the Western classics when he appeared in *The Squaw Man* and *The Virginian* in 1913. He was followed by his brother, William, who starred in the first screen adaptation of *The Spoilers*. By 1916, the top cowboy stars were William S. Hart, the Farnums, J. W. Kerrigan and Bill Russell.

Gradually, the short one and two-reelers were extended to feature-length productions. Due to its simplicity of plot, the Western became monotonous. In 1923, James Cruze directed the first large-scale cowboy classic when he made *The Covered Wagon* on location in Nevada and Utah. An outstanding masterpiece, it broke all attendance records and proved to be the cornerstone for the major Western productions that followed. Even the severest critics had to admit that the Western had finally achieved true artistic merit. It was obvious that Cruze had proven that a skillful director, working with a capable crew of players and technicians on a sound budget, could turn out a picture that would compare favorably with any heavy drama. On the other hand, not all of the Westerns rated as high as *The Covered Wagon*. Most of the cheaper productions were standard, while some of the independently made films were poor. The Western heroes became more colorful with rugged individualists such as Tom Mix, Buck Jones and Hoot Gibson. Their exceptional riding skill and flair for showmanship brought a new type of cowboy star to the screen.

Meanwhile, a steady diet of major Westerns kept the public interested in frontier adventures. In 1924, director John Ford made the first of his epic masterpieces, *The Iron Horse,* which ranks among the all-time greats. Among those that followed were *The Thundering Herd* (1925); *The Vanishing American* (1926); *White Gold* (1927); *In Old*

Arizona, the first all-outdoor talking film (1929); *The Virginian* (1929); *The Big Trail* (1930); the Oscar-winning classic *Cimarron* (1931); *Union Pacific* and *The Westerner* (1939). *Stagecoach,* directed by Ford in 1939, is regarded as the greatest western of all by many critics. Other outstanding Westerns were *Western Union* (1941); *They Died With Their Boots On, The Spoilers* and *Ox Bow Incident* (1942); *Tall in the Saddle* and *Buffalo Bill* (1944); *Fort Apache, Duel in the Sun* and *Red River* (1948); *Yellow Sky, She Wore a Yellow Ribbon* and *Three Godfathers* (1949); *The Gunfighter, Broken Arrow, Wagonmaster* and *Winchester '73* (1950); *High Noon* (1952); *Shane* (1953); *Hondo* (1954); *The Far Country* and *Wichita* (1955); *The Searchers* (1956); *Trooper Hook* (1957); *The Proud Rebel* and *The Big Country* (1958); *Rio Bravo* and *The Hanging Tree* (1959); *The Unforgiven* and *The Magnificent Seven* (1960); *Ride the High Country* and *Lonely Are the Brave* (1962); *How the West Was Won* (1963); *Cheyenne Autumn* (1964) and *The Professionals* (1966).

As the years passed, the Westerns came to be known by various names in the industry. To those of the trade, they were more familiarly called "hoss-operas," "oaters" or "sagebrush sagas." It was the B-class features which constituted the bulk of Western output and several studios owed their very existence to the manufacturing of these cheaply made features. A cowboy hero could turn out a series of seven or eight pictures per year without too much trouble providing his box-office appeal was sufficient to withstand such exposure. Many big name directors and stars had made their initial bow in this field, finding it a stepping-stone to bigger and better things. Others, however, found the B-Westerns to be a means to an end for failing careers. Basically, cowboy pictures underwent only two major changes during the history of movies—the arrival of sound and the invasion of the singing range riders. The first was regarded as a change for the better since it allowed the audience to hear the gunshots, the thunder of hoofbeats and the war cries of the Indians. As for the cowboy vocalists, public opinion was divided with most of the old-timers predicting that musical Westerns would bring down the curtain and cause the downfall of the genre. Nevertheless, the singing heroes lasted well over ten years before the B-class Western series came to an end in 1954. The following year, even the cliff-hanging serials had reached the end of the trail with the last of them, a sagebrush chapter-play entitled *Blazing the Overland Trail,* marking the finish in 1956.

During the early 1950's the film industry suffered great losses at the box-office due to the arrival of television. The public began to enjoy its screen entertainment in the comforts of home while film producers were frantically searching for a new gimmick to lure people back in the theatre. Three dimensional wide - screen projection and stereophonic sound were some of the innovations used. Although not exactly new to the industry, these processes were meant to draw the public back into the habit of attending theatres weekly as it had done throughout the 1930's and 1940's. In the meantime, television networks were gaining momentum by purchasing the screen rights to dozens of outdated films and showing them to audiences at home. The movie industry was in direct competition with itself and, ironically, the Western was once again called upon to pull the producers out of the frying pan. Unfortunately, most of the well-known cowboy stars had either passed on or were too old to carry on. Only a handful remained who could continue in the tradition the old-timers had established. The new crop of actors was either uninterested or lacked the necessary qualifications to become important in the field of Westerns. It all led to a so-called "new type" of cowboy feature termed the "adult Western." As it turned out, this was merely an excuse to introduce a greater amount of boring dialogue and an increasing portion of sex to the genre. The action so commonplace in the old features was now reduced to the last reel while a doubtful public ceased to grasp the meaning of the industry's comment that the new cowboy hero was a "thinking man." On the other hand, the bevy of modern heroines who strutted across the screen in skin-tight dungarees and open-necked blouses brazenly flaunted the fact that they were of doubtful virtue and offered little to the plot of the picture.

Fortunately, there were a few who stuck to their guns and it is noticeable that cowboy pictures have been the only surviving fad in television. Since the beginning of TV, the Westerns have outlasted themes about spies, detectives, mysteries, reporters, doctors and science-fiction. Each new season brings forth a steady diet of range riders without any signs of letting up, although none of these has been able to attain the stature of a Bill Hart, a Tom Mix or a Buck Jones.

As for the features, the theatre audiences have experienced a renewed vigor in Western productions made on a slightly higher scale than the old B-type films. A new trend has started with the import of European made Westerns which capitalize on gory violence, but this has already shown signs of dying away. In more recent years, movie fans have loudly expressed the desire to see the return of the nostalgic, tried-and-true form of cowboy adventures. Whether or not this trend will return remains to be seen, but one thing is certain—the Western will always be a major part of American screen entertainment.

"BRONCO BILLY" ANDERSON (1882-   )

Very little was known about the life of G.M. Anderson until after 1948. Up to that time it was known that he had appeared in *The Great Train Robbery* way back in 1903, and that he had been the first cowboy star of the screen in his "Bronco Billy" Westerns. But after 1920, he had so completely drifted into obscurity that many people believed him to be dead. During the late 1940's, a renewed interest in the history of motion pictures caused a nation-wide search for Anderson. In 1948, a newspaper reporter found evidence that the pioneer film actor was in Los Angeles, still involved in movies. Two years later, the Associated Press printed an article stating that Anderson was very much alive and in charge of an organization called Progressive Pictures.

Having finally been discovered after so many years, Anderson was given a long-overdue citation from the film industry when the Academy of Motion Picture Arts and Sciences awarded him a special "Oscar" for his contribution to that medium of entertainment. In June, 1958, he was further honored when he appeared as a special guest on a nation-wide TV show called "Wide Wide World," which dedicated a particular broadcast to the great cowboy stars of the screen.

Gilbert M. Anderson was born Max Aronson in Little Rock, Arkansas in 1882. He worked as a salesman for awhile, then took the name of Gilbert M. Aronson and became an actor in vaudeville. When he achieved nothing in the way of success on the stage, he became an artist's model in New York. In 1903, he visited the Edison Studio in New Jersey, where he was hired by director Edwin S. Porter to appear in a one-reel movie called *The Messenger Boy's Mistake*. When Porter decided to make a picture entitled *The Great Train Robbery*, he also included Aronson in the cast, even though the actor had never ridden a horse before. Filmed in Dover, New Jersey, years before the "star system" came into existence, the picture was a smashing success and made history as the first movie to tell a story.

Six months later, Aronson changed his name to Gilbert M. Anderson and left the Edison Company to join its chief competitor, Vitagraph. Starting as a production assistant, he eventually directed and acted in many one-reelers and, in 1905, was responsible for a big hit called *Raffles, the Amateur Cracksman*. He then left Vitagraph to make movies for Col. William H. Selig, for whom he served mostly as a director. In 1907, Anderson quit Selig to form a partnership with

George K. Spoor and organized the Essanay Film Company in Chicago, the name Essanay being derived from their last initials "S" and "A."

Early in 1908, Anderson learned that the Selig Company had started a studio in southern California and was taking advantage of ideal weather conditions for movie-making. Later that summer, he took a troupe of actors to Niles, California and directed a series of comedies starring Ben Turpin. Realizing the great possibilities the West Coast had for the film industry, he opened a new studio which eventually became the headquarters for the Essanay Company.

One day, Anderson decided to make a one-reel Western which would feature a central character upon which the audience could focus its attention. Naming this character "Broncho Billy," he looked around for someone to play the part but failed to come up with the right actor. He concluded the search by taking the role himself in a picture he called *The Bandit Makes Good*. Released in 1908, the film was a huge success and Anderson became an overnight sensation. Much to his surprise, he discovered that he had created the first movie character who could readily be identified in one film after another. Even though the "star system" was yet unknown, Anderson had invented the first idol of motion pictures.

With rapidly mounting success, G. M. Anderson continued making the "Broncho Billy" Westerns for eight years, none of them longer than two reels. A short time later, he dropped the "H" from Broncho, making the name "Bronco." Having become a national hero on the screen, he made a fortune and reached the peak of his career between 1912 and 1915. After completing over 400 films, he sold his holdings in the Essanay Company and retired in 1916. Three years later, he made a brief comeback to direct a series of two-reel comedies starring Stan Laurel for the Metro Company. But he ran into disagreements with the studio and retired permanently in 1920.

For nearly thirty years, Anderson remained lost from public life. A forgotten man, he had faded into oblivion while the industry he had helped create passed him by. When he was finally rewarded with an Academy Award in 1957, he was seventy-five years of age. In recent years, he has lived in retirement at the Motion Picture Country Home in Woodland Hills, California, where he reminisces about the good old days when he was the first movie personality.

FILMS: *The Messenger Boy's Mistake. The Great Train Robbery. The Bandit Makes Good. Broncho Billy and the Baby. The Deadline. Caught Red Handed. Bronco Billy's Reward. In the Nick of Time. Bronco Billy Escapes. Shootin' Mad. A Ride for Life.*

24

HARRY CAREY (1878-1947)

When John Ford directed his Technicolor version of *Three Godfathers* in 1949, he began the picture with a film clip showing Harry
Carey on horseback before a picturesque sunset while a footnote stated
that the feature was dedicated to the memory of that great star. Playing the leading roles were John Wayne, Pedro Armendariz and Harry
Carey, Jr. In this simple way, some of the biggest names in the movie
industry were paying tribute to a wonderful actor and beloved performer.

Born Henry DeWitt Carey in the Bronx, New York on January 16,
1878, Harry Carey was educated at the Hamilton Academy and New
York University, where he studied to be a lawyer. Stricken with pneumonia, he was forced to give up all hope of becoming an attorney. Instead, his illness led him to write a play called "Montana." Taking the
leading role, Carey had the play presented on the stage and thus began
his acting career. After this initial success, he continued with a stage
production of his second play, "Heart of Alaska." In 1909, he made
his first motion picture appearance in a two-reeler called *Bill Sharkey's
Last Game,* which was filmed on Staten Island. He began working under the supervision of director David W. Griffith, who offered him an
important part in *The Unseen Enemy,* a film which also marked the
debut of Lillian and Dorothy Gish. Shortly afterward, Griffith became
a director for the Biograph Company and induced Carey and the Gish
sisters to go along. For the next two years Carey played a wide variety
of roles from heroes to villains. Having established himself as a com-
petent actor, he left Biograph and made a series of action features and
melodramas for companies like Progressive and Pathe before signing a
contract with Universal Pictures. By 1919, he was considered one of
that studio's hottest properties and was well situated among the top
screen personalities of that period. He became famous through a long
series of Western features and continued his success until the arrival
of talking pictures in 1927. Forced into temporary retirement, Carey
took a well-earned rest before resuming his career by appearing in a few
mediocre productions. In 1930, he staged a terrific comeback in talkies
when he starred in M-G-M's *Trader Horn,* which was filmed in Africa
and Mexico. With Duncan Renaldo and Edwina Booth in featured
roles, the picture was a smash hit and became an all-time screen classic.
From then on, Carey starred in features for R-K-O, Paramount, Universal, Warners and other major studios, gaining momentum as a cow-

boy star before finally changing to character parts in 1936. With his experience and talent, he had no difficulty in keeping active in first grade productions and was soon considered to be among the finer motion picture character players. His strong, honest portrayals brought him the respect of his fellow-workers as well as admiration from the audiences. Known for his roles as the gentle, soft-spoken but firm friend whose wisdom and sense of honor always helped those in need, Carey won the hearts of moviegoers. He ably supported stars like John Wayne and James Stewart in several excellent features until his death on September 21, 1947.

In private life, Carey lived quietly in Brentwood, California with his actress wife, Olive Golden Carey. His son, Harry, Jr., also became well-known in westerns. Like William S. Hart, he was a true admirer of the real West and was happiest when working with genuine cowboys or managing his spacious ranch in the San Fernando Valley. Harry Carey may be gone forever but his name remains among the immortal stars of the silver screen.

FILMS: *Bill Sharkey's Last Game. Thieve's Gold. The Scarlet Drop. Bare Fists. Last of the Clintons. Night Rider. Hell Bent. Wagon Trails. Blue Streak McCoy. Wild Mustang. The Unseen Enemy. Graft. A Woman's Fool. Desperate Trails. The Wallop. Man to Man. Last of the Mohicans. Broken Ways. Border Devils. Silent Sanderson. The Fox. Good Men and True. The Kickback. Canyon of Fools. Crashin' Thru. Desert Driver. Miracle Baby. Lightning Rider. Night Hawk. Man From Texas. Tiger Thompson. Roaring Rails. Beyond the Border. Soft Shoes. Texas Trail. The Badlands. Prairie Pirate. Man From Red Gulch. The Seventh Bandit. Driftin' Thru. Frontier Trail. Satan Town. Desert Rose. Devil Horse. Ghost Town. Brute Island. Vanishing Legion. Straight Shootin'. Outcast of Poker Flats. Law and Order. Last Outlaw. Trail of '98. Trader Horn. Sutter's Gold. Sunset Pass. Barbary Coast. Prisoner of Shark Island. Valiant Is the Word For Carrie. Powdersmoke Range. Port of Missing Girls. Kid Galahad. Souls at Sea. Beyond Tomorrow. Mr. Smith Goes to Washington. Law West of Tombstone. Destry Rides Again. The Spoilers. Shepherd of the Hills. Sundown. Air Force. Angel and the Badman. China's Little Devils.*

PETE MORRISON (1893-   )

Pete was born George D. Morrison in Denver, Colorado in 1893. After getting his education in local schools, with a major in science, he traveled around the country working at odd jobs before he wound

26

up in Cheyenne, Wyoming as a champion rodeo rider. In 1908, he made his initial appearance in the movies by playing juvenile leads in silent one-reelers. Shortly afterwards, he became a star for the Universal Studios making serials and five-reel features.

Morrison's skill on horseback served him well and he became known as a daredevil stunt performer. His acrobatic agility never failed to thrill his fans from one film to another. When he parted company from Universal, Pete went to work for independent producer Joe Sameth in a chain of snappy little Westerns that kept him busy until the arrival of talkies.

When the movies underwent the change from silence to sound, Pete went south to make pictures for producers in Argentina, Brazil and Mexico. Returning to the U.S.A., he renewed his association with Universal and made another group of films before turning character actor. Although his pictures were comparatively short in length and low-budgeted, they were exciting features with good plots and fine action. After 1930, Pete made appearances in films for Paramount, R-K-O and Big Four until he retired from movies in 1935.

FILMS: *West Versus East. The Better Man Wins. Headin' North. Ghost City. Making Good. Rainbow Rangers. Black Gold. Triple Action. Duty First. Chasing Trouble. The Escape. Desperate Game. Blue Blazes. Bucking the Truth. The Outcasts. Beyond the Rio Grande. Ridin' the Law. Trails of Danger. One Man Ranch. Saddle War. Chinatown Nights. Courtin' Wildcats. Tong War. Trailing Trouble.*

J. WARREN KERRIGAN (1880-1947)

James Warren Kerrigan was born in Louisville, Kentucky on July 25, 1880 and educated at the local schools. While still a student, he helped increase the family income by working as a warehouse clerk and was directed toward an acting career after getting his first chance to appear on the vaudeville stage when he was thirteen. Later, he acted in repertoire and stock and even managed to enter the University of Illinois.

In 1911, Kerrigan made his motion picture debut at a time when screen players were just beginning to have their names publicly connected with the new industry. Having started on his way to fame by playing in two-reelers for the Essanay Company, he then rose to stardom as a leading man for the American Film Corporation, where he remained at the top of the roster for over a year. In 1914, Universal Studios offered him a contract and made him one of their biggest stars. To thousands of movie fans, he became known as "Jack" Kerrigan, a

1. *Pete Morrison*
2. *Harry Carey*
3. *"Broncho Billy" Anderson*
4. *James W. Kerrigan*
5. *Dustin Farnum*
6. *Tom Santschi*

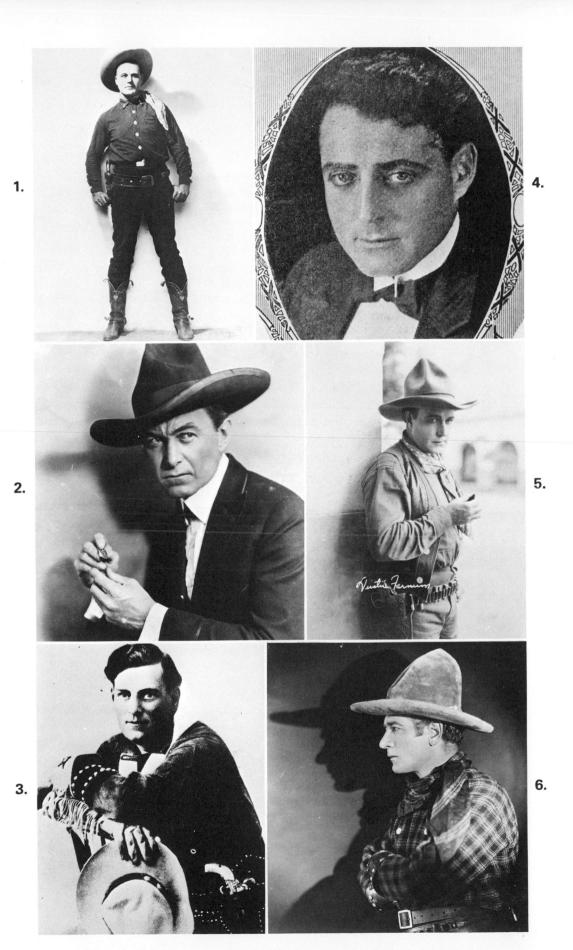

1.

4.

2.

5.

3.

6.

matinee idol of romantic and adventure dramas. About 1915, he was starred in the first five-reel feature that Universal ever made, emerging as one of the screen's highest paid actors of the silent films.

After seven years as a top celebrity, Kerrigan found his career slowly diminishing due to the lack of good roles and the growing competition. He was forced to resort to making pictures for the independent smaller companies like Paralta and Hodkinson until he began to lose his magic appeal. Longer periods of idleness and second-rate films did nothing to help his cause. Finally, director James Cruze selected him to play the leading part in a new Western movie called *The Covered Wagon,* which Paramount Studios were filming on a great scale. Photographed on location in Utah, the picture was an extraordinary spectacle that boasted a large cast and was the first "epic western" ever produced on such a big budget. Needless to say, *The Covered Wagon* became a classic.

Jack Kerrigan suddenly found himself at the top of popularity lists once again and his career took on new dimensions. In fact, everyone connected with *The Covered Wagon* became successful in one way or another. With this new lease on life, Kerrigan resumed his appearances in first-class productions by making a series of films for the Vitagraph Studio until he decided to retire while he was still at the top. Making his last starring appearance in a picture called *Captain Blood* in 1924, Kerrigan abandoned the movies to live a life of leisure. Years later, he staged a brief comeback when he played character roles in a few talkies just before his death at Balboa Island, California on June 9, 1947.

Although many moviegoers remember Kerrigan as a romantic idol, he had been associated with dozens of Western roles. Despite the fact that he reached the zenith of his career in *The Covered Wagon,* he took pride in several other pictures. He was one of those rare actors who appealed to both men and women in the audience because he was capable of portraying rugged characters, even though he had the fine physique and good looks of the stereotyped screen lover. Of all those famous stars of the silent screen, Jack Kerrigan really earned himself a high place among the immortals.

FILMS: *The Hand of Uncle Sam. The Sheriff's Sisters. Stranger at Coyote. The Sheriff's Daughter. For the Flag. The Wishing Seat. Calamity Jane's Inheritance. The Silent Battle. Adventures of Terence O'Rourke. Samson. A Man's Man. Stool Pigeon. Landon's Legacy. A White Man's Chance. Girl of the Golden West. The Man From Brodney's. The Covered Wagon. Captain Blood.*

DUSTIN FARNUM (1874-1929)

Dustin Lancy Farnum was born at Hampton Beach, New Hampshire on May 27, 1874, the son of Greenleaf and Clara Legros Farnum, professional actors. While spending his childhood in Bucksport, Maine, he was educated at the East Maine Conference Seminary and made his first stage appearance with Thomas Shea in 1889. He then entered vaudeville with his brother, William, performing athletic exhibitions throughout New England and New York. In 1897, Dustin joined the Ethel Tucker Stock Company and appeared with Margaret Mather, Chauncey Olcott and Blanche Walsh in various stage productions. His first big success on the legitimate stage came in 1901 when he played the role of "Lt. Denton" in a revival of a play called "Arizona." A short time later, he won praises for his performance in "The Virginian" and continued his rise to fame by appearing in "The Ranger," "The Rector's Garden," "The Squaw Man," "The Littlest Rebel" and "Cameo Kirby."

After playing in another revival of "Arizona" in 1913, Dustin was lured into motion pictures and went to Cuba to make his first film, *The Soldiers of Fortune*. That same year, he accepted an offer to star in a movie version of one of his former stage hits, "The Squaw Man," which was being made by a new organization named the Lasky Corporation. Directed by Cecil B. De Mille on location in California, the picture turned out to be a success and started the company on its way to becoming one of the biggest in the industry. Unfortunately, Farnum lost out on the chance to reap a fortune when he turned down an offer to take shares in the organization in payment for his work. Instead, he chose to be paid a flat salary, thus missing the opportunity of becoming one of the major stockholders. Nevertheless, he went on to make another film adapted from one of his stage hits, "The Virginian," and wound up starring in the first classic Western of screen history.

In 1914, Dustin Farnum left the Lasky Corporation to make pictures for Triangle and Bosworth. By 1917, he had joined the Fox Film Corporation where his equally famous brother, William, was one of the studio's major stars. During the first few years, Fox decided to star Dustin in films which were adapted from his old stage plays. But eventually, Farnum drifted more and more into Westerns and other outdoor adventures. Within a short time, he was associated principally with cowboy roles until audiences classified him as a Western star.

Having spent nearly thirteen years in the movie industry, Farnum decided to retire from the screen in 1926 after making his last film,

31

Flaming Frontier. He made a brief return to the stage, then retired completely. His private life was anything but dull. Dustin had married Agnes Muir Johnston in 1898 and was divorced ten years later. In 1909, he wed Mary Conwell, a marriage which also ended in a stormy divorce suit in 1924. Dustin then wed his third and last wife, leading lady Winifred Kingston, in 1926.

Dustin Farnum died on July 3, 1929, leaving behind a score of fine motion pictures and memorable stage performances as a legacy.

FILMS: *Soldiers of Fortune. The Squaw Man. The Virginian. The Buster. The Man Who Won. Yosemite Trail. Iron to Gold. The Devil Within. Oathbound. The Grail. Three Who Paid. Gentleman From Indiana. David Garrick. Scarlet Pimpernell. Cameo Kirby. Call of the Cumberland. The Corsican Brothers. Ben Blair. David Crockett. Son of Erin. Captain Courtesy. Man in the Open. Light of the Western Skies. The Spy. Strange Idols. While Justice Waits. Trail of the Axe. Bucking the Barrier. Kentucky Days. A Man's Fight. Durand of the Badlands. Flaming Frontier.*

TOM SANTSCHI (1878-1932)

Tom Santschi was the first actor to gain notoriety as a movie villain, having entered motion pictures at the dawn of their existence. Before he came along, film players were still being used to portray a wide variety of characters ranging from heroes to badmen. The "star system" had not yet arrived and directors were placing their actors in whatever part they found convenient. Although he had started making movies a few years earlier, Tom Santschi played the first identifiable screen villain in 1914, when he was cast as the conniving "McNamara" in *The Spoilers*.

Born in Kokomo, Indiana on October 14, 1878, Tom received a liberal education before spending ten years on the stage and vaudeville. When times got tough, he even doubled as an actor and piano player in order to earn his living. In 1908, he met a producer named Frank Boggs, who talked him into appearing in a filmed version of the opera "Faust." Convinced of the many possibilities of motion pictures, Tom went to California where he heard that Col. William H. Selig and G. M. Anderson were pioneering the film industry on the West Coast by establishing new headquarters for the Selig and Essanay companies.

Beginning with a variety of small parts in the early one-reelers, Tom made his official film debut in 1910. He was thus active at the time that the "star system" began, when producers started realizing that movie audiences wanted to know the identities of the actors on the

32

screen. No longer satisfied with referring to players as "Little Mary" and "Dashing Dan," people were curious concerning the names of these entertainers. Probably the most important factor for introducing the new system was an incident where one producer's biggest attraction had been reported killed in an accident. To quench the false rumors, he issued public statements saying that the actress, Florence Lawrence, was still very much alive and was in the process of filming a new picture. Within a year, almost all screen players were having their names publicized in connection with their movies.

By 1913, Tom Santschi was appearing with Kathlyn Williams in Selig's history-making serial *The Adventures of Kathlyn*. The following year, he played his most famous role as the villain opposite William Farnum in *The Spoilers*, a film based on the popular Rex Beach novel. The first screen version of this rugged story about the Klondike became a classic and was later remade four different times. The highlight of the picture was the fierce brawl staged by Farnum and Santschi which turned out to be the greatest free-for-all ever filmed.

Even though he was identified mostly as a movie badman, Tom also starred in quite a few pictures as a hero. His rugged physique was ideally suited for the outdoor roles he played, particularly in the many Westerns he made. During the span of his career, he appeared in features for Selig, Pathe, Goldwyn, First National, Universal and Fox. In many cases, he was employed as a director as well as an actor and was responsible for several screen hits.

After 1925, Tom reverted to character roles which kept him active on the screen until his death in 1932. Ironically, the name of his last picture was *The Last Ride*.

FILMS: *The Adventures of Kathlyn. The Spoilers. The Crisis. Beware of Strangers. Garden of Allah. Who Shall Take My Wife? In the Long Ago. Shadows. City of Purple Dreams. Smoldering Flame. The Still Alarm. Little Orphan Annie. Hell Cat. Her Kingdom of Dreams. Lorraine of the Timberlands. Mother of Dreams. Spirit of the Lake. A Guilty Cause. Brass Commandments. Is Divorce a Failure? Tipped Off. Hills of Kentucky. Wagonmaster. My Own Pal. Siberia. Hands Across the Border. No Man's Gold. Forlorn River. The Last Ride.*

WILLIAM FARNUM (1876-1953)

William Farnum was one of the earliest and biggest motion picture idols the screen has ever produced. By 1915, he was the highest paid actor in movies, ranking in popularity with celebrities like Mary Pick-ford, Charlie Chaplin and William S. Hart.

He was born in Bucksport, Maine on July 4, 1876, the son of Green-leaf and Clara Legros Farnum and made his first stage appearance at the age of twelve by taking part in a Shakespearean play with the Edwin Booth-Lawrence Barrett Company. From 1889 to 1891, he and his older brother Dustin toured vaudeville in an athletic act which eventually led Bill to play the part of Marc Antony in a stage production of "Julius Caesar." As a member of a stock company, he traveled for the next five years in a presentation of "Ben Hur," then organized his own troupe of thespians and played "The Prince of India" with great success in a tour that brought him to the Broadway stage.

In 1913, Bill's brother had scored a big hit when he made a motion picture called *The Squaw Man* for the Lasky Corporation. The follow-ing year, Col. William H. Selig offered Bill the lead in a film entitled *The Spoilers,* based on the famous Rex Beach novel. With a cast that included Kathlyn Williams and Tom Santschi, the picture was a huge success, breaking all attendance records and making history as one of the greatest of the silent movies.

While making *The Spoilers,* Bill Farnum and Tom Santschi were supposed to feature a fist-fight in the last reel where the hero gives the villain his come-uppance. For the sake of more realism, the two actors decided not to pull their punches and the result was the greatest knock-down brawl ever filmed. Although both stars wound up spending weeks in the hospital, the fame they received made it all seem worthwhile. It took only a short time for Bill to become one of the biggest person-alities on the silent screen. After he left Selig, he joined the Fox Studio where he was known principally for his strong outdoor roles. For awhile, he starred in a series of films adapted from the classic novels, but his masculine appeal and virility lent themselves better in pictures that characterized him as the he-man type. When he branched off into Westerns, he gained even greater heights of popularity, playing leads in films based on the books of Zane Grey. In the meantime, Bill's career was running parallel to that of his equally famous brother, Dustin, who was also a Fox star.

During 1924, Bill took a leave from motion pictures to star in a Broadway stage revival of "Ben Hur." On his return to film-making, he continued a long series of first-grade Westerns at various studios until 1929, when the death of his brother and the loss of a fortune in the stock market crash made him retire. It was not until 1931 that he made a comeback as a character actor in talkies.

Bill remained active on the screen right up until his death on June

5, 1953. Admired the world over by his fans and fellow workers, his last years had seen him portraying kindly old gentlemen in dozens of features and serials.

FILMS: *The Spoilers. If I Were King. A Tale of Two Cities. Sign of the Cross. Les Miserables. Du Barry. Woman of Passion. Maid of Salem. The Scarlet Letter. Mr. Robinson Crusoe. The Nigger. The Plunderer. Man of Sorrow. Heart of a Lion. Rough and Ready. True Blue. Rainbow Trail. Riders of the Purple Sage. Painted Desert. The Adventurer. Lone Star Ranger. Flaming Guns. A Stage Romance. Shackles of Gold. Without Compromise. The Gunfighter. The Man Who Fought Alone. Brass Commandments. Devil's Dooryard. Wolves of the Night. Last of the Duanes. When a Man Sees Red. Irish Gringo. The Conqueror. Drag Harlan. The Silver Streak. The Corsican Brothers. A Connecticut Yankee in King Arthur's Court. Custer's Last Stand. American Empire. Powdersmoke Range. The Lone Ranger. Sea Hawk. Tennessee Johnson. South of the Border. Zorro Rides Again. Samson and Delilah. Lone Star. Trail of Robin Hood.*

FRED CHURCH (1889-   )

Another pioneer performer in motion pictures was Frederick Church, who first made a name for himself as a dramatic actor and then later became equally famous as a cowboy star. Born in Quebec, Canada in 1889, he was educated in Michigan before entering upon an acting career on the stage. After spending more than six years in vaudeville and stock, he made his first screen appearance in the early single-reelers of the Selig Company. In 1914, the Essanay Studio hired him to star in some action thrillers that brought him the admiration of theatre audiences all over the country. Having once established himself as a leading dramatic actor, Fred switched to more adventurous roles by starring in Westerns and serials for companies like Universal, Lasky, Balboa, Fox and Bluebird. By 1919, he was involved in a series of outdoor two-reelers for Bell Pictures and, from 1923 to 1925, was playing leads in some independent productions for producer-director Fred J. Balshofer. Among his more important films, Fred had one of the top featured roles in the Mascot super serial of 1928, *The Vanishing West,* which had an all-star cast including Jack Daugherty, Yakima Canutt, Leo Maloney, Jack Perrin and Bill Fairbanks.

Having enjoyed a screen career that spanned nearly twenty years, Fred retired from pictures about 1929 with the contented feeling that he had at least contributed his share toward improving the Western film.

35

FILMS: *The Clever Mrs. Carfax. Glad Glory. The Blindness of Divorce. The Long Chance. The Golden West. Son of a Gun. The Vanishing West. Unknown Rider. Western Methods.*

WILLIAM S. HART (1870-1946)

The man that many film critics regard as the greatest cowboy star of all time was born William Surrey Hart in Newburgh, New York on December 6, 1870. After living in Iowa, Kansas, Minnesota and Wisconsin, the Hart family settled down near a Sioux reservation in South Dakota, where young Bill became friendly with the Indians, learning their language and customs. It was during that period of his life that he developed his great love for the West.

When Bill's father was on the verge of going blind and his mother fell ill, the family moved back to New York where Bill worked at odd jobs. At nineteen, he made his stage debut with Daniel E. Bandmann in "Romeo and Juliet" and embarked on an acting career that took him through some lean years before he won public acclaim for his role as "Messala" in the stage version of "Ben Hur" in 1899. Then came a series of other hits like "The Squaw Man," "The Barrier," "Dead or Alive," "The Virginian" and "Trail of the Lonesome Pine."

In 1914, Hart met movie director Thomas Ince, who offered him a chance to play villains in a couple of two-reelers. This led to the leads in two other films, *On the Night Stage* and *His Hour of Manhood*. Almost overnight, the new cowboy was skyrocketed to fame and succeeded in replacing the fabulous Bronco Billy Anderson as the outstanding Western movie star. Hart was immediately signed to a contract, whereby he would make a series of cowboy features for Ince which would be released through the Mutual Film Studios. Beginning with short two-reelers, he slowly graduated to five-reel features and was left in complete charge of making Westerns as he thought they should be made. In these films, Hart always portrayed a character type which came to be known as the "good badman," the outlaw who found a way to redeem himself by the end of the picture when he performed some fine and noble deed. When Ince left Mutual in 1915, he took Hart along with him and joined Triangle Films. There, the two men continued their business relationship for two more years until, after mounting disagreement with Ince, Hart went to work for the Artcraft Company. During the latter months of their association, hard feelings had developed between them and Hart came to believe that Ince was taking advantage of him. Although the star's films had been reaping big profits at the box-office, his salary reportedly had increased very little. With Artcraft, Hart was still in charge of his own pictures, producing, directing and sometimes writing as well as acting.

By 1920, Hart's audience had grown weary of the monotonous, overdone plots of his pictures and moviegoers started favoring more exciting personalities like Tom Mix and Buck Jones in their Westerns. Bill's insistence on detail and authenticity were the chief causes for his loss of popularity, as he stubbornly refused to compromise with his studio bosses who advised him to change the repetitious pattern of his stories. Instead, he went so far as to poke fun at the crop of "streamlined" cowboys who were rapidly edging him off his throne. When he was finally given a choice of either changing his pictures or losing his status as a producer-director and star, Hart refused to give an inch and made his last film for Artcraft in 1922.

After a deal with Famous Players-Lasky ended in a lawsuit over contract difficulties, Hart accepted an offer to make pictures for United Artists in 1924. The following year, he released a film called *Tumbleweeds,* which turned out to be his last. Bitterly disappointed over the reception the picture had, he filed suit against United Artists, claiming that the studio had failed to properly publicize and distribute the film. The act resulted in his being "blacklisted" throughout the industry and Hart's career came to an end. Eventually, he won his case in court when he was awarded $278,000 in damages in 1940, but the star had lost much more than that over a period of years, even though he had firmly stuck to his principles.

When it came to making Westerns, probably no other cowboy star was as enthusiastic as William S. Hart. He dearly loved the Western frontier life and despised any phoney misrepresentations of how the real-life cowboys lived. He was the first Western star to feature his horse (a Pinto pony called "Fritz") in the cast of his pictures and he was a noted individualist.

Except for a brief marriage to one of his leading ladies, Winifred Westover, Hart lived a quiet, secluded life at his fabulous Horseshoe Ranch in Newhall, California. Although the marriage did result in a son, William, Jr., the majority of his life was spent with his devoted sister, Mary. When she died in 1943, Hart spent his last years in lonely solitude until his death on January 23, 1946. He was buried in Greenwood Cemetery, Brooklyn, New York and left his $1,000,000 estate to charities.

Among his many hobbies, Bill wrote a series of books: *Pinto Ben, Injun and Whitey, O'Malley of the Mounted* and his autobiography, *My Life, East and West.*

FILMS: *The Bargain. On the Night Stage. His Hour of Manhood. The Passing of Two Gun Hicks. Scourge of the Desert. Mr. Silent Haskins. The Sheriff's Streak of Yellow. The Taking of Luke McVane. The Ruse. Darkening Trail. The Patriot. Dawn Maker. Conversion of Frosty Blake. Cash Parrish's Pal. The Bloodhound. Keno Bates, Liar. The Disciple. Hell's Hinges. The Aryan. Border Wireless. Truthful Tulliver. The Primal Lure. The Gunfighter. Devil's Double. Square Deal Man. The Last Card. Silent Man. Wolves of the Trail. His Last Errand. The Avenger. Blue Blazes Rawden. Tiger Man. Wolf Lowry. The Cold Deck. Narrow Trail. Selfish Yates. Shark Monroe. Caravan. Riddle Gawne. Breed of Men. Branding Broadway. Redressor of Wrongs. Wagon Tracks. Square Deal Sanderson. Sand. Toll Gate. Cradle of Courage. Testing Block. The Sheriff. O'Malley of the Mounted. Return of Draw Egan. The Whistle. White Oak. Travelin' On. Singer Jim McKee. Wild Bill Hickock. Tumbleweeds.*

WILLIAM DUNCAN (1880-1961)

William H. Duncan was born in Dundee, Scotland in 1880, and, when his family came to live in New York City, he arrived in America at the age of ten. After completing a modest education, he became interested in athletics and joined the Bernarr McFadden Physical Culture Academy. Before long, he was employed as an instructor for the school, rising to the position of branch manager. After two years, he set out on his own, opening an academy that went bankrupt four months later.

In 1906, Bill entered vaudeville, giving exhibitions of strength with the great Sandow, the strong man. Having decided on a career in show business, he joined the Forepaugh Stock Company of Philadelphia and took part in several theatricals before being spotted by motion picture talent scouts for the Selig Studios. He made his initial screen appearance in 1910 when he starred in a series of one-reelers, most of them outdoor adventures. Five years later, he was regarded as one of the foremost action stars in the business. Leaving the Selig organization, Bill then went to work making pictures for Vitagraph Studios, where he rose to even greater heights as one of filmdom's top ten Western players. Although he made various types of adventure features, the fans came to know him best for his cowboy roles, especially in serials. Directing, writing and starring in most of his work, he made a genuine effort to better himself and his productions.

In 1921, Bill married his beautiful leading lady, Edith Johnson, to whom he was devoted. He terminated his association with Vitagraph the following year to sign a contract with Universal, where he continued to turn out exciting serials and features. He and Edith together appeared in no less than ten serials, making them one of the most popular teams on the screen. By 1925, Bill decided that his fortune had been made and retired from pictures to enjoy life with his wife and three children. The family undertook a nation-wide tour, seeing all the sights that they had read and dreamed about until Bill's wife suddenly fell ill and died. Grief-stricken, the famous star went into seclusion until some friends persuaded him to return to his work. He immediately undertook a new series of features and chapter plays for various studios and independent producers until he regained the stature he had once abandoned.

Later, Bill married actress Edith Roberts, with whom he lived happily until his death. Having turned to character roles after the arrival of the talkies, he remained active in pictures until he was stricken ill and confined to his home several years before his death on February 8, 1961. He was buried at Inglewood Cemetery near Hollywood and was survived by his wife, two sons, a daughter and three grandchildren. During the silent film era, he had been regarded as an exciting personality, well-known for his skill at performing the most dangerous stunts. An able writer, he was responsible for several good screenplays, such as "The Fifth Generation" and "The Sporting Editor." Admired by his co-workers as well as by his fans, Bill reaped the praise and affection which he so richly deserved.

FILMS: *Alladin of Broadway. Dead Shot Baker. The Fighting Trail. Wolfville. The Tenderfoot. The Last Man. Vengeance and the Woman. A Fight for Millions. Man of Might. Smashing Barriers. The Fighting Guide. The Silent Vow. When Danger Smiles. The Silent Avenger. The Steel Trail. Playing It Wild. The Unforeseen Hand. Love and Honor. Fast Express. Wolves of the North. Steel Heart. Where Men Are Men. Shadows of the North. The Farmer's Daughter.*

TOM MIX (1880-1940)

Without a doubt, the most colorful cowboy star of them all was Tom Mix, whose sense of showmanship, wealth and exploits made him the idol of an era. Contrary to the reports that he came from Texas, Thomas Edwin Mix was born at Mix Run near Dubois, Pennsylvania on January 6, 1880, the son of Calvary officer Edward E. Mix and Elizabeth Smith Mix. After attending the Virginia Military Institute, he joined the Army and saw service in Cuba during the Spanish-American War. In 1900, he took part in the Boxer Rebellion in China, was wounded and returned to America to recover. A short time later, he was involved in the Boer War in Africa, fighting first with the British and then with the Boers.

Next, having had his fill of warfare, he served as guide on one of President Theodore Roosevelt's hunting trips before taking the job of sheriff in Montgomery County, Kansas. From there, Tom went on to serve as a deputy sheriff and U. S. Marshal in Oklahoma and as a member of the Texas Rangers. The year 1906 found him at Fort Bliss, Oklahoma, where he was employed as livestock foreman for the Miller 101 Ranch. It was at that time that he took part in rodeo competitions, winning his first national riding championship in 1909 at Prescott, Arizona, and his second at Canon City, Colorado in 1911.

Tom's first appearance in motion pictures came in 1910 when he was sorted out from the Miller Ranch to play in Col. William Selig's *Ranch Life in the Great Southwest*. He continued to make one- and two-reelers for the Selig Studio until 1917, when he left to join the Fox Film Company, where he received a substantial raise in salary and a long-term contract. At Fox, Tom's popularity grew with each new picture he made and it was only a short time before the public was clamoring for more of his films. Eventually, he headed his own company, releasing under the Fox banner, writing and directing many of his features. By 1921, he was nudging William S. Hart from the throne as King of the Cowboys and was well on his way to becoming the idol of millions all over the world. Unlike Bill Hart, Tom refused to stick to realism in his screen adventures. Instead, he introduced a more colorful character whose reckless, devil-may-care attitude seemed more exciting to Western fans. His daredevil stunts and expert horsemanship had audiences sitting on the edge of their seats and the public was only too quick to grasp this new type of cowboy hero.

At the peak of his career, Tom was reportedly earning as much as $20,000 per week at a time when taxes were almost nil compared to modern times. With his picturesque style and freedom of manner, the press found him a natural for publicity purposes, and his private life proved to be almost as colorful. While indulging his flair for extravagance, Tom lived in a huge $40,000 mansion, which boasted a mile-long driveway with gates that flashed his initials in neon lights. His spectacular wardrobe included dozens of white cowboy suits, ten-gallon hats, hand-tooled boots, diamond studded belts and pearl-inlaid pistols. He owned six of the flashiest automobiles in the world, one of which was a white chrome-decorated Rolls Royce that could also be driven atop a silver-inlaid saddle on the hood. He tossed lavish parties, gave away expensive gifts and hob-nobbed with elite society. But, in spite of this,

40

he openly announced that he was a lonely man. Having divorced his first wife, the former Olive Stokes, in 1917, Tom won custody of a daughter, Ruth. A year later, he wed Victoria Forde, a marriage that also ended in a stormy divorce in 1930 and resulted in another daughter, Thomasina. In 1932, Tom married a former circus aerialist named Mabel Hubbard Ward.

When talkies disrupted the movie industry in 1927, Tom ended his association with Fox to make a series of features for F.B.O. Studios. He then undertook a personal appearance tour with the Sells-Floto Circus which lasted three seasons, culminating when he signed a contract with Universal Pictures in 1932. Beginning with his first talkie, *Christmas Eve at Pilot Butte,* he made several sound Westerns before terminating his contract with *Rustler's Roundup.* His last screen appearance came in 1934, when he starred in a Mascot serial called *The Miracle Rider.*

Bidding his farewell to the film industry, Tom bought an interest in the Sam B. Dill Circus, which later became known as the Tom Mix Circus, and made annual nation-wide tours throughout America, Canada and Mexico. In 1938, he merged with the larger Sells-Floto menagerie, traveling all over the country and meeting his fans in person. For young and old alike, one of the highlights of summer was to see Tom Mix and his fabulous horse, Tony, do their tricks under the big top. Even audiences in many of the countries of Europe had been treated to performances.

It was during an advance publicity campaign trip that Tom met his death in an auto crash at Florence, Arizona on October 12, 1940. He was buried in a silver casket at Forest Lawn Memorial Park, Los Angeles, under a simple tablet inscribed "Tom Mix 1880-1940." Looking back at the pages of Hollywood history, Tom stands out as a classic example of the Golden Age of the movie industry. Having starred in over 370 pictures, his name had been linked with noted personalities all over the world. Dozens of manufacturers had paid him royalties for the use of his name on their products and a popular radio series known as "The Tom Mix Show," continued to captivate audiences even after his death.

FILMS: *Ranch Life in the Great Southwest. Western Blood. The Law and the Outlaw. A Child of the Prairie. Back to the Primitive. The Escape of Jim Dolan. Why the Sheriff Is a Bachelor. Slim Higgins. Chip of the Flying U. The Heart of Texas Ryan. Durand of the Badlands. Cupid's Roundup. Pony Express Rider. Six Shooter Andy. Ace High. Fame and Fortune. Mr. Logan, U.S.A. The Trimming of Paradise Gulch. In the Days of the Thundering Herd. King Cowboy. Hidden*

Gold. Up and Coming. Sky High. Rough Diamond. Do and Dare. Tom Mix in Arabia. Just Tony. Catch My Smoke. Circus Ace. Flaming Guns. Lone Star Ranger. Steppin' Fast. Soft Boiled. Romance Land. Three Jumps Ahead. North of Hudson Bay. Oh You Tony. Mile a Minute Romeo. Eyes of the Forest. Trouble Shooter. Lucky Horseshoe. For Big Stakes. Best of the Badmen. Riders of the Purple Sage. Dick Turpin. Deadwood Coach. The Yankee Senor. The Great K and A Train Robbery. Canyon of Light. No Man's Gold. The Lost Trail. Outlaws of Red River. Arizona Wildcat. Hello Cheyenne. Christmas Eve at Pilot Butte. Destry Rides Again. Rider of Death Valley. My Pal the King. Hidden Gold. Flaming Guns. The Fourth Horseman. Terror Trail. Rustler's Roundup. The Miracle Rider.

FRANKLYN FARNUM (1883-1961)

Another pioneer actor in movie Westerns was Franklyn Farnum. Born in Boston, Massachusetts on June 5, 1883 and educated in the local schools, he was a boyhood pal of a certain James M. Curley, who later became one of Boston's most popular mayors. At the early age of twelve, Franklyn made his debut in vaudeville and decided on an acting career. Years later, he made numerous appearances in dramatic and musical stage productions, playing leading roles in hits such as "The Dollar Princess," "Madame Sherry" and "The Only Girl." He was a popular star for the well-known Broadway producers Charles Frohman, George Lederer, Henry W. Savage and George Webber before entering moving pictures.

In 1914, Franklyn began his film career when he starred in *Love Never Dies* for Universal Pictures. Cast as a romantic leading man, he made a series of one- and two-reelers for Bluebird, Lasky, Metro, Mutual and Triangle before branching off into Westerns about 1917. Having graduated to three- and five-reel features, he starred in a number of cowboy pictures for Fox and Selig. By that time, two other actors named Farnum were also enjoying successful careers in movies. William and Dustin Farnum were brothers and many people thought that Franklyn was a relation. In spite of the fact that he was not, there proved to be plenty of room at the top for three successful Farnums in Westerns.

Among Franklyn's most important work on the screen during those early years were the serials. In 1920, he starred in *The Vanishing Trail* for Selig's Canyon Productions, a chapter-play which ranked among the best of that period. In 1924, he co-starred with serial-queen Helen Holmes in Rayart's first cliff-hanger, *Battling Brewster*. These and a long list of thrilling features kept Franklyn active during the silent film era. When the threat of talking pictures loomed near, the major studios cut down production so he went to work for the independent companies like Goldstone, I.P.C. and Arrow.

With the arrival of sound, Franklyn's career as a star came to an end. Turning to character roles, he remained on the screen in many supporting parts until illness forced him to retire in 1960. He died of cancer at the Motion Picture Country Hospital in Woodland Hills, California on July 4, 1961. He was survived by a daughter, Rose, and three grandchildren. His wife, Edith, had passed away a few years prior to his death. A closely devoted couple, they had been married since 1921.

FILMS: *Love Never Dies. Little Partner. Face Value. The Lash. Empty Cab. Winged Mystery. Breeze Bolton Blows In. Human Targets. The Fighting Grin. The Clock. Rough Lover. Brother Bill. Uphill Climb. Desert Rat. Anything Once. The Cub. The Vanishing Trail. Fighting Stranger. Mark of the Spur. The Last Chance. The Raiders. Honor of the Press. So This Is Arizona. Battling Brewster. White Masks. In Judgement Of. Gold Grabber. Trail's End. Two Fisted Tenderfoot. A Desperate Adventure. Calibre '45. The Gambling Fool. Drugstore Cowboy. Border Intrigue. Crossroads. The Firebrand. Shackles of Gold. Gun Shy. Wolves of the Border. Two Gun Sap. When Love is Young. Beyond the Rio Grande. Texas Badman. Honor of the Range. Powdersmoke Range. Hopalong Cassidy of the Bar 20. Frontier Justice. The Crusaders. Deadwood Dick. Sunset Boulevard.*

WILLIAM DESMOND (1878-1949)

William Desmond was born in Dublin, Ireland on January 23, 1878. While still in his youth, he came to live in New York City, where he completed his education and entered vaudeville as an entertainer and writer of his own sketches. Having worked his way to California, he became a member of the Burbank Stock Company and appeared in a stage version of "Quo Vadis," in which he was cited for his fine performance. Soon after that, he toured the Keith-Orpheum circuit in hits like "Romeo and Juliet," "The Lion and the Mouse," "If I Were King," "Midsummer Night's Dream," "The Bird of Paradise," "The Sign of the Cross," "Ben Hur," "Alias Jimmy Valentine" and "Raffles."

Bill had organized his own troupe of actors and had just finished a tour of America, Canada and Australia when he was selected to play Billie Burke's leading man in a movie called *Peggy* in 1915. The first studio to make use of his talents was Triangle, which billed him as "The

43

1. *William S. Hart*
2. *William Farnum*
3. *Bill Duncan*
4. *Franklyn Farnum*
5. *Fred Church*
6. *Tom Mix*

1.

2.

3.

4.

5.

6.

Romantic Adventurer." While establishing himself in films, he created the image of being the ideal hero of feminine dreams and became one of the leading matinee idols of the silent screen. To add to his popularity, he also portrayed rugged, two-fisted he-men which also appealed to the male audience. After leaving Triangle, Bill made a few pictures for Hampton Productions then joined Pathe in 1920. Two years later, he went under contract to Universal, where he earned the title of "King of the Silent Serials." During the 1920's he expressed a particular liking for Westerns, emerging as one of the top cowboy stars of that period. The greater part of his popularity came from the exciting chapter-plays he made at Universal and his success continued until the end of the silent picture era.

In the early 1920's, Bill married one of William S. Hart's leading ladies, an actress named Mary McIvor, and when the talkies brought a temporary slump to their careers, the couple took the opportunity to make a nation-wide tour on the stage from 1927 to 1929. Returning to motion pictures, Bill starred in his first sound film, *No Defense* for Warners, then made a series of independent features before turning character actor.

By 1932, Bill Desmond had stepped down to make room for newer and younger cowboy stars. He continued appearing in Westerns as a supporting player right up until the time of his death on November 2, 1949. Sometimes called "The Typical Cowboy," he made a lasting impression on audiences as one of the finest action stars of a bygone era.

FILMS: *Peggy. Not My Sister. The Captive God. Deuce Duncan. The Pretender. Wild Life. Hell's End. Old Hartwell's Club. Beyond the Shadow. Paws of the Bear. Flying Colors. Society For Sale. An Honest Man. A Sudden Gentleman. The Sea Panther. Life's a Funny Proposition. The Prodigal Liar. A Romance in Overalls. Man From Make Believe. The Prince and Betty. Fargo Express. Perils of the Yukon. Around the World in 80 Days. The Riddle Rider. Shadows of the North. Her Code of Honor. Broadway Cowboy. Muffled Drums. Ace of Spades. The Winking Idol. Beasts of Paradise. Big Timber. Breathless Moment. Return of the Riddle Rider. Measure of a Man. Burning Trail. The Vanishing Trail. Fighting Mad. Vanishing Rider. The Meddler. Mystery Rider. No Defense. McGuire of the Mounted. Sunset Trail. Ridin' Pretty. Blood and Steel. Tongues of Scandal. Phantom Fortune. Perils of the Wild. Strings of Steel. Phantom of the West. Courage of the North. Timber Terrors. Powdersmoke Range. The Way of the West. Custer's Last Stand.*

WILLIAM RUSSELL (1884-1929)

The life of Bill Russell is a perfect example of the classic Horatio Alger story where a poor, young crippled boy rises from rags to riches. He was born William Lerche in the Bronx, New York in 1884 and made his first theatrical appearance at the age of eight, when he was chosen to replace an ailing child actor in a play called "Chimmie Fadden." When Bill was not attending public school, he sold newspapers and spent his summer vacations swimming in the East River. When he was twelve, he was involved in an accident which forced him to spend fourteen months in a hospital bed with a broken hip and it was through sheer determination and courage that he ever walked again. By exercising more each day, he was able to attend a Bernarr McFadden school of Physical Culture and by the time he reached eighteen, he was playing football while studying at Fordham University.

In 1905, Bill won a boxing championship. After competing in several athletic events, he suddenly decided he would like to be an actor. He appeared with headliners such as Ethel Barrymore, Chauncey Olcott, Blanche Bates and David Higgins before finally getting a chance to play leads with the Poli Stock Company of Philadelphia. Then came the starring role in a Broadway stage success called "St. Elmo," which kept him busy for no less than two years. After that, Bill toured in vaudeville, giving a series of boxing exhibitions, until 1912 when he entered the movies.

Getting his start at the old Biograph Studio, he took part in some of the early silent flickers until he had the opportunity to join the Thanhauser Company where he first played leading roles. By 1915, Bill was considered one of the top action stars in movies. His ability to perform daring stunts was unparalled and he continuously amazed his fans and co-workers with his feats of danger.

It was in 1915 that Bill appeared in what was probably his greatest film. This was a serial in which he starred for American Films called *Diamond in the Sky* and resulted in a screen masterpiece. It was chiefly through the serials that Bill became famous, for he was an expert at action and suspense. Some of his best chapter-plays were made for Biograph, Thanhauser, American, Famous Players and Mutual. By 1918, he was heading his own production company, releasing under the distributorship of Pathe and working as a star and director.

In July of 1919, William Fox, head of the Fox Film Company, had decided to enlarge his roster of male stars by hiring some new talent.

His first act was to offer Bill Russell a contract to make features and serials. Taking the offer, Bill made a series of pictures which alternated between Western and other types of adventure stories. His hair-raising stunts completely delighted his fans and his success in silent films continued until his untimely death in 1929, when he was only forty-five years of age.

Survived by his wife, the former Helen Ferguson, Bill Russell left a saddened public when he vanished from the screen. His long list of pictures were the most fitting monument for a star who helped bring screen entertainment to a high level.

FILMS: *Sands of Sacrifice. The Sea Master. Temporary Peter. His Arabian Night. Snap Judgement. Aladdin's Lamp. Diamond in the Sky. Robin Hood. The Straight Road. Sequel to Diamond in the Sky. The Midnight Trail. Hearts or Diamonds. Up Romance Road. Hobbs in a Hurry. Garden of Lies. Pride of the Man. The Man Who Dared. Shod With Fire. Lincoln Highwayman. Twins of Suffering Creek. Brass Buttons. This Hero Stuff. Singing River. The Roof Tree. Lady From Longacre. Strength of the Pines. Self Made Man. Money to Burn. Men of Zanzibar. Desert Blossoms. The Great Night. Mixed Faces. The Crusader. Alias the Night Wind. Boston Blackie. Goodbye Girls. Man Size. Times Have Changed. When Odds Are Even. Anna Christie. Before Midnite. The Still Alarm. Blue Eagle. Wings of the Storm. Big Pal. The Passing of Wolf McLean. In Bad. Girls Gone Wild. The Beloved Brute.*

JACK HOLT (1888-1951)

One of the greatest adventure stars of all time was Jack Holt, who enjoyed fame on the screen during both the silent and sound eras of motion pictures. Born Charles John Holt in Winchester, Virginia on May 31, 1888, the son of an Episcopal minister, he was educated at the Trinity School in New York and the Virginia Military Institute. After studying law, he abandoned the idea of becoming an attorney and took up engineering. His first job with a railroad proved to be a disappointment so he followed the urge to go prospecting for gold in Alaska. Meeting with failure, Jack went to Oregon and worked as a cowpuncher, and for the next few years was employed on ranches throughout the Northwest.

In 1909, Jack joined a traveling troupe of actors and appeared in stage presentations for the next four years, until he entered motion pictures as a bit player in 1913. It was in 1915 that he astonished film directors by riding a horse over a thirty-foot cliff into a river, a stunt

48

that brought him his first important acting assignment in a picture called *Salomy Jane*. Having finally reached stardom, he made a long list of two- and three-reelers for companies like Ince, Universal, Vitagraph, Select and Famous Players. During that early period of his career, Jack was portraying all types of roles ranging from villains to heroes.

In 1916, Universal Studios made the first chapter-play that contained a completely Western theme. Entitled *Liberty, a Daughter of the U.S.A.*, it starred Marie Walcamp, Jack Holt, Eddie Polo, Roy Stewart and Neal Hart, and became a huge success at a time when serials were very popular. Early in the 1920's, Jack Holt joined Paramount's impressive roster of stars when he was selected to play the leads in a new series of Western features based on the popular novels of Zane Grey. After the tremendous box-office appeal of these pictures, he was considered one of the studio's leading personalities. His portrayals of rugged he-men became his trademark and, before long, the name of Jack Holt was synonymous with the word "adventure."

When the movies underwent the change from silence to sound, Jack had very little difficulty in remaining actively employed. His rich, clear voice proved adaptable for talkies and his popularity was still at its peak. He left Paramount and made a few films for Realart and Artcraft before joining Columbia Studios, where he continued his successful career. Although Jack had been primarily classified as a cowboy star, he later broadened his repertoire to include all sorts of outdoor adventures. But it was in Westerns that he really hit his stride. Among the major studios that made use of his talents were Columbia, R-K-O, Republic and M-G-M.

In 1943, Jack left motion pictures temporarily when General George C. Marshall invited him to serve as a horse buyer for the U.S. Cavalry. A recognized authority on horseflesh, he spent four years at the remount stations in El Rena, Oklahoma and Fort Warren, Colorado before returning to Hollywood. He had just completed his last film, *Across the Wide Missouri* with Clark Gable, when he died of a heart attack on January 18, 1951. He had been married to Margaret Woods Holt since 1916 and was the father of two sons, Tim and David, and a daughter, Jennifer, that were also active in Westerns. One of the all-time greats, Jack Holt's absence from the screen left an important vacancy which no one has ever been able to fill.

FILMS: *Salomy Jane. A Cigarette, That's All. White Man's Law. Liberty, a Daughter of the U.S.A. One More American. The Honor of His House. A Desert Wooing. Love Me. Green Eyes. The Marriage Ring. Enchanted Hill. Little American. Victory. The Claw. The Woman*

1. *Bill Russell*
2. *"Shorty" Hamilton*
3. *Art Acord*
4. *Fred Burns*
5. *William Desmond*
6. *Jack Holt*

1.

2.

3.

4.

5.

6.

Thou Gavest Me. Squaw Man. Lifeline. Held by the Enemy. Bought and Paid For. Call of the North. While Satan Sleeps. The Man Unconquerable. The Cheat. The Tiger's Claw. Mysterious Rider. Lord Raa. Empty Hands. The Lone Wolf. Light of the Western Stars. Making a Man. Nobody's Money. Marriage Maker. Wanderer of the Wasteland. North of '36. In the Days of the Thundering Herd. Wild Horse Mesa. Border Legion. Born to the West. Red River Valley. Riders of the Purple Sage. Water Hole. Blind Goddess. Forlorn River. Vanishing Pioneer. Over the Andes. The Woman I Stole. Crash Donovan. Dirigible. Avalanche. Submarine. Dangerous Waters. Sunset Pass. Sorrel and Son. The Donovan Affair. Fugitive From a Prison Camp. North of Nome. Father and Son. Curly Top. San Francisco. Under Suspicion. House of Mystery. End of the Trail. Sea Horses. A Gentleman of Leisure. Flight. Ancient Highway. Vengeance. Arizona Ranger. They Were Expendable. My Pal Trigger. Return of the Frontiersman. Across the Wide Missouri.

FRED BURNS (1878-?)

Fred Burns was an original character from the West whose authentic background started him off as a broncho-buster for the Buffalo Bill Cody Wild West Show. Born at Fort Keogh, Montana in 1878, he grew up on a ranch and worked with horses all his life. After his job of breaking wild horses for the Cody show ended, Fred went to work at the famous Miller 101 Ranch in Oklahoma and toured with the "101 Ranch Wild West Show," giving exhibitions of fancy riding and roping throughout the U.S.A. and Europe.

In 1916, he entered motion pictures by starring in some single-reelers for Selig and Reliance. These were followed by another series of cowboy adventures for companies like Majestic, Pallas, Fine Arts, Clune and Artcraft. His last starring roles were played during 1918-19 when the Vitagraph Company hired him to make a chain of silent two-reelers. After that, Fred became a "heavy," portraying villains opposite stars like Bill Duncan, Bill Cody, Neal Hart and Hoot Gibson. Among his most notable films were *Fancy Jim Sherwood* and a role in support of Ruth Roland in the 1920 serial thriller, *Ruth of the Rockies*.

By the mid-1920's the screen had become overcrowded with cowboy stars so Fred turned to character roles, usually playing the sheriff or town marshal, in dozens of features which kept him active well into the late 1930's. When he died, sometime in the mid-1940's, he passed away silently as so many had before him who had belonged to that roster of unsung Western heroes of the screen.

52

FILMS: *Birth of a Nation. Ben Blair. Sold For Marriage. Eyes of the World. Fancy Jim Sherwood. Sunlight's Last Raid. The Fighting Trail. Bound in Morocco. Vengeance and the Woman. Ruth of the Rockies. California Mail. The Scarlet Brand. Unknown Rider.*

SHORTY HAMILTON

John "Shorty" Hamilton was a pioneer film actor who started his career way back in 1912 as a vaudeville comedian. After three years of barnstorming around the country, he ended up making two-reel comedies for the old Vitagraph Company, working his way up to stardom in 1915. It was at that time that he began his long series of silent Western featurettes. During the six years that he remained a star, Hamilton worked for Pathe, Universal and a string of independent producers. Unfortunately, he was criticized for letting his brand of slapstick comedy take priority over the action in his pictures and he lasted only a short time.

He eventually wound up as a supporting comic in a number of productions, but the demand for his talents grew rapidly scarce with each passing year. By the time the talkies rolled around, he had vanished from the scene. His most memorable role was in a Pathe serial of 1927 called *The Masked Menace.*

It is truly unfortunate that Hamilton was wasted in second-rate films, for he was capable of much better things on the screen. Had he received better backing, he could have lasted much longer in major productions. In spite of his short height, he could handle action scenes well when he was not too busy clowning before the camera. He seemed thoroughly at home in cowboy costumes and the manner in which he handled his horse was a pleasure to watch. As was the case with many other talented performers, Shorty lacked the foresight to engage himself a good agent who would have seen to it that better opportunities came along to further his career.

ART ACORD (1890-1931)

One of the earliest and most authentic cowboys that ever appeared in motion pictures was Art Acord. Although his career ended tragically, he had been among the most popular Western players of the 1920's. Born in Stillwater, Oklahoma in 1890, when it was known as Indian Territory, Art became an accomplished horseman at an early age. He worked as a cowpuncher while competing in rodeos all over the West and won a trunkload of trophies and cash prizes. An all-around champ who specialized in bronco-busting, calf-roping and bulldogging, he distinguished himself by being one of the very few men who rode a wild mustang named "Cyclone," known to rodeo cowboys as the toughest bronc in the business.

In 1909, Art was appearing with the Dick Stanley-Bud Atkinson Wild West Show in New York when he met a man named Adam Kessel, who was in the process of organizing a new movie studio called the Bison Film Company in New Jersey. Kessel gave him a job as a stuntman and player in some of the earliest one-reelers the company ever made. But after a year, Art decided to accept a better offer to perform with "Buffalo Bill" Cody's Wild West Show on a tour of America, Canada and Europe. While he was competing in a rodeo at Salt Lake City, Utah, Art married an actress named Edythe Sterling in July, 1913. The following year, he returned to motion pictures when the Mutual Film Corporation hired him to star in a group of two-reel Westerns under the name of Buck Parvin. A short while later, he made another string of horse-operas for the American Film Company and quickly rose to fame as a top-notch performer.

When his marriage ended in divorce in 1916, Art seemed to go to pieces. He joined the U.S. Army in 1917 and saw service in France during the First World War. Released in 1919, he made a tour of the U.S. and Australia with the Stanley-Atkinson Wild West Show and then made a screen comeback when Universal Studios gave him the leading role in his first serial, *The Moon Riders*. Having scored a big hit, Art signed a contract with Universal to star in five more chapter-plays besides a group of three- and five-reel features. Known as the "Blue Streak" series, these five-reelers were among the best little Westerns made during the 1920's and they contained plenty of trick riding and fancy stunts by Art.

By 1924, the three leading cowboy stars at Universal were Harry Carey, Hoot Gibson and Art Acord. The profits their pictures made brought a fortune to the studio and themselves at a time when it was said that Westerns were suffering a slump period. Three years later, the talkies arrived and Art Acord was suddenly told that his voice was unsuitable for sound. He tried working for the cheaper independent companies, but even they turned him down. After repeated unsuccessful attempts to remain in pictures, he fell into a state of melancholy and took to drink. Dejected and despondent, Art left Hollywood and became involved in illegal bootlegging, which resulted in his arrest and a jail sentence. On his release from prison, he organized an act and went to Mexico in 1930, where he went broke from his heavy gambling and

54

drinking. Early in January, 1931, he was found dead in his Mexican hotel room, his body reportedly filled with a large amount of cyanide. Although officials termed it suicide, there were many circumstances which made his death a mystery and many of his old friends believed he had met with foul play.

Regardless of his tragic end, the fact remained that Art could have solved his original problem by taking voice lessons which undoubtedly would have helped him continue his career. As it turned out, his death marked the end of a bright personality who had flashed like a meteor across the silent screen.

FILMS: *The Squaw Man. The Moon Riders. North of the Rio. Winners of the West. The White Horseman. In the Days of Buffalo Bill. The Oregon Trail. The Scrappin' Kid. The Call of Courage. Three in Exile. Circus Cyclone. Rustler's Ranch. Man From the West. Lazy Lightning. The Terror. The Riding Rascal. Sky High Corral. The Set Up. Western Pluck. Loco Luck. Cactus Cyclone.*

THE WESTERN SERIAL

The first movie serial started way back in 1912 when the Edison Film Company made a deal with a magazine publication called *The Ladies' World*. The contract called for Edison to make a series of short one-reelers which would be released in conjunction with the magazine stories. The result was a chain of episodes, each containing a different plot, known as *What Happened to Mary?* In 1913, the *Chicago Tribune* joined in the competition with several other newspapers by signing a similar contract with the Selig Studios. The only difference was that Selig came up with an entry that had one continuous story with the same characters and ended each episode with the star in a perilous predicament. It was named *The Adventures of Kathlyn* and featured Kathlyn Williams with Tom Santschi.

With the outstanding success of Selig's serial, all the other film companies followed suit and adopted the same format of ending each chapter with suspense. Week after week, the public was drawn back to see how the star could be saved from a dangerous situation until, in the last episode, good finally overpowered evil. By 1915, the serials had achieved great public appeal. With practically every major studio involved in at least one chapter-play, the companies that turned out the best were Universal, Vitagraph and Pathe. Names like Kathlyn Williams, Pearl White, Helen Holmes, Ruth Roland, Bill Duncan, Art Acord, William

Russell, Jack Holt, Allene Ray and Walter Miller were among the most prominent in serials.

During its history, the serial always had the adventure story for its theme. The type of adventures ran in cycles. In the beginning, the mystery melodramas had been the fashion, then the fad changed to cycles involving railroads, the circus, firefighters, jungle stories, spies, aviation and, finally, science-fiction. The only type of chapter-plays that never seemed to run out of style was the Western. In 1916, the first completely Western serial was produced and called *Liberty, a Daughter of the U.S.A.* It co-starred Marie Walcamp and Jack Holt with Neal Hart, Eddie Polo and Roy Stewart and, from that time on, Western chapter-plays were a major portion of serial production. Among the leaders in this category were *The Fighting Trail* (1917); *Lightning Bryce* (1919); *The Moon Riders* (1920); *Winners of the West* (1921); *The Riddle Rider* (1924); *Hawk of the Hills* (1927); *The Vanishing West* (1928); *The Mystery Rider* (1928) and *The Indians Are Coming* (1930). Although the latter-named serial was distributed in both silent and sound versions, these were the outstanding Western cliff-hangers of the silent picture era.

As the movies found a voice, the studios that turned out the largest portion of serials were Universal, Mascot, Columbia and Republic. By the year 1940, Republic had absorbed Mascot and the entire production of chapter-plays was left up to only three companies. The most popular of the Western serials were *Gordon of Ghost City* (1932); *Phantom Empire* (1934); *Rustlers of Red Dog* (1935); *The Vigilantes Are Coming* (1936); *The Lone Ranger* (1937); *The Great Adventures of Wild Bill Hickock* (1938); *Flaming Frontiers* (1938); *The Oregon Trail* (1939); *The Adventures of Red Ryder* (1940); *White Eagle* (1940); *Riders of Death Valley* (1941); *The Ghost of Zorro* (1948) and *Cody of the Pony Express* (1949). Among the names that were most prominent were Buck Jones, Tom Tyler, John Wayne, Johnny Mack Brown, Bill Elliott, Bob Livingston, Allan Lane, Clayton Moore, Ray Corrigan and Rod Cameron.

Down through the years, dozens of players had found a beginning to their careers in serials, discovering that weekly exposure, that lasted from twelve to fifteen consecutive weeks, was just what an upcoming young performer needed to rise to stardom. During the silent film period, Bill Desmond had held the crown of "King of the Silent Serials" while Walter Miller and Bill Duncan had competed for the title of "Crown Prince." When the talkies arrived, Buster Crabbe had become the undisputed "King of the Sound Serials" and the "Crown Prince" was a toss-up between Bob Livingston, Johnny Mack Brown and Clayton

56

Moore. Apart from the Western chapter-plays, there were dozens of excellent serials of various themes and the total number of releases from 1913 to 1956 came to nearly four hundred.

Similar to the full-length Western features, the serials had a basic content of action. This was undoubtedly the reason for their universal appeal. The stories were simple, the characters clearly identifiable and the suspense was almost unbearable. After awhile, the endings seemed to be repeated when the hero found himself trapped in a burning mine or sent careening over a cliff in a wagon, but it was still a thrill to see how each individual came out unscathed. There was always plenty of fighting and hard riding. One of the sure-fire gimmicks was to introduce a mystery man—either the hero or the chief villain. In all but the last chapter the mystery man would appear behind a disguise and keep the fans guessing until his final unmasking in the last reel. Sometimes, only the audience knew who the mystery man was, thus giving the fans the extra thrill of being one step ahead of the players. In 1937, the mystery man theme reached its zenith when Republic Studios decided to feature no less than five leading heroes in *The Lone Ranger*. One of the group turned out to be the heroic masked man, but not until the final episode did the audience discover which one.

Another favorite attraction was to make an "All-Star Serial," whereby producers would combine several well-known stars in the same production. Universal had led the way in 1916 when it made *Liberty, a Daughter of the U.S.A.*, using an all-star cast. In 1924, *The Iron Man* and *Perils of the Wild* in 1925 were two more Universal releases that featured impressive rosters of players. Three years later, Mascot outdid all previous serials by combining Jack Daugherty, Leo Maloney, Yakima Canutt, Jack Perrin, Bill Fairbanks, Fred Church and Eileen Sedgwick in *The Vanishing West*. In 1929, Mascot had been the first to release a chapter-play in both silent and sound versions when it came up with a non-Western serial named *King of the Kongo,* starring Walter Miller. The first Western cliff-hanger to be issued with and without sound was Universal's *The Indians Are Coming,* which also boasted an impressive cast that included Allene Ray, Tim McCoy, Ed Cobb, Francis Ford and Bud Osborne.

After the arrival of sound pictures, Mascot brought an excellent serial into production called *The Phantom Empire,* which contained a combination of Western theme and science-fiction. Released in 1934, it introduced a new singing cowboy star named Gene Autry, along with a cast that consisted of Smiley Burnette, Frankie Darro, Betsy King Ross, Wheeler Oakman and John Merton. That same year saw the arrival of an independently produced serial called *Custer's Last Stand,* which had

57

1. *(Left to right) "Big Boy" Williams, William Desmond and Bob Livingston in Republic's "The Vigilantes Are Coming" (1936)*

2. *Buck Jones and Russell Simpson in Columbia's "White Eagle" (1940)*

3. *Don Barry and Tommy (Little Beaver) Cook in "The Adventures of Red Ryder" (Republic, 1940)*

4. *Buck Jones, Noah Beery, Jr., Dick Foran, "Big Boy" Williams and Leo Carrillo in Universal's "Riders of Death Valley" (1941)*

5. *Ray (Crash) Corrigan faces up to LeRoy Mason and his henchman in "The Painted Stallion" (Republic, 1937)*

6. *(Left to right) Lane Chandler, Lee Powell, Herman (Bruce Bennett) Brix, George (Montgomery) Letz and Hal (Wally Wales) Taliaferro listen to Chief (Tonto) Thundercloud in "The Lone Ranger" (Republic, 1937)*

1.

4.

5.

6.

Rex Lease, Reed Howes, Bill Farnum, Dorothy Gulliver, Bobby Nelson, George Chesebro and Bill Desmond in leading roles. However, its production value was unfortunately below standards. The next important all-star serial was the previously-mentioned Republic release of 1937, *The Lone Ranger,* which was followed closely by *The Painted Stallion,* an action-packed thriller that had Ray Corrigan, Hoot Gibson, Jack Perrin, Julia (Jeanne Carmen) Thayer, Leroy Mason, Noah Beery, Sr. and Charlie King heading its cast. Finally, the last of the all-star serials came in 1941 when Universal released its "million-dollar production" *Riders of Death Valley,* with a cast headed by Dick Foran, Buck Jones, Leo Carrillo, "Big Boy" Williams, Noah Beery, Jr., Charles Bickford, Anne Gwynne, Monte Blue, William Hall, Lon Chaney, Jr. and Glenn Strange. After that, it seemed as though rising production costs were too high for studios to invest in expensive chapter-plays and a steady decline in popularity marked the closing of another era in motion picture history.

Having made their exit after forty-three years of providing countless thrills to screen audiences, the serials became a thing of the past when Columbia released *Blazing the Overland Trail* in 1956. It rang down the curtain on one of the most popular forms of motion picture entertainment—one which fans had come to identify as synonymous with spectacular thrills and excitement. Somehow, it seems sadly regrettable that the modern generations must do without the extra sensation of attending weekly cinema episodes where they could meet such fabulous characters as the serials brought us. Although they are all gone, those of us who saw them will never forget them. Despite the fact that we knew the hero would somehow escape unharmed through each episode, it was always comforting to see him give the villain his just reward at the conclusion of the last chapter. Briefly, most of us experienced moments of sadness when the finale flashed across the screen, bringing to an end a particular thriller that appealed to us. Fortunately, the following week always seemed to bring another exciting cliff-hanger that promised to be even more appealing. It is with a sense of nostalgia that some of us can look back and remember such colorful characters as "Craig Kennedy," "Tarzan," "Pauline," "The Lion Man," "The Riddle Rider," "White Eagle," "The Green Archer," "Hawk of the Hills," "Chandu," "The Eagle," "Flash Gordon," "Buck Rogers," "The Shadow," "Zorro," "The Spider," "Dick Tracy," "The Scorpion," "Red Ryder," "Frank Merriwell," "Jungle Jim," "Ace Drummond" and "Captain Marvel."

HOOT GIBSON (1892-1962)

Hoot Gibson was another perennial cowboy favorite of Western movies, whose career lasted for many years throughout the silent and sound eras of motion pictures. Sometimes called "The Dean of Cowboy Stars," he played a major part in modernizing horse-operas by breaking away from the old standards set by Bronco Billy Anderson and William S. Hart. Along with Tom Mix and Buck Jones, Hoot completely transformed Westerns into a new streamlined version of the old West.

He was born Edmund Richard Gibson in Tekamah, Nebraska on August 6, 1892. At the age of thirteen, he ran away from home to join a circus and wound up working as a cowpuncher in Wyoming and Colorado. In 1906, he took a job as a performer with the Miller 101 Ranch at Fort Bliss, Oklahoma until a year later when he started a four-year tour with the Dick Stanley-Bud Atkinson Wild West Show. After traveling throughout America and Australia, Hoot made his first motion picture appearance in 1911 as a player for Col. William Selig in *Shotgun Jones*. Having competed in rodeos ever since his youth, he found time to win the title of "World's Champion Cowboy" in 1912, adding to the many trophies he already had in his collection.

For the next few years, Hoot played in many one-reelers, but failed to gather any attention until 1916. By that time, his wife Helen (the former Helen Wenger, whom he had married in 1913) was on her way to fame as Helen Gibson, star of serials and Westerns. Almost simultaneously, Hoot hit the big time when Universal Studios starred him in a series of two-reelers which offered him a real chance at success. Suddenly, the U.S. entered World War I and in 1917 the cowboy left pictures to serve with the Tank Corps of the Army. He reached the rank of sergeant before being discharged in 1919, and then resumed his career in silent movies.

Returning to the Universal lot, Hoot became friendly with Harry Carey, who was then one of the studio's major stars. In 1921, Carey helped the young veteran land the lead in a picture called *Action*, which skyrocketed him to fame. Hoot Gibson went on to make dozens of features for Universal until he was regarded as one of the leading cowboy actors of the screen. By the mid-1920's, he was producing his own films under Universal distributorship and earning as much as $14,500 per week.

When time came for Hoot to make talkies, his association with

61

Universal had ended. He had suffered a bad year in 1929, when he lost a fortune in the stock market crash and witnessed the failure of his circus. In 1930, he started all over again by appearing in a list of independent features for companies like Allied, First Division and Diversion, while also starring in major Westerns for Warner Brothers. Along with Ken Maynard and Tim McCoy, he was the third important cowboy star to make pictures for both the major studios and the independent market. Although his films were turned out in quick succession, Hoot managed to keep some noticeable amount of production value in them. However, his chief interest was to make money and, unfortunately, this affected the overall quality of his Westerns. Even though he enjoyed his work, he lacked any emotional feeling for the real West and after being one of the top ten for many years, he took leave from picture-making to tour with a circus from 1936 to 1938. The following year, he retired.

In 1941, Hoot staged a comeback when Monogram Pictures co-starred him with Ken Maynard and Bob Steele in the *Trail Blazers* series. These features lasted until the latter part of 1943, at which time he returned to retirement. As a man of leisure, he spent his time managing his business affairs, which included the sub-division of his many real estate holdings in California. His last leading role was played in a Western comedy called *The Marshal's Daughter* in 1953. Six years later, he appeared in two minor parts in *The Horse Soldiers* and *Oceans 11,* before ill health forced him to undergo several serious operations. While being treated at the Motion Picture Country Hospital in Woodland Hills, California, Hoot Gibson died of cancer on August 23, 1962. His first marriage, which ended in 1920, had resulted in a daughter. Gibson's second wife was actress Sally Eilers and, after what seemed to be an ideal union, they were divorced in the late 1930's. Finally, on July 3, 1942, the cowboy star wed a young rodeo performer named Dorothy Dunstan at Las Vegas, Nevada.

During the peak of his fabulous career, Hoot had followed the style of Tom Mix in living an extravagant life. His flair for showmanship was evident even when he was off the screen. His taste for flashy automobiles and expensive clothes went hand-in-hand with his custom of throwing lavish parties and mixing with Hollywood's so-called "high society." Belonging to a lost era of glamorous stars earning high salaries, Hoot Gibson was among the leading personalities in the "Golden Age of Motion Pictures."

FILMS: *Shotgun Jones. The Hazards of Helen. Knight of the Range. The Cowboy Girl. Judge Not. Lass of the Lowries. Texas Sphinx. The*

Secret Man. Frustrated Holdup. Smilin' Guns. Burning the Wind. Bear Cat. Fire Eater. Headin' West. Step on It. Sure Fire. Trimmed. Riding Wild. The Gallopin' Kid. The Loaded Door. Lone Hand. Double Dealing. Gentleman From Arizona. Courtin' Calamity. Kindled Courage. Out of Luck. The Ramblin' Kid. Shootin' For Love. Single Handed. The Thrill Chaser. Hit and Run. Ride For Your Life. Sawdust Trail. Hook and Ladder. Broadway or Bust. 40 Horse Hawkins. The Ridin' Kid From Powder River. Taming the West. Spook Ranch. Saddle Hawk. Hurricane Kid. Let 'Er Buck. Calgary Stampede. Arizona Sweepstakes. The Phantom Bullet. Flaming Frontier. Chip of the Flying U. Man in the Saddle. Buckaroo Kid. King of the Rodeo. The Lariat Kid. Points West. Mounted Stranger. Winged Horseman. The Cactus Kid. The Texas Streak. Red Courage. Painted Ponies. The Last Outlaw. Hero on Horseback. Clearing the Range. Hard Hombre. Wild Horse. Cowboy Counsellor. A Man's Land. Swifty. Courtin' Wildcats. Trailing Trouble. Roaring Ranch. The Denver Dude. Hey Hey Cowboy. Silent Rider. The Texas Steer. Powdersmoke Range. Feud of the West. Frontier Justice. The Painted Stallion. Sonora Stagecoach. The Utah Kid. Marked Trails. Trigger Law. Wild Horse Stampede. Death Valley Rangers. The Marshal's Daughter. The Horse Soldiers. Oceans 11.

ROY STEWART (1884-1933)

Roy Stewart was another favorite among the pioneering cowboy stars of the early silent picture days. He was born in San Diego, California on October 17, 1884 and was later a student at the University of California, where he won a reputation for excelling in sports. After winning the West Coast single-sculls championship, he decided to take up an acting career by joining a stock company and appearing on the stage in a variety of productions. He performed as a member of the Pacific Coast "Floradora" troupe before finally entering moving pictures in 1915.

For his first year in films, Roy was active as a leading man opposite stars like Lillian Gish and Bessie Love, until 1916 saw him featured in the first all-Western serial, *Liberty, a Daughter of the U.S.A.* with Jack Holt and Marie Walcamp. His career took a turn for the better when Triangle Productions signed him to star in a series of Western features which brought him success and popularity. By 1918, he was among the most important players on his studio's roster where he remained active for a period of four years.

In 1921, Hollywood was undergoing a slump in movie production and many actors found themselves unemployed. Having left Triangle Studios, Roy went to work for the independent companies like Majestic, American, Fine Arts, Radio and Sunset, turning out an equally large number of films. He then organized his own Roy Stewart Productions, releasing his pictures under Universal's label and also finding time to star in that studio's first ten-episode serial in 1922.

A tall, husky athlete, Roy was ideally suited for the cowboy heroes he portrayed on the screen. He could ride and fight with the best of them and he developed a genuine fondness for horses and outdoor roles. When the talkies arrived, he was active in pictures for Pathe Studios, but the revolutionary movement to sound caused him to turn character actor. His last few years in movies saw him as a supporting player before he died at the age of forty-nine in 1933.

FILMS: *Liberty, a Daughter of the U.S.A. The Law's Outlaw. Boss of the Lazy Y. Paying His Debt. By Proxy. Untamed. The House Built on Sand. Daughter of the Poor. Faith Endurin'. The Doll Shop. Keith of the Border. The Fugitive. Cactus Crandall. Radio King. Wolves of the Border. Silent Raider. Back to the Yellow Jacket. Innocent Cheat. Life's Greatest Question. A Motion to Adjourn. One Eighth Apache. Burning Words. Love Brand. Lady From Hell. With Gen. Custer at Little Big Horn. Kit Carson Over the Great Divide. Buffalo Bill on the Union Pacific Trail. With Daniel Boone Through the Wilderness. Sundown. Pure Grit. Fighting Gringo. The Viking. In Old Arizona. Lone Star Ranger. Men Without Women. Mystery Ranch. Come on Tarzan. Fargo Express. Zoo in Budapest.*

LESTER CUNEO (1888-   )

Lester Cuneo was born in Oklahoma in 1888, when it was still known as Indian Territory. After attending the Northwestern University he took up acting and appeared on the stage until 1909, when he was hired to direct some early one-reel flickers for Col. William Selig. When Selig pioneered the film industry's move to California in 1906, Cuneo went along as a player and director. Five years later, he joined the Essanay Film Company for which he acted and directed in a series of short films known as the *George Ade Comedies*. At that time, G.M. (Bronco Billy) Anderson, part owner of Essanay, was ruling the movie industry with his Westerns. Along with a few others, Cuneo became one of the early pioneers of cowboy pictures.

During World War I, Cuneo entered the U.S. Army and went overseas to France, where he saw service until the Armistice in 1918.

Returning to America in 1919, he resumed his career in the movies by starring in a number of silent features for Metro and building himself a reputation for playing tough, red-blooded characters in Westerns. Since he had been raised on the real frontier, he had no trouble portraying heroes of the range.

In the early 1920's, Cuneo was starring in a series of five-reel features for producer Ward Lascelle. After that, he made pictures for Fox, Realart and Capital before finally turning to character roles. By the late 1920's, he was regarded as one of the screen's leading villains until the talkies put an end to his career.

FILMS: *George Ade Comedies. Graustark. Mr. 44. Big Tremaine. Pidjin Island. Haunted Pajamas. Under Handicap. Paradise Garden. Love Me For Myself Alone. Blue Blazes. Food For Scandal. Masked Avenger. Blazing Arrows. The Ranger and the Law.*

JACK HOXIE (1890-1965)

No list of cowboy stars would ever be complete without the name of Jack Hoxie. For years this Western favorite held his fans spellbound with a score of action-packed features in both the silent and talkie eras. He was born in Oklahoma on January 24, 1890 and learned to ride a horse while he was still very young. Hoping to make a better living, his father took the family to live in Iowa, where the boy took a job as soon as he was able to work. When he was not busy laboring as a farmhand, he competed in rodeos and became the proud winner of at least a dozen trophies before he reached the age of eighteen.

After being awarded the title of National Riding Champion in 1914, Hoxie accepted an offer to appear with a Wild West Show that toured the U.S.A. Eventually, he wound up in California where he made his debut in motion pictures as a stuntman in 1917. Using the name of Hartford Hoxie, he gradually rose to more important parts until he was finally given his first starring role in a silent serial called *Lightning Bryce* in 1919. Scoring a success, he then signed a contract with independent producer Anthony Xydias, who changed his name to Art Hoxie and gave him the leads in a group of fast-moving features.

In 1921, Universal Studios decided to enlarge its growing stable of Western stars and offered Hoxie a chance at being associated with a major company. Taking the name of Jack Hoxie, he graduated to five-reel features and quickly rose to fame along with other Universal cowboys such as Harry Carey, Hoot Gibson, Peter Morrison and Neal Hart.

Being adept at handling action came comparatively easy to him since he had a genuine background as a cowhand.

With the arrival of talking pictures, Jack Hoxie's career was momentarily interrupted while the movie industry reorganized itself. He took the time to tour the country with a circus and did not return to picture-making until 1932. After completing a few good features with sound for Universal, it became increasingly evident that Jack was poorly suited for talkies. He performed well when it came to riding and fighting, but his ability to handle scripts or dialogue was sorely lacking. Some critics even went as far as to label him illiterate. No matter what the reason, Jack was through in movies.

After making his last picture in 1934, he formed a partnership with Cly Newton and organized the Jack Hoxie Circus in 1937. He then spent a year of personal appearances all over the U.S.A., before he finally retired from public life and went to live with his mother on his spacious ranch in Oklahoma. Except for a few loyal fans who will always remember him, Jack was completely forgotten and was never heard of again. He died in Oklahoma in 1965.

FILMS: *Lightning Bryce. Dumb Girl of Portici. Thunderbolt Jack. Backfire. The Forbidden Trail. Men of Daring. Barbed Wire. Two Fisted Jefferson. Desert's Crucible. Don Quickshot of the Rio Grande. Crow's Nest. The Double O. Men in the Raw. Where Is the West? Red Warning. Galloping Ace. Western Wallop. Daring Chances. Ridgeway of Montana. Fighting Fury. Back Trail. Man From Wyoming. Phantom Horseman. White Outlaw. Sign of the Cactus. Open Trail. Roaring Adventure. Riding Thunder. Two Fisted Jones. Hidden Loot. Flying Hooves. Bustin' Thru. Don Daredevil. The Demon. Border Sheriff. Lookin' For Trouble. Fighting Peacemaker. Wild Horse Stampede. Red Hot Leather. Six Shootin' Romance. The Last Frontier. Heroes of the Wild. Phantom Express. Law and Lawless. Gold. Via Pony Express. Gun Law. Trouble Buster. Rough and Ready. The Fighting Three. Outlaw Justice.*

BUCK JONES (1891-1942)

On the afternoon of November 28, 1942, cowboy star Buck Jones had been a special guest of the city of Boston, Massachusetts, where he attended a parade and Thanksgiving season football game. Nearing the end of a War Bond tour, he celebrated the signing of a new contract with Monogram Studios that evening at a Boston nightclub called the "Coconut Grove." Suddenly, a fire broke out which took the lives of nearly 500 people and two days later, Jones died of burns received in that disaster. Thus perished one of Hollywood's most beloved screen personalities.

Buck was born Charles Frederick Gebhart at Vincennes, Indiana on December 12, 1891, the son of Charles and Evelyn Showers Gebhart. While still a boy, he was nicknamed "Buck" (which derived from Chuck) after he had been tossed by a cantankerous mule. His father having taken the family to live on a ranch near Red Rock, Oklahoma, Buck became an expert with horses at an early age. At sixteen, he decided to strike out on his own and went to Indianapolis, where he worked as a mechanic on the early racing cars. Shortly afterwards, he opened his own garage but went bankrupt four months later. At seventeen, he joined the U.S. Army, received his training at Nogales, Arizona, and saw action on the Mexican border with the Cavalry at the time when Pancho Villa and his revolutionists were terrorizing the area.

On completing his first three-year hitch, Buck re-enlisted and was sent to the Philippines, where he fought in the Moro Insurrection. While in the Philippines, he was wounded in the thigh by a sniper and sent back to the States to recover. In 1913, discharged from the Army with the rank of top sergeant, he returned to Oklahoma to work for the famous Miller 101 Ranch. When the Miller family decided to organize the "101 Ranch Wild West Show," Buck became one of the featured trick riders that toured with the outfit all over the country.

It was while appearing with the show at Madison Square Garden, New York in 1914 that Buck met a circus rider named Odelle Osborne, daughter of a New York civil engineer. On August 11, 1915, they were married in the ring during an actual performance at Lima, Ohio. A year later, Buck went to Indianapolis where he took a job as a test driver for the Stutz Motor Company until he was offered more money to train horses for the French government in Chicago. In 1917, after accumulating enough to start his own circus, he toured the Northwest. He later accepted an offer to perform with the famous Ringling Brothers Circus.

While the show was in California, Buck was forced to quit due to his wife's pregnancy. Therefore, he decided to try the movies. At first, he worked as a $5-a-day extra at Universal Studios, gradually rising to featured parts. Then he became a stuntman for the Fox Studios, where he graduated to stardom. In 1919, William Fox, head of the Fox Company, decided to add a new cowboy star to his list when he gave Buck his first leading role in a film called *The Last Straw*. At that time Tom Mix was Fox's most important celebrity, but Mix was constantly demanding more money and the producers thought that a possible substitute would keep him in line. What they had not figured on

1. *Jack Hoxie*
2. *Roy Stewart*
3. *Buck Jones*
4. *Leo Maloney is having a rough time showing Billy Butts who is boss*
5. *Hoot Gibson*
6. *Lester Cuneo*

1.

4.

2.

5.

6.

was that Buck Jones would become such a big hit. By 1921, Mix and Jones were the two biggest money-makers at Fox and both stars were hot after William S. Hart's crown as "King of the Westerns."

Although Tom Mix was a more flamboyant showman, Buck remained his closest competitor throughout the 1920's and, by 1928, even surpassed him. For eight years, Buck made pictures for Fox, each one a profit-making success. In 1928, he set out to produce his own films. But the untimely arrival of talkies forced him to postpone his plans. The following year, having lost a fortune in the stock market crash and in an unsuccessful circus venture, he returned to the film capital to make a series of Westerns for producer Sol Lesser at a fraction of the salary he had received at Fox. In 1931, Buck started his association with Columbia Studios, making action features until 1934, when he joined Universal as a producer-director and star of his own movies. By that time, he was the "King of the Cowboys" and one of the leading personalities of the screen.

During the years that followed, Buck starred in films for Universal, Columbia, Paramount and Republic. But the arrival of the singing cowboys caused a major change in Westerns that seriously affected his position. By 1940, he was no longer listed among the top ten. In 1941, he started a new series for Monogram called *The Rough Riders,* which co-starred Tim McCoy and Ray Hatton. These features were well-received by the public and the trio of old-timers held their own despite stiff competition from the musical cowboys.

Having completed his last picture, *Dawn on the Great Divide,* Buck undertook the Bond-selling tour which ended in his tragic death. On December 7, 1942, various delegates attended the high Episcopal services at the Washington Boulevard Chapel in Hollywood, where the flagdraped casket containing the star's remains was commemorated before cremation. During a career that had spanned twenty-three years, Buck had averaged eight pictures per year and had never been linked with a scandal of any kind. He held the rare distinction in Hollywood of having been married to only one woman throughout his life and was the proud father of a daughter, Maxine, who wed cowboy actor Noah Beery, Jr. in 1940. Being extremely loyal to his younger fans, Buck had often played host to his "Buck Jones Rangers" fan club, an organization which once boasted of its 4,000,000 members.

Among the most appealing features of Buck Jones' pictures was the presence of his white stallion, Silver. An animal of high intelligence, the horse seemed to sense when the camera was focused on him and he would perform at the drop of a hat.

Another highlight of Buck's pictures was his ability to inject humor into his roles without seeming ridiculous. Unlike most cowboy stars, he often poked fun at himself rather than at a sidekick. He was among the first to break away from the grim, poker-faced heroes continuously portrayed by William S. Hart, and the fact that he once received more fan mail than matinee idol Clark Gable is a proper example of the wide popularity he enjoyed.

FILMS: *The Last Straw. Firebrand Trevision. Square Shooter. Just Pals. Sunset Sprague. Trail of Two Moons. The Big Punch. One Man Trail. Riding With Death. Get Your Man. Straight From the Shoulder. Roughshod. Fast Mail. Bells of San Juan. Boss of Camp Four. Hell's Hole. Snowdrift. Trooper O'Neill. Footlight Ranger. Crimson Trail. Second Hand Love. Skidproof. Big Dan. Cupid's Fireman. Western Luck. Vagabond Trail. Against All Odds. Winner Take All. The Man Who Played Square. Gold and the Girl. Hearts and Spurs. Timber Wolf. Lazybones. Durand of the Badlands. Gentle Cyclone. Outlawed Guns. For the Service. Fighting Buckaroo. Cowboy and the Countess. Thirty Below Zero. Branded Sombrero. War Horse. Silver Valley. Lone Rider. Sandflow. When a Man Sees Red. Ranger of the Big Pines. Dawn Trail. The Avenger. The Cowboy and the Kid. Empty Saddles. Range Feud. Ride 'Em Cowboy. Boss of Gun Creek. White Eagle. Hello Trouble. McKenna of the Mounted. Sundown Rider. California Trail. Black Aces. Stone of Silver Creek. Border Brigands. Sunset of Power. High Speed. Child of Manhattan. Gordon of Ghost City. Rocky Rhodes. The Roaring West. Stranger from Arizona. Phantom Rider. Unmarried. Wagons Westward. Riders of Death Valley. The Rough Riders. Arizona Bound. Gunman from Bodie. Forbidden Trails. Ghost Town Law. Down Texas Way. West of the Law. Dawn on the Great Divide.*

LEO MALONEY (1888-1929)

Leo Daniel Maloney was born in San Jose, California in 1888 and was educated at Santa Clara College. He made his motion picture debut in 1914, when the industry was still in its infancy. As a star for the Mutual Film Corporation, he appeared in a group of serials and features in which he displayed a zest for outdoor adventure roles.

By 1920, Leo had finished his association with Mutual and began a period where he made pictures for various independent producers that included Nestor, N.Y.M.P., Signal and Steiner. After that, he became exclusively connected with Pathe Films and reached the peak of his career. While he was with that organization, Leo produced, directed, wrote and starred in a score of pictures which were classified as being well above the average horse-opera. While seeking to avoid unnecessary violence, he managed to make interesting films without detracting from the action. His popularity throughout the 1920's was due to the fact that he could captivate his audiences with exciting screen adventures. Since Pathe had one of the largest stables of cowboy stars on its payroll, the competition was keen, but Leo managed to hold his place without too much effort. His best movie role was undoubtedly in Mascot's super-serial of 1928, *The Vanishing West*, which also boasted of a cast that included Jack Daugherty, Jack Perrin and Yakima Canutt.

In 1929, Leo was arranging for the release and distribution of his first all-talking picture, *Overland Bound*, in which he again appeared with Jack Perrin, when he died suddenly in New York City at the age of forty-one.

FILMS: *The Girl and the Game. Whispering Smith. Medicine Bend. Diamond Runners. Lost Express. Railroad Raiders. Judith, Lass of the Lumberlands. Overland Disaster. A Fight For Millions. Arizona Catclaw. His Enemy's Friend. One Jump Ahead. The Fatal Sign. Under Suspicion. 100% Nerve. Manager of the B and A. Double Cinched. Perfect Alibi. Payable on Demand. Riding Double. Not Built For Running. King's Creek Law. Headin' Thru. Huntin' Trouble. Loser's End. Across the Deadline. Win, Lose or Draw. Outlaw Express. Luck and Sand. The High Hand. Smoked Out. The Extra Seven. Trouble Buster. Border Blackbirds. The Devil's Twin. The Long Loop. Don Desperado. The Man From Hardpan. Two Guns of Tumbleweed. The Vanishing West. Law and Order. Fire Detective. Overland Bound.*

JACK PERRIN (1896-)

Jack Perrin was born at Three Rivers, Michigan on July 26, 1896. When he was six years of age, his family moved to Los Angeles, California, where he received his education. After leaving school, Jack entered motion pictures as a bit player in some of the early Mack Sennett comedies, rising steadily to bigger and better roles until 1917, when he won the leading part in a film entitled *Toton the Apache*. Soon after that, he entered the U.S. Navy and saw service with the submarine force during World War I.

Returning to Hollywood after the war, Jack scored a successful comeback in films when Universal hired him to play the male lead in a chapter-play called *The Lion Man* in 1919. His stature as an actor rose to new heights when critics singled out his performance in a movie called *Pink Tights* in 1920, which established him as a first-rate artist.

He was then called upon to star in several important features before he decided to accept an offer from the Rayart Company to make Westerns. Later, he became associated with Universal, Pathe and F.B.O. successively, starring in dozens of outdoor adventures and serials that made him a leading contender for the roster of Hollywood's most popular cowboy stars.

When talkies arrived, Jack experienced little ill-effects in his career on the screen, for his voice seemed well suited for sound pictures. He completed a series for First National Studios and, in 1928, co-starred in Mascot's super-serial *The Vanishing West* opposite Jack Daugherty, Yakima Canutt and Leo Maloney. His next work on the screen was a series of action features that had him portraying Canadian Mounted Policemen, which delighted his fans to a high degree. His work seems to have been equally distributed among independent producers and Universal during those early years of talking pictures. Having made films for Aywon, Rayart, Albee and Hodkinson, he was then given the lead in Universal's first serial to be released in both silent and sound versions, *The Jade Box*.

During the early 1930's, Jack teamed up with screen comic Ben Corbett in order to make a series of three-reel Westerns for Astor Pictures. Known as the "Bud and Ben Westerns," these short featurettes became extremely popular with fans all over the country and enabled Jack to remain active at a time when most film performers were seeking to ward off unemployment. Later, he was employed as the star of a long list of features for Big Four, Syndicate and Reliable, all independent releases which somehow lacked the production value of his earlier work. In 1936, Jack appeared in his last series as a star when he made a string of Westerns for producer William Berke under the banner of Atlantic Pictures. After 1938, he became involved in character roles, remaining active until his eventual retirement during the early 1940's.

An able performer, Jack took pride in his choice of stories for his Westerns. In spite of the fact that most of them were done for independent producers, he strived to keep them up to standards and disliked the tired overdone scripts on which most horse-operas depended. Having started his screen career at a time when the majority of performers did all their own stunt work, he obtained his share of injuries while making dangerous scenes. For awhile, he featured himself with his wonder horse, Starlight, a beautiful white steed that had a few tricks of its own.

FILMS: *Toton the Apache. Pink Tights. Blind Husbands. The Lion Man. Harvest of Hate. Hoofbeats of Vengeance. Plunging Hoofs. Santa Fe Trail. Beyond the Rio Grande. Fighting Skipper. Trails of Danger.*

73

Riders of the Plains. The Lone Horseman. Border Vengeance. Coyote Fangs. Gray Devil. Starlight's Revenge. A Ridin' Gent. Man From Oklahoma. West of the Rainbow's End. Hijacking Rustlers. Double Fisted. Ridin' Law. Overland Bound. Girl Trouble. Loser's End. The Cactus Kid. Wolf Riders. Rawhide Mail. Texas Jack. The Vanishing West. Fire and Steel. North of Arizona. Border Ranger. Song of the Gun. Thunderbolt Tracks. Romance of the West. Rainbow Riders. Phantom of the Plains. A Real Pal. '45 Calibre Echo. Hellfire Austin. The Kid From the West. Lariats and Six Shooters. Hair Trigger Casey. Gun Grit. Wildcat Saunders. Desert Justice. Dynamite Ranch.

"LEFTY" FLYNN (1890-   )

Maurice Flynn was born in 1890 and became a graduate of Yale University, where he won nation-wide popularity as a top athlete in football, baseball and track. After completing his education, he turned to professional football, becoming one of America's foremost gridiron stars. In 1921, he accepted an offer from producer Sam Goldwyn to enter motion pictures as the star of some outdoor adventure films. When these had been completed, Goldwyn proceeded to feature Flynn in a series of melodramas, which proved unsuitable for the actor-athlete. With the background and ability to handle rough action, Flynn expressed his desire to return to adventure roles. After some convincing, Goldwyn finally agreed that his new star was more at home in outdoor features and proceeded to give "Lefty" the kind of parts he wanted. For the next four years, movie fans were treated to a steady diet of Flynn's he-man characterizations in dozens of Goldwyn films.

During the mid-1920's, Lefty ended his association with Goldwyn to work for the Fox Film Studios. His reputation as a virile, outdoor type was carried through in a number of pictures that saw him as a cowboy. It was then that he really hit his stride, as he portrayed the rugged man of the West at ease with nature and at home in the saddle. His pictures high-lighted his excellent physical prowess, making use of his rough exterior appearance and gentle manner. His fans enjoyed many exciting moments when they chanced to witness exceptional films like *Breed of the Border, Glenister of the Mounted, Roughshod* and a smashing hit serial called *The Golden Stallion.*

Shortly after the talkies came into being, Lefty found his career on the decline. Producers wanted stage actors with trained voices for talking pictures and, therefore, many silent film players were let go. For awhile, he took parts as a character actor, gradually descending to smal-

74

ler roles until he retired from the screen around 1934. Like many other Western stars, he seemed to have completely disappeared from public view. On the other hand, his list of fine films remains as a legacy to his many fans.

FILMS: *The Silver Horde. Going Some. The Great Accident. Officer 666. Just Out of College. Roads of Destiny. Smiles Are Trumps. Bucking the Line. The No Gun Man. Breed of the Border. Speed Wild. High and Handsome. The Traffic Cop. Sir Lumberjack. Smilin' at Trouble. The College Boob. Glenister of the Mounted. Dangerous Curves Ahead. Night Rose. Voice of the City. Roughshod. O. U. West. Salomy Jane. Drums of Fate. Oathbound. Omar the Tentmaker. Snow Bride. The Golden Stallion. Open All Night.*

NEAL HART (1887-   )

Neal Hart was another cowboy star of the screen who could boast of an authentic Western background. Born in Wyoming in 1887, he spent some time as a cowpuncher before working as a performer with the Miller "101 Ranch Wild West Show." Like several other top riders who had found the Miller organization a means of entering the movies, Neal followed in the footsteps of Tom Mix, Buck Jones and Bud Osborne by accepting an offer to play in Westerns for Universal Pictures. Making his debut in 1915, he starred in some two-reelers which enabled him to astonish his fans with his expert horsemanship. Big and husky in physique, he found it easy to fill the boots of a cowboy hero.

In 1916, Neal's big break came when Universal decided to feature him opposite Jack Holt and Marie Walcamp in a chapter-play entitled *Liberty, a Daughter of the U.S.A.* The first serial to have a completely Western theme, it was one of the most successful cliff-hangers of that period. Since Universal was then the source of the top serials, Neal found himself in an ideal position. Billed as "America's Pal," he was given the lead in a series of outdoor features that made him popular throughout the country. He gained enough stature to allow him to leave Universal and to produce and star in his own productions.

By the late 1920's, Neal's career had passed it zenith. He made several cheap productions for independent outfits like Anchor and Sunset before finally retiring from the screen at the arrival of the talkies. After a brief tour of the United States, he tried a couple of unsuccessful comebacks but the fans had already forgotten him.

FILMS: *Liberty, a Daughter of the U.S.A. West of the Pecos. Rangeland. Butterfly Range. The Lure of Gold. Left Hand Brand. South of the Northern Lights. Tucker's Top Hand. The Scarlet Brand.*

FRED THOMSON (1890-1928)

Christmas night, December 25, 1928, saw the end of one of film-dom's most beloved personalities when Fred Thomson died after a short illness. His passing marked the finish of a career that had lasted a mere six years, yet, had reached the point where he had become the idol of millions all over the world.

Frederick Clifton Thomson was born in Pasadena, California on February 26, 1890, the son of Reverend and Mrs. Williel Thomson. He entered Occidental College in Los Angeles and graduated with a B.A. degree in 1910. An excellent athlete, Fred participated in college football, baseball and track and took first place in the National Track and Field competition in 1910 with a total score of 7,009 points. The following year, he repeated his victory by winning with 6,709 points.

While attending the Princeton Theological Seminary, Fred took part in the Track and Field events at Princeton, New Jersey in the Spring of 1913 and shattered the great Jim Thorpe's world record by scoring 7,499 points. This record withstood until Fred's own brother, S. Harrison Thomson, topped it in 1921.

After being ordained a Presbyterian minister in the latter part of 1913, Fred was appointed pastor of the Hope Chapel in Los Angeles. That same year, he married a girl named Gail Dubois Jepson. In 1915, the couple traveled to Goldfield, Nevada, where Fred served as pastor of the local Presbyterian church and was appointed the State Commissioner of the Boy Scouts. After a short illness, his wife died in 1916 and the young minister decided to enter the U.S. Army as chaplain of the 143rd Field Artillery Regiment at Camp Kearney, San Diego, California. It was during an inter-service exhibition football game that he broke a leg and was forced to recuperate in an Army hospital bed. During his confinement, he met visiting actress Mary Pickford and screenwriter Frances Marion, who were greatly impressed by the cheerfulness and good looks of the young invalid. After his recovery, Fred went to France with his regiment when World War I was still raging strong.

Following the Armistice in 1918, Fred was detached to the inter-Allied Athletic games where he and his brother took first and second place in the hand-grenade throwing event. Returning to the U.S., Fred resumed his friendship with Frances Marion, which blossomed into marriage in September, 1919. While living in California, he met some of his wife's movie friends who coaxed him into entering motion pictures. In 1921, he left the ministry and made his screen debut the following year as the leading man opposite Mary Pickford in *The Love Light*. After that, Fred was launched into stardom when Universal gave him the lead in a serial entitled *The Eagle's Talons*.

Having started as a performer earning $2,000 per week, Fred Thomson made a long list of Westerns for F.B.O. Studios until he ranked among the top five cowboy stars of the silent screen. Although he received offers from several major companies, one for as much as $17,000 per week, he decided to organize his own Fred Thomson Productions. Needless to say, his athletic ability proved to be a valuable asset when making his thrill-packed features. Like Tom Mix, Fred knew that his fans came to see him perform spectacular stunts and he made sure to give them what they wanted. His pictures always highlighted his acrobatics, as he characterized the noble, humane type of hero who possessed a genuine fondness for animals. Featured with Fred was his horse, Silver King, who gave performances just like any other member of the cast.

On the technical side of film-making, due to his deep scientific interest, Fred Thomson was regarded as an expert on lenses and lighting techniques. Many professional cameramen sought his advice and his pictures were noted for their fine quality of photography and trick optical effects.

During the 1920's, Hollywood was in its heyday and movie stars lived up to their reputations as kings and queens of the entertainment world. Fred was no different. He bought a fabulous estate on the heights of Beverly Hills. It reportedly cost him $650,000 and included a luxurious twenty-room mansion. Next to the house was an adjoining $25,000 stable where the star kept his famous horse and a pet bull named "Pansy."

Shortly after completing his last picture, *Jesse James*, for Paramount, Fred fell seriously ill during the early part of December, 1928. He died on the night of the 25th, at the age of thirty-eight, and was survived by his wife, two sons (Fred, Jr. and Richard), his mother and a brother. He was buried at Forest Lawn Memorial Park, Los Angeles, California.

FILMS: *The Love Light. The Eagle's Talons. The Mask of Lopez. Silent Stranger. Dangerous Coward. The Fighting Sap. Galloping Gallagher. North of Nevada. Thundering Hooves. Quemado. Wild Bull's Lair. The Bandit's Baby. That Devil Quemado. The All Around Frying Pan. Riding the Wind. Tough Guy. Two Gun Man. Lone Hand Saunders. Kit Carson, Pioneer Scout. Desert Legion. Arizona Nights. Don Mike. Silver King Comes Through. Silent Valley. The Sheriff of Tombstone. Sunset Legion. A Regular Scout. Hands Across the Border. Jesse James.*

1. *Edmund Cobb seems to have finally caught villain Paul Hurst*

2. *"Lefty" Flynn*

3. *Bill Fairbanks*

4. *Neal Hart*

5. *Fred Thomson*

6. *Jack Perrin (at right) comes to the rescue of a young pal*

1.

4.

5.

6.

BILL FAIRBANKS (1889-   )

Although the roster of cowboy stars seems endless to the movie fan, only a handful of names ever really hit the big time. Most of the others achieved comparatively milder success simply because their films lacked real production value. Among those who worked strictly for the independent producers was William Fairbanks. Throughout the 1920's, he seemed to have accepted the fact that he would never reach the top rung of the popularity ladder but, nevertheless, was content with the secondary degree of fame that he achieved.

Bill was born in St. Louis, Missouri around 1889 and went West at an early age. His work experience extended from that of being an Oklahoma cowpuncher to riding the rodeo circuit as far north as Oregon. Around 1919, he entered motion pictures as a stuntman and bit-player and, after two years, rose to the position where he was playing leads in a series of action features for Arrow Productions. Although cheaply made, the majority of his films never lacked excitement due to his capabilities as a rider and roper. Compared to Tom Mix or Hoot Gibson, his career as a star was short, but he was able to chalk up a number of Westerns to his credit under the banners of Arrow, Anchor and Sunset Productions.

In 1926, Bill made a few features for Columbia, but his most important role came in 1928 when he appeared in Mascot's super serial *The Vanishing West*. After that, the arrival of the talkies seems to have steadily diminished his popularity until he had completely disappeared from the screen by 1932.

FILMS: *Hell's Border. Peaceful Peters. Devil's Door Yard. Marry in Haste. Spawn of the Desert. Law Rustlers. Do It Now. Sheriff of Sundog. Sundog Trails. Tainted Money. Speed Mad. Great Sensation. The Winning Wallop. The Mile a Minute Man. A Fight to the Finish. The Handsome Brute. New Champion. Vanishing Millions. Through Thick and Thin. The Vanishing West. Spoilers of the West. Under the Black Eagle. Western Demon. The Western Adventure.*

EDMUND COBB (1892-   )

Edmund Fessenden Cobb was born in Albuquerque, New Mexico in 1892, grew up on a ranch and became an expert horseman by the time he was sixteen. On learning that movie-makers were searching for real cowboys in California, he went to the West Coast and made his debut as a bit player in 1910. It was during those early years of motion pictures that Ed made appearances in one-reelers for companies like Essanay, Selig and Mutual. In 1913, he was featured in the history-making serial *The Adventures of Kathlyn.*

By 1918, Arrow Productions were starring Ed Cobb in a series of two-fisted Westerns that earned him a reputation for being one of the most exciting cowboy stars on the silent screen. Two years later, he graduated to bigger productions when Universal placed him under contract, making a long list of features for that company until the arrival of talkies. From there, Ed went to work for various independent producers. He continued as a star of Westerns until the early 1930's, after which he resorted to character roles.

For many years, Ed could be seen in horse-operas as a villain. But he was too familiar a figure to remain in that type of undesirable role. Producers started giving him better parts as a sheriff or a deputy, much to the relief of Ed's loyal fans. As a supporting player, he made too many film appearances to list in this short biography, but most of his activity was in Westerns for Republic, Monogram, R-K-O, Universal, Columbia and United Artists. His career terminated when he retired in 1952, but the long list of pictures he left behind is a fine tribute to a wonderful performer.

FILMS: *The Adventures of Kathlyn. Sting of the Scorpion. At Devil's Gorge. Western Yesterdays. Rodeo Mixup. Range Blood. Fighting With Buffalo Bill. The Days of '49. The Strange Case of Mary Page. The Indians Are Coming. Twin Fates. Money to Burn. Western Feud. Fangs of Destiny. Four Footed Ranger. Gunners and Guns. Fighting Forester. The Missing Juror. Law of the Valley. Cherokee Flash. Song of Arizona. In the Days of Buffalo Bill. Roaring Ranger. The Last Frontier. Rustler's Roundup. Prairie Schooners. Rusty Rides Alone. Red River Renegades. Deadwood Pass. Lone Trail. Santa Fe Uprising. The El Paso Kid. Tangled Fortunes. Stagecoach to Denver. Comanche Territory.*

WALLACE MACDONALD (1891-   )

Wallace MacDonald was born in Mulgrave, Nova Scotia, Canada in 1891. Having received his education in Canadian schools, he entered upon an acting career by playing in summer stock, until he answered the call of military service in 1916 and joined the British Army. After seeing action in France during the First World War, he returned to America where he continued his career on the stage. In 1919, Wallace made his debut in motion pictures by becoming a featured player for

81

1. *Art Mix*
2. *Wally Wales*
3. *Wallace MacDonald*
4. *Bill Patton*
5. *Reed Howes*
6. *Jack Daugherty*

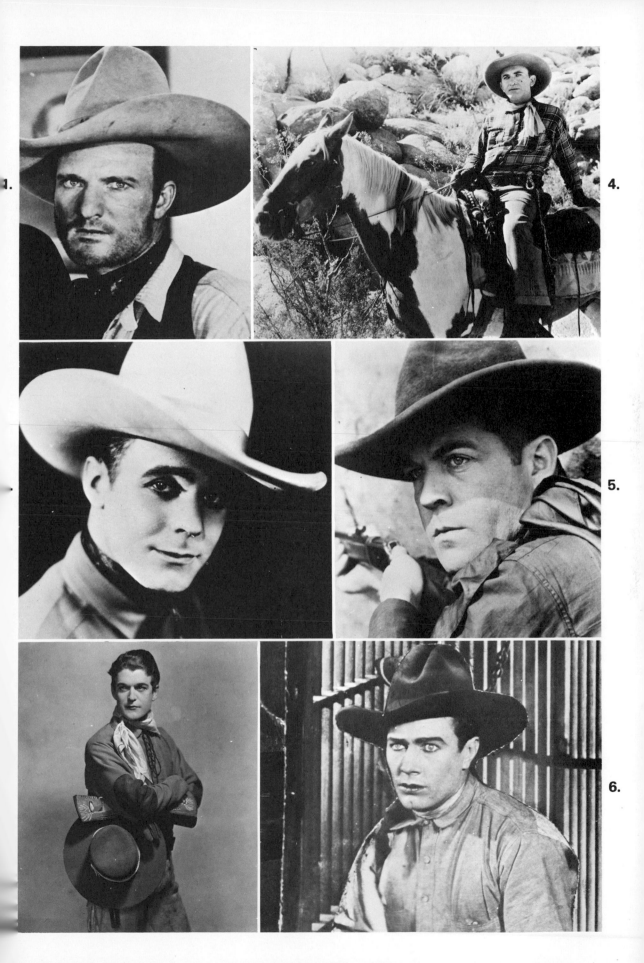

1.

4.

5.

6.

the Triangle Studios. After completing a few films, he joined producer Samuel Goldwyn and starred in a series of melodramas, until he was offered a contract with the Vitagraph Company.

During the early 1920's, MacDonald was cast for the most part in mysteries and romantic dramas. Not until 1925 was he given the opportunity to star in outdoor adventures. That year, he signed with Pathe Studios and made several exciting serials and Westerns which completely changed his career in movies. Possessing the athletic ability for rugged action, he soon became associated with cowboy roles for companies like Pathe, Universal, First National and Metro.

For several years before the arrival of the talkies, Wallace was enjoying a measure of popularity from his Westerns. When sound came to the movies, he went through a period of unemployment and then made a comeback as a character actor. By the mid-1930's, he had abandoned acting in favor of writing for the screen. In 1935, Wallace became a supervisor of writers at Republic Studios, a new company which had been formed by the merger of Lone Star, Mascot and Consolidated. The following year, he left Republic to work as a writer and producer at Columbia Pictures, where he has been active ever since. Leaning more toward Westerns, he has produced such films as *The Nebraskan, Apache Ambush, White Squaw, Phantom Stagecoach, Return to Warbow* and *Gunmen From Laredo.*

Looking back on MacDonald's career in motion pictures, one can only come to the conclusion that his years of hard work contributed a great share towards the success of his movies. Having gone from romantic actor to cowboy star, and from writer to producer, he certainly has earned a place in this book.

FILMS: *Marked Cards. The Shoes That Danced. Mlle. Paulette. The Saintly Showgirl. Madame Sphinx. Princess of Park Row. Next Door to Nancy. An Investment in Petticoats. The Checkered Flag. Two Can Play. The Bar C Mystery. Hell's 400. Casey of the Coast Guard. Fighting With Buffalo Bill. Breaking Thru. Whispering Smith Rides. The Spoilers. Day of Faith. Thy Name Is Woman. Maytime. The Sea Hawk. Darkened Rooms. Sweetie. Fancy Baggage. Gunmen From Laredo.*

JACK DAUGHERTY

Among the dozens of stars who reached the heights of fame through the Serials was a young athlete named Jack Daugherty. He had first entered motion pictures somewhere around 1920, after having spent several years in vaudeville and stock. During the early part of his career in films, he had been cast as a romantic leading man without too much fanfare. It was in 1923 that he came into his own after appearing with Ruth Roland in a Pathe serial called *Haunted Valley*.

Signed to an exclusive contract with Universal Studios, Jack rose to stardom quickly, reaching a high degree of popularity through a series of spellbinding chapter-plays and action features. By 1928, he and William Desmond were ranked as Universal's top serial stars. For the most part, Jack made his fortune chiefly from Westerns. It was while he was playing cowboy roles that he seemed to be at his best. Unfortunately, he arrived at a time when the roster of sagebrush heroes was at its peak, thus accounting for a career that was cut short by the arrival of the revolutionary talkies. He did, however, manage to appear in a few sound features, but his popularity waned until he finally decided to retire in the early 1930's. Among his best-known films were *The Vanishing West, Haunted Valley, The Body Punch* and *Scarlet Streak.*

FILMS: *Haunted Valley. Fighting Ranger. Scarlet Streak. Trail of the Tiger. Radio Detective. Haunted Island. The Firefighters. Perils of the Range. The Vanishing West. The Body Punch. Special Delivery. The Iron Man.*

REED HOWES (1901-1964)

To thousands of movie fans, Reed Howes was a familiar figure in the collegiate films of the 1920's and the Westerns of the 1930's. Born around 1901, he started out as an actor in stock companies and vaudeville before entering motion pictures in 1923. It was in that year that he was acclaimed "The Handsomest Man in America," after winning a nation-wide search for the "Arrow Collar Man." His photograph appeared in periodicals all over the country, advertising the man in the Arrow shirt.

Brought to Hollywood by a talent scout, Reed made his debut as a star for F.B.O. following a big publicity campaign. For the remainder of the 1920's, he appeared in dozens of films as the handsome young leading man of the "flaming youth" era. In 1927, one of his most important roles was in *Rough House Rosie* opposite Clara Bow. Although he had made several Westerns earlier, he really broke away from his "pretty boy" image in 1930, when he starred in one of the last silent serials, *Terry of the Times*. By then, Reed had completed a number of pictures for F.B.O., Rayart, Arrow, Sono-Art, Paramount and Warners.

Having established himself in the talkies, Reed was given the leads in a series of action features for the major studios in Hollywood. He eventually wound up at Republic, where he chalked up over fifty full-length films and serials. By the late 1930's, he was usually seen as the hero's closest pal. When the 40's rolled around, Reed turned to less likeable characters, playing villains opposite Republic's impressive stable of cowboy stars. He was active until ill health forced him to retire around 1950. He died on August 6, 1964.

FILMS: *Lightning Romance. Youth's Gamble. The Snob Buster. Cyclone Cavalier. Gentle Cyclone. Wings of the Storm. Racing Romance. The Self Starter. Kentucky Handicap. Night Owl. The High Flyer. Dangerous Dude. The Danger Quest. Moran of the Mounted. High Speed Lee. Come Across. Stolen Kisses. Super Speed. Bobbed Hair. The Devil on Deck. Rough House Rosie. Terry of the Times. Custer's Last Stand. A Million to One. Zorro's Fighting Legion. Zorro Rides Again. Six Gun Rhythm.*

ART MIX

Although the name "Art Mix" was well-known to Western fans from the early 1920's to the late '40's, it was quite controversial and caused lots of confusion. To begin with, the first actor to appear on the screen as Art Mix was a silent screen player named Victor Adamson, who produced and starred in a series of Art Mix Westerns during the early 1920's. Shortly afterward, Adamson became popular as Denver Dixon while another player named George Kesterson took over the title Art Mix. Later, still another actor appeared with the name on the screen for the Adamson productions. But for the sake of avoiding confusion, it was Kesterson who kept the name throughout his career.

Kesterson had been hired by Adamson in 1924 to succeed him in a group of silent action features about "Art Mix." After some contract difficulties, Kesterson abandoned the original series to make another group of films for producer J. Charles Davis, using the same name. Although there were damage suits and counter-suits in the courts, Kesterson remained on the screen as Art Mix. Due to a combination of poor productions, lack of public interest and no particular appeal, his career as a cowboy hero was short-lived and he was soon forced into outlaw roles. The late 1920's saw him menacing such stalwart heroes as Hoot Gibson, Don Coleman and Buddy Roosevelt before the arrival of talkies caused a temporary lapse in his career. When sound pictures became established, he continued to oppose the leading Western stars such as Tom Tyler, Bob Steele and Ken Maynard. His activity in "hoss-operas"

86

continued until the late 1940's, after which he completely disappeared from the screen.

FILMS: *Ace of Cactus Range. Below the Border. South of Santa Fe. Sagebrush Trail. Fighting Ranger. Powdersmoke Range. Blinky.*

BILL PATTON

Born in Amarillo, Texas, Bill Patton was no stranger to the saddle when he entered motion pictures in 1924. He was raised on a ranch, worked as a cowpuncher, rode wild broncos on the rodeo circuit and performed with a Wild West show before finally ending up in Hollywood. For awhile, he stood among the dozens of real cowboys who tramped from studio to studio trying to earn a day's pay by playing a bit part in Westerns. He started out by taking obscure roles in non-important features, gradually rising to leading parts in independently produced two-reelers for the Tennek Corporation. In 1926, Bill went to work for F.B.O. as the star of some comedy Westerns which did fairly well at the box-office. A natural-born clown, he was able to inject humor into his characterizations of a Western hero without losing his dignity and, although he never rose to great heights as a star, managed to continue his successful career well into the 1930's.

By the time the talkies had overtaken the film industry, Bill had played leads in dozens of Westerns for F.B.O., Radio, Capital, Chesterfield and Universal. After 1931, he turned to character roles, usually as a comedy sidekick or as a villain. He gradually descended into the realm of bit players again, lasting until the late 1930's.

FILMS: *The Last Chance. Lucky Spurs. Western Trails. Under Fire. Beyond the Trail. Freckled Rascal. One Man Dog. Below the Deadline. The Flying U Ranch. The Pinto Kid. Strawberry Roan. Five Badmen. Desert Mesa.*

HAL (WALLY WALES) TALIAFERRO (1895-)

This rip-roaring bronc-buster of the screen was born in Sheridan, Wyoming on November 13, 1895 and was christened Floyd T. Alperson. Raised on a ranch, he acquired a skill with horses that landed him a job as a wrangler for the famous Three Circle Ranch. From there, he went to work for the Brown Land and Cattle Company in Montana until 1916, when he made his debut in motion pictures as an "extra." Spotted by cowboy star Tom Mix, he was given a few featured roles in

Westerns and had all the earmarks of becoming a big name in horse-operas until World War I changed all that.

Entering the U.S. Army, Floyd served with the American Expeditionary Forces in France during 1917-18, returning home after the Armistice to resume his career in the movies. He succeeded in getting a few acting assignments at Universal until 1924, when a producer at Pathe changed his name to Wally Wales and starred him in a series of Westerns that went over big with cowboy fans. With his authentic background and a genuine talent for handling action, Wally rose to the ranks of the most prominent heroes of the sagebrush. He became one of Pathe's biggest money-makers during the 1920's, making pictures that highlighted his riding skill and performing daring stunts that continually delighted his fans.

When the talkies arrived, the change had no apparent effect on Wally's career because he continued making Westerns throughout the transition period. He did, however, end his association with Pathe Studios and went to work for independent film-makers such as Artclass, Rayart and Arrow Productions. Although somewhat lacking the production value of his Pathe features, these pictures were fairly well done and, as a whole, were highly entertaining.

About 1936, Wally started realizing that his career as a star was practically at an end since he had spent a couple of years as a supporting player. Changing his name to Hal Taliaferro, he resorted to character parts which kept him equally active for the many years that followed. His last important role was in Republic's classic serial of 1937, *The Lone Ranger,* in which he appeared with Lee Powell, Herman Brix, Lane Chandler, George (Montgomery) Letz and Chief Thundercloud. After that, he was more familiar to Western fans as an outlaw in dozens of features and serials for Republic, Monogram, Universal, Columbia, Warners and United Artists.

Having retired around the late 1950's, he left behind an almost endless number of screen credits. To those who were fortunate enough to see him perform, either as Wally Wales or Hal Taliaferro, he will never be forgotten.

FILMS: *Twisted Triggers. Double Daring. Riding Rivals. Vanishing Hooves. Tearin' Loose. The Fighting Cheat. Galloping On. Desert of the Lost. Hurricane Horseman. Soda Water Cowboy. Meddlin' Stranger. Cyclone Cowboy. Skedaddle Gold. Tearin' into Trouble. Saddlemates. Trail of Danger. White Pebbles. Carrying the Mail. Arizona Cyclone. Lone Rider. Law and the Lawless. Roaring Ranger. Heir to Trouble. Powdersmoke Range. Gun Play. Hair Trigger Casey. The Traitor.*

Avenging Waters. Red Fork. Riders of the Cactus. Hell's Valley. Black Bandit. Guilty Trails. Flying Buckaroo. Bar L Ranch. Canyon Hawks. Overland Bound. The Lone Ranger. Cherokee Strip. Colorado. Border Legion. Red River. The Fallen Angel. Ramrod. Brimstone. The Savage Horde. West of Sonora. Junction City.

FRED GILMAN

Unfortunately, Fred Gilman never quite made the grade as a star of full-length Western features. Similar to other screen cowboys, he was agile enough to handle himself well in action scenes and he was an accomplished rider. But he was limited to playing leads in a series of shorter featurettes for Universal called *Mustang Westerns.* Nevertheless, Fred scored well above average in these snappy little thrillers of the late 1920's. His pleasing personality and good looks proved advantageous in a field that was highly competitive.

After starring in the "Mustangs" from 1926 to 1929, Fred finally graduated to full-length features by playing supporting roles opposite Universal's top echelon stars such as Hoot Gibson, Ken Maynard and Fred Humes. He managed to keep active until the mid-1930's, remaining a familiar figure in hoss-operas for various studios until his retirement around 1936.

FILMS: *Dangerous Waters. The Night Riders. God's Law. The Outlaw and the Lady. Roped and Tied. Lonesome Luck. Naked Fists. Forgetting the Law. Blinky. Senor Daredevil. Man in the Saddle.*

PEE WEE HOLMES

Pee Wee Holmes first made his entrance into motion pictures around 1924 playing "The Clown of the Saddle," a title that he considered flattering. Having risen from the ranks of cowpunchers who sought to strike it rich in the movies, he was a former daredevil rider with a circus. When film producer W. C. Tuttle hired him to star in a series of Westerns, Holmes jumped at the chance to gain recognition through the flickers. A skilled horseman, he astonished his audiences with a never-ending bag of stunts until his name became fairly prominent during the 1920's.

Having started his career in two-reelers, Holmes eventually graduated to full-length features for Universal Studios. His flair for comedy blended well with his skill for handling action and, much to the delight of his younger fans, he was able to continue his success as a star right up

1. *Bob Reeves*
2. *Fred Gilman*
3. *"Pee Wee" Holmes*
4. *Tom Tyler*
5. *Fred Humes*
6. *Buffalo Bill, Jr.*

1.

4.

5.

Sincerely Fred Gilman

6.

until the arrival of the talkies. By 1929, he had finally turned to character roles, supporting more prominent names at studios like Paramount, Universal, Fox and Warners. After 1935, he dropped out of sight and was never heard of again.

FILMS: *One Horse Play. Double Cinched. When Fighting's Necessary. Right of Way Casey. A Fight For a Mine. Sunset Pass.*

TOM TYLER (1903-1954)

One of Hollywood's most tragic stories is that of Tom Tyler, who rose from the depths of the Pennsylvania coal mines to become a champion athlete and an all-time great among cowboy stars, then died in desolate poverty. He was born Vincent Markowski at Port Henry, New York, on August 9, 1903 and raised in Detroit, Michigan, where he attended school. While still in his youth, he struck out on his own by taking a job as a miner in Pittsburgh, Pennsylvania, but after awhile decided to give that up in favor of working as an able-bodied seaman aboard a tramp steamer. During the years that followed, he spent some time as a professional football player, lumberjack, prizefighter and sculptor's model before he finally entered motion pictures as a bit player and stuntman in 1924.

While playing a small part in the 1925 screen version of *Ben Hur,* Tom was spotted by an agent for F.B.O. Studios, who recognized him as a potential leading man for action features. For years, he had been a prominent weight-lifter and his marvelous physique fitted well into cowboy costumes. Signed to an F.B.O. contract, Tom made his debut as a Western star in *Galloping Gallagher* and was an instant hit. Meanwhile, his activities in athletics had not been overlooked, for he established a new world's record in weight-lifting in the Senior Heavyweight Class (unlimited) by lifting a total of 760 pounds in 1928. As the years rolled by, Tom was to remain a champion weight-lifter for fourteen years with several of his record-breaking lifts going unbroken.

By 1929, Tom Tyler and Bob Steele were considered F.B.O.'s most important cowboy stars. But the arrival of talking pictures caused the firm to be reorganized into another company called R-K-O. In 1931, Tom made his first all-talking Western, *West of Cheyenne,* for an independent outfit known as Syndicate Pictures. It marked the beginning of his association with independent producers such as Reliable, Freuler, Bell and Victory, and although these features were not quite up to the standards of his earlier films for F.B.O., they were extremely good in action content. In spite of working for these individual producers, Tom was constantly employed and his turn-out of pictures even exceeded that of some of the major cowboy stars. During the early 1930's, he found time to include a few hair-raising serials to his credit which also went over big with his thousands of fans. But when R-K-O made the mistake of casting him as a misguided outlaw opposite Harry Carey, Bob Steele, Hoot Gibson and Big Boy Williams in *Powdersmoke Range* in 1935, his fans protested violently that the unsympathetic role was not in keeping with his usual heroics. After that incident, Tom returned to his customary characterizations by starring in a series of features for Universal, which were followed by another string of Westerns at Monogram.

In 1939, Tom played another unusual role in John Ford's classic *Stagecoach,* opposite John Wayne, when he took the part of the villainous "Luke Plummer." Although it was a comparatively small assignment, Tom deemed it a pleasure to work for the award-winning director and his performance was a vital one. However, this departure from likeable roles was again only temporary for, in 1941, Tom joined Republic Studios where he replaced Bob Livingston as "Stony Brooke" in the popular *Three Mesquiteers* series alongside his old pal, Bob Steele, and comedian Rufe Davis. To top this, he was chosen to star in a serial entitled *The Adventures of Captain Marvel,* which became one of the most successful chapter plays ever produced.

From 1941 to 1943, Tom appeared in thirteen "Mesquiteers" features at a time when the famous cowboy trio was listed among the ten most popular Western heroes. If one were superstitious, the number of these films that Tom made might signify something for, immediately after the series ended in 1943, he was taken seriously ill and was forced to remain out of pictures for over two years. When he returned, he was a mere shadow of his former self and it became visibly evident to his fans that his sickness had taken a heavy toll. Reduced to taking minor roles as a cowboy villain, Tom's career descended rapidly to the point where he was included among the ranks of film extras who live from day to day hoping to get some small acting assignment. Finding himself badly crippled with arthritis, ill and penniless, Tom left the movie colony where he had once earned a fortune as a top-notch action star and went to live with a sister in the Hamtranck section of Detroit, where he died of a heart attack on May 1, 1954. Once married to his leading lady, Jeanne Martel, Tom was one of the dozens of cowboy performers who lacked the foresight to reserve the television exhibiting rights to his old pictures. Had he done so, he would have reaped a fortune when TV revived his features for home viewing. Regardless of his tragic ending, Tom Tyler will forever be remembered by the thousands of film fans who were fortunate enough to see him on the screen.

FILMS: *The Only Thing. Ben Hur. Galloping Gallagher. Masquerade Bandit. Cowboy Musketeer. Born to Battle. Arizona Streak. Red Hot Hoofs. Out of the West. Wide to Go. Cowboy Cop. Gun Law. The Sonora Kid. Lightning Lariats. Phantom Rider. Pioneers of the West. Man From Nevada. Lone Horseman. 'Neath Western Skies. Law of the Plains. Canyon of Missing Men. Call of the Desert. Idaho Red. Pride of Pawnee. Man From New Mexico. Three Weeks. When a Man Rides Alone. Deadwood Pass. Cheyenne Rides Again. Fast Bullets. Riding With Buffalo Bill. Roamin' Wild. The Last Outlaw. The Forty Niners. Honor of the Mounted. Phantom of the Air. Clancy of the Mounted. Phantom of the West. Rio Rattler. Jungle Mystery. War of the Range. Single Handed Saunders. Riders of the Plains. Feud of the Trail. Powdersmoke Range. Brothers of the West. Rip Roarin' Buckaroo. Orphan of the Pecos. Stagecoach. Gone With the Wind. Grapes of Wrath. The Adventures of Captain Marvel. Outlaws of Cherokee Trail. Gauchos of Eldorado. West of Cimarron. Code of the Outlaw. Raiders of the Range. Westward Ho. Phantom Plainsmen. Shadows on the Sage. Valley of Hunted Men. Thundering Trails. Blocked Trail. Santa Fe Scouts. Riders of the Rio Grande. The Phantom. The Mummy's Hand. The Younger Brothers. Valley of the Sun. Trail of Robin Hood. Badman's Territory. Blood on the Moon. I Shot Jesse James. Cow Country.*

"BUFFALO BILL, JR." (1902-)

Jay Wilsey was born in Cheyenne, Wyoming in 1902 and, by the time he reached the age of eighteen, he had already won his first rodeo trophy. While working as a cowpuncher, he acquired great skill as a horseman and trick roper and always took time to appear at rodeos where he usually came away with some prize money. After following the rodeo circuit throughout Wyoming, Colorado, Texas and Canada, he accepted an offer to perform with a Wild West show that toured the U.S.A. In 1921, he entered motion pictures as a featured player for Artclass Productions and was gradually promoted to starring roles in a series of Westerns under the name of Buffalo Bill, Jr.

As a cowboy star, Bill appeared in many features for independent producers such as Artclass, Rayart and Arrow but, in 1924, he left that field to join Pathe Studios where his brand of pictures greatly improved. With increased production value, better direction and bigger budgets, his films took on more lustre and he became one of the upcoming personalities of the screen. By 1926, he was starring in Westerns for Universal, producing and directing many of his own features while thrilling his fans with a steady diet of action and excitement.

94

Despite the stiff competition from the large array of cowboy stars on the screen during the 1920's, Bill managed to hold his own by turning out a group of highly entertaining films. He had no difficulty in making the change from silent to sound pictures, although the switch did cause him to return to the independent market. His career as a star lasted until about 1933, after which he turned to character roles. His last important part on the screen was in R-K-O's all-star Western of 1935, *Powdersmoke Range,* which contained an impressive cast that included Harry Carey, Bob Steele, Hoot Gibson, Tom Tyler and "Big Boy" Williams. After that, Bill appeared as a supporting player in a few more features until his retirement in 1938.

FILMS: *Rarin' to Go. Hard Hittin' Hamilton. Fast and Fearless. On the Go. Quicker Than Lightnin'. Deuces High. Trumpin' Trouble. Speedy Spurs. Saddle Cyclone. Desert Demon. Streak of Luck. Rawhide Romance. Bonanza Buckaroo. Galloping Gobs. Rawhide. Badman's Bluff. Ballyhoo Buster. Interferin' Gent. Pals in Peril. Obliging Buckaroo. Riding Rowdy. Lady From Hell. The Texan. Riders of Golden Gulch. Lightning Bill. Riding Speed. Union Pacific Trail. The Fighting Comeback. Pirates of Panama. Final Reckoning. Through the Wilderness. Rainbow Valley. Powdersmoke Range. Daniel Boone.*

BOB REEVES (1899-)

Bob Reeves is another example of how quickly some cowboy stars of the screen were forgotten completely. At one time, he had been starring in Westerns for independent companies before his popularity declined, forcing him to turn character actor and gradually descending to bit roles.

Not much is known of his history except that he came into motion pictures around 1920, after having been a noted rodeo and circus performer. By 1922, he was playing leads in silent horse-operas for the Anchor Distributing Corporation, a series of films which lacked production value but contained plenty of action. A little while later, he became associated with independent producers releasing pictures through the Rayart Corporation which fortunately added more quality to his features. Although an able performer, he lacked something in personality and failed to go over with Western fans.

Bob appeared in a few serials besides the string of feature-length films he made at Rayart, but he never rose to the ranks of the major stars. By the time the talkies came, he was already playing villains opposite some of the bigger names in Westerns. He was last seen in 1939 por-

95

traying a badman in a Johnny Mack Brown feature, *The Son of Roaring Dan.*

FILMS: *Fighting Luck. The Iron Fist. Narrow Escape. Riding For Life. Desperate Chance. The Son of Roaring Dan.*

FRED HUMES

Fred Humes was another cowboy star who came on the scene at an inopportune time and, as a result, lasted only a few years on the screen. Having first achieved fame as an expert rider with rodeos and Wild West shows, he made his entrance into motion pictures around 1923, when he took bit parts in Westerns and also filled in as a stunt-man. A year later, he was working at Universal Studios supporting Hoot Gibson in several features and serials until the front office decided to try him out as a lead.

By 1926, Fred was starring in a series of five-reelers for Universal called the "Blue Streak" Westerns, which caught on quickly with the public. Despite the fact that these films were quickly made and lacked any real production value, the action content was sufficient to warrant another string of features with a little more class. Fred was quite capable of performing his own stunts and, although he never reached major status as a cowboy star, he did manage to turn out some good action pictures. At the time that he reached the peak of his career, Westerns were going into a slump. However, it was only a short while before the horse-operas came back with renewed vigor, as the screen introduced a host of new heroes.

Having made many features during his stay at Universal, Fred endured his success throughout the late 1920's and, when the talkies arrived, he switched to character roles, continuing in that capacity until he retired from the movies in the early '30's.

FILMS: *Hurricane Kid. Smilin' Sam. Loco Weed. True Blue. Prowlers of the Night. The Yellow Back. Stolen Ranch. One Man Game. Duke of Black Buttes. The Border Cavalier.*

GEORGE O'BRIEN (1900-)

George O'Brien was born in San Francisco, California on April 19, 1900, the son of Margaret Donohue and police chief Daniel O'Brien. While he was a student at Polytechnic High, he excelled in all kinds of sports, especially boxing, football and baseball. When the U.S. entered

World War I, he joined the Navy, finding time to win the light-heavy-weight boxing championship of the Pacific Fleet before being released from the service in 1919. After studying medicine at Santa Clara College, he took part in a few school dramatics and decided to become an actor.

In 1922, George's father was in charge of escorting visiting cowboy star Tom Mix, when their meeting turned out to be the start of a new career. Tom helped George get a job at Fox Studios as an assistant cameraman and later hired him for stunt work in his own productions. After awhile, George graduated to featured roles in a number of pictures for Fox. In 1924, director John Ford selected him to play the lead in an epic Western called *The Iron Horse,* which elevated him to stardom.

As a major contract player at Fox Studios, George was starred in dozens of first-grade films throughout the 1920's. But he was not yet considered to be a Western idol. He made several fine cowboy features, but the majority of his pictures were a combined variety of action-dramas and he was regarded more as an all-around he-man during the silent movie period of his career. He had a special talent for handling rugged parts and possessed a strong, powerful physique. Many times, he was referred to by publicity agents and gossip columnists as "The Chest."

Even though George had made his reputation as a virile, manly hero, he proved he could act in heavy dramas when given the chance, particularly in 1927 when he appeared with Janet Gaynor in *Sunrise.* Directed by F. W. Murneau, and also featuring Margaret Livingston, *Sunrise* turned out to be a screen classic. Another example of George's dramatic ability came two years later when he was loaned out to Warner Brothers for the lead in *Noah's Ark,* a screen spectacle with a biblical background that was regarded as one of the best of 1929.

By 1931, talkies had definitely replaced silent movies and George left Fox Studios to join the new R-K-O organization. It was with R-K-O that he made himself known in Westerns and quickly became the studio's top cowboy star. Having occupied second place for several years, George remained on the list of top ten sagebrush heroes from 1932 to 1940. He could play a two-fisted lumberjack, a tough sailor or a gallant Canadian Mountie with equal vigor, but always retained a devil-may-care attitude which his fans admired. Like his colleagues Buck Jones and Hoot Gibson, George could add humor to his roles without losing dignity and he often seemed to play his parts with tongue-in-cheek.

When the Japanese bombing of Pearl Harbor brought the U.S. into World War II, George took leave from motion pictures to accept a commission in the Navy and serve in another war. Absent from the screen for five years, he made a short comeback in 1946, only to retire in 1950 to work as a film supervisor for the U.S. Government. In 1965, he returned to motion pictures when his old friend, director John Ford, gave him a role in *Cheyenne Autumn*. In private life, George was divorced from actress Marguerite Churchill in 1949 and is the father of a grown son.

FILMS: *The Iron Horse. The Man Who Came Back. Painted Lady. The Dancers. The Roughneck. Fighting Heart. The Johnstown Flood. Rustling for Cupid. Fig Leaves. Blue Eagle. Three Bad Men. Silver Treasure. Havoc. Is Zat So? Thank You. Sunrise. Paid to Love. Rough Romance. The Golden West. East Side West Side. Sharpshooters. Noah's Ark. Salute. Blindfold. Honor Bound. Masked Emotions. True Heaven. Lone Star Ranger. Last of the Duanes. The Seas Beneath. Holy Terror. Gay Caballero. Mystery Ranch. Robber's Roost. Smoke Lightning. Life in the Raw. The Last Trail. O'Malley of the Mounted. Hard Rock Harrigan. Cowboy Millionaire. Park Avenue Logger. Daniel Boone. When a Man's a Man. Hollywood Cowboy. The Windjammer. Tall Timber. The Painted Desert. Renegade Ranger. Lawless Valley. Border G-Man. Arizona Legion. Gun Law. Fighting Gringo. Legion of the Lawless. Marshal of Mesa City. Racketeers of the Range. Trouble in Sundown. Timber Stampede. Triple Justice. Stage to Chino. Prairie Law. Bullet Code. The Dude Ranger. Whispering Smith Speaks. The Rainbow Trail. Shine on Harvest Moon. Fort Apache. Cheyenne Autumn.*

"BIG BOY" WILLIAMS (1900-1962)

Guinn Williams was born in Decatur, Texas on April 26, 1900. He attended the Decatur Military Academy before becoming a student at the Texas Normal University. His father, a U.S. Congressman, had wanted him to be a lawyer, but an active interest in sports sidetracked him from his course when he sought a career as a professional baseball player. After practically being disowned by his dad, Guinn left home in order to lead his own life, wandering to California while working at odd jobs.

It was in 1919 that he entered movies as a bit player in a Will Rogers film called *Almost a Husband*. Impressed by his size and talent, Rogers nicknamed the young newcomer "Big Boy" and helped him get along further in his career. The name stuck to Williams for the rest of his life and he never forgot the kind and generous help Rogers had given him.

After appearing in supporting roles for Goldwyn, Pathe, Universal

98

and Fox, Big Boy finally reached stardom in 1922, when he started making Westerns for the Al Film Corporation. An independent company, Al Film kept him busy for a few years with no less than thirty-six features. By the time talkies came around, he was playing in comedies with his old friend, Will Rogers, with whom he was associated for two years. During the early 1930's he was actively employed as a cowboy star in Westerns and as a comedy support in major productions.

Big Boy played his last leading roles in a series of horse-operas in 1935, making his final bow as a star in *Powdersmoke Range* in which he shared top billing with Harry Carey, Bob Steele, Hoot Gibson and Tom Tyler. After that, he resorted to character parts in dozens of films for Universal, Republic, Columbia, R-K-O and Warners. He was a familiar figure to movie fans and displayed an unusual flair for comedy. While versatile enough to take a variety of roles, he was better known for his portrayals of a confused but happy-go-lucky cowhand. When producers tried to cast him as a villain, audiences reacted by refusing to accept Big Boy in anything but "good guy" roles. His infectious grin and likeable personality were too well-known for him to play heavies, so he continued to portray the hero's pal in many pictures. Among his many screen appearances, Big Boy gave his best performances in rip-roaring Westerns. But he also showed his skills as an actor in top-grade films like *Swamp Water* and *Dodge City*.

Besides taking part in feature pictures, he entered the field of television in 1960 by playing opposite Noah Beery, Jr. in a series called "Circus Boy." His long career in films came to an end when he died of uremic poisoning at his home in Van Nuys, California on June 6, 1962.

FILMS: *Almost a Husband. Polly of the Circus. Quarantined Rivals. Western Firebrands. Trail of Hate. Across the Border. Blazing Away. Rounding Up the Law. Freshie. End of the Rope. Cyclone Jones. Red Blood and Blue. Whistling Jim. Noah's Ark. Lightnin'. Ladies of the Jury. 70,000 Witnesses. Driftin' Soul. Dulcy. Singin' in the Corn. Black Cyclone. Rex, King of the Wild Horses. Rose of the Desert. Brown of Harvard. Blackmail. Slide Kelly Slide. Burning Daylight. The Big Fight. From Headquarters. Lucky Star. Vanishing Venus. My Man. City Girl. Forward Pass. College Widow. Lucky Boots. The Avenger. Cowboy Holiday. Big Boy Rides Again. Danger Trails. Our Daily Bread. Mystery Squadron. Thunder Over Texas. Law of the '45's. Powdersmoke Range. Heritage of the Desert. Belle of the Yukon. The Marines Are Here. Phantom Broadcast. The Vigilantes Are Coming. Dodge City. The Fighting 69th. Virginia City. Swamp Water. Castle on the Hudson. Al Jennings of Oklahoma. Rocky Mountain. Man in the Saddle. Five Bold Women. Springfield Rifle. The Alamo. Hangman's Knot.*

BUDDY ROOSEVELT (1898-)

Buddy Roosevelt was born in Meeker, Colorado on June 25, 1898. He was educated at schools in Massachusetts, then traveled West, working at a variety of jobs as a salesman, ranch-hand, lumberjack and miner. In 1922, he landed in the movies as a bit player, gradually rising to leading roles in 1924, when he starred in Westerns for Artclass Productions. A year later, he joined Pathe Studios, where he made a string of features and serials which earned him a degree of popularity with cowboy fans.

After completing his films for Pathe, Buddy went to work for Universal making features that combined his flair for comedy with a natural skill for handling action. By 1927, he was among the more notable cowboy stars of the silent screen and was actively participating in pictures for Universal, Associated Exhibitors and Paramount. As a whole, his films contributed a good share in keeping up with the standards of the Western. Yet, the untimely arrival of sound brought his career as a star to an end.

Buddy played leads in a few talkies for an organization called Superior Pictures until 1933, then reverted to supporting roles. Since then he has been active as a character player in Westerns for various studios.

FILMS: *Rarin' to Go. Walloping Wallace. Biff Bang Buddy. Rough Riding. Battling Buddy. Rip Roarin' Roberts. Reckless Courage. Gold and Grit. Hoodoo Ranch. Tangled Herds. Thundering Thru. Action Galore. Galloping Jinx. Twin Triggers. Easy Going. The Dangerous Dub. Bandit Buster. Code of the Cow Country. Fighting Comeback. Phantom Buster. Between Dangers. Ride 'Em High. Pals in Peril. The Fourth Horseman. Trail Riders. Circle Canyon. Mystery Valley. The Riding Kid. Devil's Tower. Wild Horse Mesa. Boss Cowboy. Powder-smoke Range. Fury at Showdown. Flesh and the Spur.*

DON COLEMAN (1897-)

During the history of motion pictures, many stars of the silver screen experienced a meteoric rise to fame for a brief period, after which they plunged into obscurity. Another cowboy actor that went through such a career was Don Coleman. He was born in the mid-West around 1897 and raised on a ranch, where he learned his skill at riding and roping at an early age. After a few years of competing in rodeos, he won

100

a handful of trophies for trick riding and was engaged to go on tour with a circus.

Without any previous experience, Don made his entrance into motion pictures in 1924, when he was hired to make a series of cheap, low-budgeted horse-operas for an independent producer. It wasn't until two years later that he became associated with Pathe Studios, where he graduated to films of a higher calibre. These features were fast little Westerns produced in a limited time, but placing their importance on Don's ability to handle action well. Although his personality was pleasing enough, he never quite made the grade to major status. By the time he had reached stardom, the movies were swamped with newcomers. In spite of this, Don made an impressive list of Westerns for Pathe and enjoyed a sizeable measure of popularity throughout the silent film era.

By 1930, the talkies were definitely established and most of the theatres in the country were equipped to show sound pictures. Having barely survived the transition, Don Coleman starred in a few more Westerns before he turned to character roles in 1932. A year later, he vanished from the screen and was never heard of again.

FILMS: *The Bronc Stomper. The Black Ace. '45 Calibre War. Rough Riding Country. The Lost Trail. Saddles and Guns.*

BOB CUSTER (1898-)

Bob Custer was born in Frankfort, Kentucky, on October 18, 1898. Not much is known about his early life, except that he worked as a cowpuncher and performed in rodeos as a trick rider. In 1924, he made his first appearance in motion pictures when he started a series of Westerns for F.B.O. An excellent horseman, Bob seemed to fit well in the role of a cowboy hero and his films enjoyed success throughout the 1920's.

When the coming of the talkies ended his association with F.B.O., he starred in action features for independent producers like Bell, Syndicate and El Dorado, and later began his career in talkies by making a series for Big Four Productions. In these tight little sound Westerns, the plots were good and the action was not overdone. After two years with the company, Bob left Big Four in 1932 to make two chapter plays for Mascot. These turned out to be his best work on the screen. The serials were called *The Adventures of Rin Tin Tin* and *Law of the Wild* and featured the dog star, Rin Tin Tin, Jr. and Rex, King of the Wild Horses. The productions were smash hits and gave Bob's career a much-needed boost. By 1936, Reliable Pictures was featuring Bob in a new series of

101

1. *Yakima Canutt*
2. *Don Coleman lands a right to the jaw of badman Bud Osborne*
3. *"Big Boy" Williams*
4. *George O'Brien helps Irene Hervey make a getaway*
5. *Bob Custer*
6. *Buddy Roosevelt (at left) seems a bit outnumbered by Charles "Slim" Whittaker (in black hat) and his henchmen*

1.

2.

4.

5.

6.

cowboy films and serials. To take advantage of the team's previous drawing power at the box-office, the producers again combined the cowboy star and Rin Tin Tin, Jr. in a feature entitled *Vengeance of Rannah*. After that Bob's career lasted until his retirement from the screen in 1938.

Although he had been active for many years and had never reached the heights of the all-time greats, his horsemanship and fighting ability thrilled his fans and enabled him to attain a permanent place in the Western Hall of Fame.

FILMS: *Flashing Spurs. Range Terror. Texas Bearcat. That Man Jack. The Bloodhound. No Man's Law. A Man of Nerve. Beyond the Rockies. The Ridin' Streak. The Fighting Boob. Man Rustlin'. Dude Cowboy. Border Whirlwind. Hair Trigger Baxter. The Deadline. Valley of Bravery. Galloping Vengeance. Cactus Trails. Last Roundup. The Fighting Terror. Riders of the Rio Grande. Parting of the Trails. Code of the West. Covered Wagon Trails. O'Malley Rides Alone. The Oklahoma Kid. Arizona Days. Law of the Mounted. The Adventures of Rin Tin Tin. Mark of the Spur. Quick Trigger Lee. Scarlet Brand. Law of the Wild. Vengeance of Rannah. Santa Fe Rides. Ambush Valley. The Prowler. Will of the North. Loose Rein. Yucca Bar. Blood Trail. Polka Dot Bandit.*

YAKIMA CANUTT (1896-)

One of the most admired and respected members of the movie industry, Yakima Canutt has certainly earned his high place among the cowboy favorites of the screen. His work in pictures, both in front and behind the cameras, has been of great value and there certainly is no doubt that he contributed a large share toward the advancement of the Western.

Yakima was born Enos Edward Canutt in Colfax, Washington on November 29, 1896. Contrary to popular belief that he was a full-blooded Indian, he came from Scottish, Irish, Dutch and German descent. It was because of his many Indian portrayals on the screen that fans believed him to be genuine.

Canutt first learned to ride and rope while he was still a boy and, by the time he was thirteen, he was working as a ranch-hand. At seventeen, he joined a Wild West show, touring the country as a trick rider and roper and participating in rodeos at every opportunity. In a short time, he had a collection of trophies that was the envy of all cowboys. In 1917, he won the title of "World's Champion All-Around Cowboy" and held it for seven consecutive years. In addition, he was awarded the coveted Police Gazette Cowboy Championship Belt in 1917, 1918, 1919, 1921 and 1923, besides winning the famous Roosevelt Trophy for 1923, thus becoming one of the greatest rodeo cowboys of all time.

In 1924, Canutt made his motion picture debut in a film called *Romance and Rustlers* for the F.B.O. Studios. After that, he starred in a number of Westerns for independent companies such as Arrow, Bell, Big Four, Syndicate and Goodwill. Shunning the use of doubles for his action scenes, he performed all his own tricks and thus branched off into stunt work. Before long, Canutt was operating in the triple capacity of star, stuntman and character actor.

When the talkies arrived, Canutt's soft, mellow voice proved unsuitable for Western heroes and he played his last leading role in 1929. Concentrating on his stunt work and character acting, he kept active with one picture after another. For years, he portrayed cowboy villains opposite many of the top names in Westerns while doubling for John Wayne, Tom Keene, Bob Livingston, Gene Autry and many more. By 1937, he was the undisputed "King of the Hollywood Stuntmen."

A short while later, Republic Studios became the leading producer of Westerns and serials and it was there that Canutt accepted the chance to become an assistant director in charge of action scenes. Organizing his own group of accomplished stuntmen, he started a stable of specially trained horses to perform the dangerous feats that were required. Being a lover of animals, he began a crusade to eliminate all unnecessary cruelty during the filming of action sequences and probably did more to achieve this purpose than any other individual in the business. Devising new tricks with special equipment and split-second timing, he helped prevent injury to actors and animals alike. Before long, Canutt had risen to the position of second unit director and was handling the action for dozens of features and serials. Among the best of these were *Stagecoach* (1939), *The Dark Command* (1940), *In Old Oklahoma* (1943), *Manhunt of Mystery Island* (1945), *Ivanhoe* (1950), *Knights of the Round Table* (1954), *Helen of Troy* (1956), *El Cid* (1961), *Spartacus* (1962), *Fall of the Roman Empire* (1963) and *How the West Was Won* (1964). Probably the most famous directing job that Canutt has ever done was the sensational chariot race for the 1959 version of *Ben Hur* which highlighted the stunt work of his son, Yakima Canutt, Jr.

Having since given up the actual performing of stunts because of his age, Yakima remains constantly active as a director for various producers involved in making action features.

FILMS: *Romance and Rustlers. Days of '49. Ridin' Comet. White Thunder. The Human Tornado. Outlaw Breaker. Hellhound of the*

Plains. *The Fighting Stallion. Desert Greed. Scar Hanan. Riders of the Storm. Sell 'Em Cowboy. Captain Cowboy. Bar L Ranch. Badmen's Money. Three Outcasts. Wild Horse Canyon. The Devil Horse. Canyon Hawks. Firebrand Jordan. The Vanishing West. Wyoming Outlaw. Ridin' Law. Fighting Texans. Sagebrush Trail. West of the Divide. Blue Steel. Lucky Texan. Randy Rides Alone. Three Musketeers. Hurricane Express. Lawless Frontier. King of the Pecos. Hurricane Horseman. Winds of the Wasteland. Cheyenne Cyclone. Secret of Treasure Island. The Vigilantes Are Coming. Man of Conquest. Zorro Rides Again. Dakota. In Old Oklahoma. The Dark Command. Under Texas Skies. Cowboys From Texas. Shooting High. Heart of the Rockies. The Angel and the Badman. Oklahoma Badlands. Carson City Raiders. Sons of Adventure.*

TED WELLS

Among the many authentic cowboys and rodeo performers that swamped the movie industry during the 1920's was tall, handsome Ted Wells. Having worked as a cowpuncher, he became known throughout the rodeo circuits as a champion rider and roper before finally entering motion pictures in 1921. At Universal Studios, the producers were competing for first place in the production of Westerns when they added Ted to their growing roster of cowboy stars.

Making his debut in a picture called *Straight Shootin',* he climbed steadily to popularity through a series of exciting features and emerged as one of the busiest action heroes of the late 1920's. Ted was able to combine his riding skill with a boundless energy and romped with natural ease through one Western after another, always insisting on good plots. Unfortunately, a few of his films were poorly produced and lacked the action that most of his pictures had. But, as a whole, his productions were good. He fared pretty well considering that Hollywood was undergoing a drastic change at the time when he was at his peak. Possessing a tall, husky frame and good looks, Ted survived the transition to talkies without too much effort and he scored in a number of successful pictures until he retired from the screen in 1933. For awhile afterwards, he made personal appearances with a circus then dropped completely out of sight.

FILMS: *Straight Shootin'. Desert Dust. The Smiling Terror. Beauty and Bullets. Border Wildcat. Grit Wins. Born to the Saddle. The Ridin' Demon.*

BOB CURWOOD (1899-)

Bob Curwood held the rare distinction of being one of the few European born actors who became famous as a cowboy star in American Westerns. He first saw the light of day in Romania on March 17, 1899, and was christened John Balas Belasco, the son of Russen and Maria Belasco. Arriving in America when he was still in his childhood, his family settled in New York where young John received his education. After two years of college, he decided on an acting career and appeared in vaudeville and summer stock. His travels finally took him to California where in 1925 he entered motion pictures under the name of Bob Curwood. Starting out as a supporting player, he reached stardom when Universal Studios gave him the leads in a series of Westerns. These silent features were good action films in spite of the fact that they were quickly made and had little production value. Although Curwood never quite became a major cowboy star, by 1929 he was in charge of his own Bob Curwood Productions, releasing his pictures under the Darmour banner. Unaffected by the movie industry's transition from silent to sound films, he continued to star in Westerns until 1933. His strong characterizations stressed the rough-and-ready action that delighted his fans and, even though his career lasted a short time, Curwood managed to win a place for himself among the sagebrush heroes of the screen.

Following his descent from starring in horse-operas, Curwood played supporting roles in a few pictures and then retired from the movies. Like many other former Western heroes, he faded out of sight and was never heard of again.

FILMS: *The Looters. Dangerous Double. Brand of Courage. Hidden Money. The Valiant Rider. Payroll Roundup. Frame Up Man. The Scrappin' Fool.*

COLONEL TIM McCOY (1891-)

Timothy John Fitzgerald McCoy was born in Saginaw, Michigan on April 10, 1891, the son of police chief Timothy H. McCoy, and was educated at St. Ignatius College in Chicago. After inheriting a large Wyoming ranch which bordered on a Sioux Indian reservation, Tim became friendly with the redmen, learning their customs and dialects until he was considered an expert. He was assigned to the U.S. Department of the Interior, working as a translator-interpreter for the Bureau of Indian Affairs, until World War I called him into service. During the war, he became attached to the Adjutant General of the Army until his release in 1919 with the rank of lieutenant-colonel.

Returning to Wyoming, Tim became an appointed U.S. Indian agent, supervising the various tribes and managing their legal affairs. In 1923, he was assigned to act as technical advisor to film director James Cruze who was then making a super-Western picture called *The Covered Wagon*. In addition, Tim helped recruit some of the authentic Indians for the film and even took a small obscure part as an actor. Needless to say, *The Covered Wagon* made movie history as an outstanding success and when the Indians were sent on a publicity tour of premiere showings in New York, Washington, D.C. and London, Tim was assigned to go along to watch over them.

It was not until 1925 that Tim McCoy really made an impression on movie audiences. That year he played a supporting role opposite Jack Holt in Paramount's *The Thundering Herd,* a film based on one of Zane Grey's best novels. It eventually led to an exclusive contract with M-G-M Studios, where Tim appeared in a series of high-budgeted historical Westerns. Within a short time, he was regarded as one of the top ten cowboy stars of the screen.

In 1930, Tim starred in a super-serial called *The Indians Are Coming* for Universal Studios, a chapter-play that was released in both silent and sound versions. As it turned out, the silent version became the last of its kind. In 1931, he went to work making pictures for Columbia and starred in a string of features that kept him among the top-ranking Western stars of the early 1930's. At the same time, he was involved in a number of independent productions for Puritan, Victory and other small companies which, despite their lack of true quality, kept him active through the lean years of the early '30's when cowboy stars were a dime a dozen.

In 1935, Tim left motion pictures temporarily to tour with the Ringling Brothers-Barnum and Bailey Circus. In 1938, he decided to organize his own Circus and Wild West Show, which made its initial performance at Chicago in April. After a quick succession of unfortunate incidents and bad luck, the show folded following its final appearance in Washington, D.C. on May 4, 1938. As history later recorded, it was a black year for circuses all over the country, and particularly so for Tim Mc-Coy who had sunk nearly a half-million dollars in the tragic failure. But in spite of its bad timing, the show had been extremely well-organized and went down in circus history as one of the last of its kind to travel the country by railroad.

Shortly afterward, Tim took up where he left off in pictures by starring in a string of features for P.R.C. and Monogram. By then, the singing cowboys were firmly entrenched in Westerns and he found it a bit difficult to rise to any stature of importance. Finally, in 1940, Monogram came up with the idea of teaming him with veteran stars Buck Jones and Ray Hatton in a series called *The Rough Riders* which quickly caught on. It was also the time when Westerns were featuring a trio of names in order to draw the fans back to the box-office, for example, "The Three Mesquiteers," "The Range Busters" and several other popular trios. With Jones, McCoy and Hatton as "The Rough Riders," the series came up with some extremely good features until 1942 when Buck Jones was killed in a Boston fire and Tim was called back into Army service.

Following World War II, Tim returned to his Wyoming ranch to live a life of leisure until he came out of retirement in 1949 to star in a television series. Shortly afterwards, he was coaxed into appearing in a small "cameo role" for Mike Todd's *Around the World in Eighty Days* and found himself in the spotlight once again. He did more TV work and several guest shots in Westerns besides squeezing in a tour with the Carson-Barnes Circus. In recent years, Tim has been content to live as a Wyoming rancher. In private life, he was divorced from his first wife, the former Agnes Miller, and married Inga Arvad in 1946. He is the proud father of four sons, two from each marriage, and still maintains his beautiful ranch in Wyoming.

On the screen, Tim was regarded as one of the handsomest cowboy stars of the 1930's, his trademark being a striking black cowboy costume that was unusual in those days. He rode a spotless white horse named "Starlight," which he later turned over to Bob Livingston, and found himself a pitch-black stallion called "Midnight" for the latter part of his film career. To cowboy fans, Tim's outstanding feature was his icy, cold stare—a look which lasted only a moment, but was able to set terror into the hearts of all badmen. With his weakness to over-act a bit, Tim made use of that look at least once in every picture when he made his entrance into the den of outlaws. In other scenes, he indulged himself by disguising his appearance when he wanted to gain access to the outlaw hangout. For this he would dress as a wily Mexican bandit and carry through with a phony accent that fooled everyone but the audience. Contrary to Western custom, Tim usually found an excuse to appear in everyday street clothes in the opening scenes of his pictures. This was to let the audience know that he was really a government agent or private investigator taking up a new case out west. The gimmick worked well for it delighted the fans to see him finally dress in cowboy costume in the next scenes. This meant that he was really getting down to business. One thing that Tim McCoy's films never lacked was action

109

1. *Ted Wells*
2. *Bob Curwood*
3. *Col. Tim McCoy*
4. *Rex Lease*
5. *Ken Maynard*
6. *Bill Cody*

4.

5.

6.

and when it came to the final showdown, none could beat him on the draw with a six-shooter.

FILMS: *The Covered Wagon. The Thundering Herd. Wyoming. Spoilers of the West. Winners of the Wilderness. War Paint. Law of the Range. The Frontiersman. California. Sioux Blood. Morgan's Last Raid. Masked Stranger. Beyond the Sierras. Bush Ranger. Desert Rider. Overland Telegraph. Gentle Cyclone. Eyes of the Totem. Under the Black Eagle. The Indians Are Coming. Fighting Fool. Code of the Rangers. One Way Trail. The Westerner. Square Shooter. Revenge Rider. Fighting Shadows. The Man from Guntown. Ghost Patrol. Police Car 17. Heroes of the Flames. Aces and Eights. Lightning Bill Carson. Border Caballero. Lightning Bill Carson Returns. Forbidden Trails. Below the Border. Gunman From Bodie. Down Texas Way. Riders of the West. Arizona Bound. Gun Trouble. West of the Law. Ghost Town Law. Around the World in Eighty Days. Run of the Arrow. Requiem For a Gunfighter.*

REX LEASE (1903-1966)

Rex Lease was born in Central City, Virginia on February 11, 1903, He studied to become a minister at the Wesleyan College in Ohio until he decided he would rather be an actor. Gaining his first experience from amateur theatricals, he joined a stock company of players and took part in several stage productions before entering motion pictures as a featured actor in 1922. After a few minor roles, he was finally given his first important part as the lead in *Clancy's Kosher Wedding* in 1925, which brought him stardom. The following year, Rex scored another success in a serial called *The Mystery Pilot,* for the Rayart Company, which earned him a contract with F.B.O. Studios.

In 1929, Rex was cast in the first serious role of his career when he played in a film entitled *The Younger Generation.* Before long, he was type-cast as a romantic lead in a group of drawing-room dramas and mysteries. Realizing that his career was not improving, he sought out more adventuresome parts and persuaded his studio to give him a chance at Westerns. After successfully proving himself in a couple of films, he became popular as a cowboy star.

Around 1930, F.B.O. was reorganized into the new R-K-O Studio and the changes in policy forced the company to dismiss a large number of its contract players due to the arrival of talking films. Unfortunately, Rex was one of the actors released. Undaunted, by going to work for independent producers like Trinity, Monogram and Supreme, he managed to keep active in horse-operas. His career as a star lasted until 1934, when he played his final leading role opposite Reed Howes and Bill Farnum in Mascot's all-star serial, *Custer's Last Stand*. It was a fine ending to what had been a promising screen career.

After completing his years as a star, Rex made a series of pictures in which he played featured roles opposite Hoot Gibson, Bob Steele and Buster Crabbe. These were followed by a long string of supporting parts in Westerns for studios like Republic, Monogram, P.R.C. and Universal. He remained an active performer in motion pictures and television until his death on January 3, 1966, when he was found dead in his Hollywood home. Cause of death was never determined.

In private life, Rex had been divorced from Eleanor Hunt since 1931 and had two sons. He was an avid sports fan, spending most of his leisure hours following football, boxing and baseball. To his colleagues, he was known as a quiet, soft-spoken chap whose friendly nature projected off the screen to his many followers.

FILMS: *Moulders of Men. A Woman Who Sinned. Ten Laps to Go. Two Sisters. Sunny Skies. When Dreams Come True. Girls Who Dare. Clancy's Kosher Wedding. Cancelled Debts. Mystery Pilot. The Younger Generation. Chinatown After Dark. Fury Below. Hot Curves. So This Is Mexico. Why Marry? Is There Justice? The Crimson Ghost. Custer's Last Stand. Troopers Three. Land of the Fighting Men. Heroes of the Alamo. The Texas Ranger. Code of the Rangers. Fighting Caballero. Desert Patrol. Cyclone of the Saddle. Rough Riding Ranger. Pals of the Range. Ghost Rider. The Cowboy and the Bandit. Inside Information. The Clutching Hand. Law of the Range. Aces and Eights. Silver Trail. Fast Bullets. Roaring Guns. Cavalcade of the West. South of the Border. Code of the Silver Sage. Sunrise Trail. Hills of Oklahoma. Outlaws of Texas. Ma and Pa Kettle. Ma and Pa Kettle at the Fair.*

KEN MAYNARD (1895-)

If any authority on movies were asked to compile a list of the ten greatest cowboy stars of all time, he would most certainly have to include Ken Maynard. One of the most popular of all sagebrush heroes, Ken starred in over 125 pictures during a career that spanned almost twenty years.

Ken Maynard was born in Mission, Texas on July 21, 1895, the son of Mr. and Mrs. William H. Maynard. At the tender age of fourteen, he ran away from home to join a traveling medicine show, only to find the going real rough on his own. When he returned home, his angry father enrolled him at the Virginia Military Institute in order that he learn discipline. Ken buckled down in his studies while learning engineering and entered the U.S. Army during World War I as the youngest engineer in the service.

After leaving the Army, Ken toured the country as a rodeo rider and, in 1920, won the National Trick Riding Championship. Three years later, he was a featured performer for the Ringling Bros. Circus when a movie talent scout spotted him during a performance. Arranging an exhibition, Ken did his tricks before such distinguished personalities as Tom Mix, Dustin Farnum and several film producers who sent him to Hollywood.

In 1924, Ken played his first screen role when he portrayed Paul Revere in *Janice Meredith,* a part that earned him the lead in his next film, *$50,000 Reward.* During the next two years, he made a series of cheaply-produced Westerns for the Davis Film Corporation, which landed him a contract with First National Studios in 1926. Having graduated to pictures with higher production value, he soon became one of the leading stars in Westerns. Imitating the grand style of Tom Mix, Ken played his heroes with much bravado, making certain to show off his excellent ability as a horseman. When it came to excitement and hair-raising thrills, his pictures offered large quantities of both. By 1930, he was producing his own features and releasing them under the Universal title.

Ken was one of the few stars who had little difficulty making the change from silent movies to talkies. In the early 1930's, he was making Westerns for major companies like Universal and Columbia, besides appearing in independent productions for Spectrum, Victory and Tiffany. As far as his own productions, he was kept active serving as producer, director, star and sometimes writer. He and two other cowboy stars, Hoot Gibson and Tim McCoy, were the only sagebrush heroes that managed to make pictures for both the major and independent studios at the same time.

It was Ken who first laid the groundwork for the musical Western. Many times, he included scenes in his pictures where he would personally vocalize a tune or feature a singing group of cowboys in order to break up the constant diet of action. Although these short musical interruptions were of minor importance, they did serve as a link to the singing cowboy craze. When Gene Autry and his pal, Smiley Burnette, first made their debuts in Ken's *Mystery Mountain* and *In Old Santa Fe,* the craze was definitely on its way to success.

Among the best performers in Ken Maynard's pictures was his famous horse, "Tarzan." To the audience, the handsome Palomino was as much a part of the plot as any of the human actors and Ken always made certain to include some scenes in which Tarzan could show off his bag of tricks. Unfortunately, Ken was indifferent when it came to his pictures. Admittedly, he made Westerns for the sole purpose of reaping a profit at the box-office and lacked the desire to even try to produce films that were true to the real West. In many cases, he substituted quantity for quality in spite of the fact that he had the means of turning out some first-grade films that would have compared with those of Tom Mix, Buck Jones and Harry Carey. Instead, he chose to make a parade of quickie, streamlined horse-operas patterned in the style of Hoot Gibson's Westerns. Nevertheless, some of Ken's films ranked high among the best Westerns ever made as far as real production value was concerned.

To take advantage of his immense popularity, Ken organized his Diamond K Ranch Wild West Show in 1936 with plans of touring the nation. Unfortunately, he failed to obtain proper financial backing and the show never left its home quarters. In less than a month, Ken was forced to abandon the idea. Returning to pictures, he starred in another chain of action Westerns until he temporarily retired from the screen in 1938.

By the early 1940's, two types of Westerns were enjoying great popularity, the musical horse-operas and the cowboy "trios." In the first group, Gene Autry, Roy Rogers, Tex Ritter and many other singers were at the top of the heap. In the second group, Westerns featuring three main characters were very popular—*The Three Mesquiteers, The Rough Riders, The Range Busters* and the *Hopalong Cassidy* series. In 1941, Monogram Pictures decided to add another trio to the competition when Hoot Gibson, Ken Maynard and Bob Steele made their bow as the "Trail Blazers." Having arrived somewhat late, the series lasted until 1943 when Monogram decided to cease production. After that, Ken made only one more picture, *The White Stallion* in 1946, before he left the screen permanently. Four years later he was in England, appearing in television while campaigning for the British Labor Party and taking part in the first televised general election in the British Isles. Returning to California, he made a tour with the Cole Bros. Circus and has since been active in personal appearances at rodeos and Wild West shows and also an occasional spot on TV. Ken was married to Bertha Rowland Denham on October 22, 1940, and has a younger brother, Kermit, who was also a popular cowboy star.

FILMS: *Janice Meredith. $50,000 Reward. The Gray Vulture. Haunted Ranch. Demon Rider. North Star. Fighting Courage. Unknown Cava-*

lier. Senor Daredevil. California Mail. Cheyenne. The Glorious Trail. Lawless Legion. The Royal Rider. Parade of the West. Kettle Creek. Senor Americano. Lucky Larkin. Wagonmaster. Fighting Legion. Arizona Frontier. Between Fighting Men. Code of the Mounted. Texas Gunfighter. Branded Men. Red Raiders. Whistling Dan. King of the Range. Mountain Justice. Hell Fire Austin. Drum Taps. Range Fighter. Come On Tarzan. Dynamite Ranch. Fargo Express. Fighting Thru. Flaming Lead. Santa Fe Trail. The Lone Avenger. The Pocatello Kid. Phantom Thunderbolt. Lawless Riders. Avenging Waters. Range Law. Heroes of the Range. Sunset Trail. Tombstone Canyon. Two Gun Man. King of the Arena. Strawberry Roan. Mystery Mountain. In Old Santa Fe. Song of the Saddle. Overland Stage. Arizona Whirlwind. Death Valley Rangers. White Stallion.

BILL CODY (1891-1948)

Contrary to popular belief, Bill Cody was no relation to "Buffalo Bill" Cody, the famous showman and Indian scout. Born William Joseph Cody, Jr. in Winnipeg, Canada on January 5, 1891, he was educated at the St. Thomas Military Academy and St. John's University in Minnesota. While fresh out of college, he joined the Metropolitan Stock Company and toured the U.S.A. in stage theatricals. In 1924, he wound up in California making his debut in movies as a featured player in Pathe Westerns. When fans demanded to see more of him, he quickly rose to leading roles in his own series of horse-operas.

Bill belonged to the old school of Western heroes patterned after the style of William S. Hart. He played the strong, silent type with a sense of nobility and unbending willpower. Always quick to avenge the wrongs done to others, he stood for all that was good and honorable in the Wild West. His keen ability to portray rugged characters of action enabled him to gain an enviable position among the cowboy favorites of the 1920's and early '30's.

Having left Pathe around 1926, Bill went under contract to Universal Studios, where he continued his career with even greater success. He made the jump from silent to sound pictures without any apparent difficulties, proving himself equally popular in talkies. Between the period of 1931-1933, he completed his work at Universal and starred in a series of independent features for Associated, Sono-Art and Spectrum Productions. Although generally good as far as the cheaper films went, they lacked the production value of his earlier pictures. In 1934-35, Bill made his last series of Westerns for Monogram before retiring from the screen in 1936.

116

Bill went on nation-wide tours with the Cole Bros. Circus during 1937 and 1938. The following year, he quit public life to manage his private interests while living a peaceful existence with his wife, the former Evelyn Hastings, and their son, Bill, Jr., who was also active in pictures. On New Year's Day, 1948, Bill died at his home in Santa Monica, California, four days before his fifty-seventh birthday.

FILMS: *Border Justice. Riders of Mystery. The Fighting Sheriff. Galloping Cowboy. Riders of Destiny. Arizona Whirlwind. Born to Battle. Pirates of Panama. Slim Fingers. Eyes of the Underworld. The Tip Off. Western Racketeers. Ghost City. Border Menace. Land of Wanted Men. Texas Pioneers. Mason of the Mounted. Law of the North. Blazing Justice. Oklahoma Jim. Border Guns. Cyclone Ranger. Frontier Days. Outlaws of the Range. Deadwood Pass. Vanishing Riders. Lawless Border. The Ranger's Luck. Under Texas Skies. Texas Ramblers.*

THE WONDER HORSE

Needless to say, horses have always played an important part in the production of motion pictures, particularly in Westerns. When film director Edwin S. Porter made *The Great Train Robbery* back in 1903, he arranged for the rental of a few animals for the chase scenes at the finale. It was the first time that horses actually took part in a screenplay. As the years rolled by, it became increasingly evident to the producers, directors and stars involved in movies just how much the Westerner had really depended on his horse for survival.

The first cowboy star to show special attention to his mount was William S. Hart, who decided to feature his Pinto pony, "Fritz," in a few important scenes. With the intention of revealing to the audience how the cowboy had relied on his horse, Hart made "Fritz" a key subject to the plot. Almost immediately, movie fans swamped the star with hundreds of requests to see more of the faithful pony. From that time on, Hart never made a picture without sharing the spotlight with his horse and, years later, when the animal died, the star had him buried at his famous ranch in Newhall, California with a large stone marking the spot. In an interview with the press, Hart once claimed that "Fritz" had saved him from drowning while filming a picture and his love for the animal was expressed many times during his life.

Soon afterward, an array of cowboy stars began to feature their favorite mounts in every film they made. Most of them were handsome, well-trained animals that could sometimes steal a scene from the human actors. In Westerns, many a hero was saved from a fatal end by the intervention of his horse in the nick of time and the audiences loved it. To the young fans, these amazing animals took second billing only to the hero in order of importance, even to the point where the horses received an abundance of fan mail. Before long, it became apparent that any self-respecting cowboy star would sooner die than appear without his "Wonder Horse" in pictures or in public appearance tours.

Following close on Bill Hart's heels, the next star to feature his horse in Westerns was Tom Mix, who started out originally with a white steed called "Old Blue." Early in Tom's career, the animal died and was replaced with a beautiful chestnut stallion named "Tony." Marked with four white stockings and a bright blaze on its face, the animal had been raised by Mix from the time it was a colt. Within a short time, "Tony" became the most famous horse in the movies. In picture after picture, the team of Tom Mix and "Tony" was the center of attraction for millions of fans all over the world. A genuine performer, the horse even accompanied his master on a tour of America and Europe, appearing before crowned heads and delighting the audiences of many nations. In rare instances when Tom was neither making a picture nor traveling on tours, he housed the horse in a luxurious stable which reportedly cost $50,000 without including the riding tack of silver-inlaid saddles and jewel-encrusted bridles.

Long before The Lone Ranger shouted "Hi-yo Silver" over the airwaves of radio and TV, Buck Jones had introduced his famous white horse "Silver" to his millions of fans all over the world. A true lover of animals, Buck had raised the stallion from colthood since 1921 and had done the major part of training him personally. A prominent horse-breeder, the star had also featured another steed called "White Eagle" in a few pictures until "Silver" took over. Highly intelligent and extremely photogenic, the animal became an important part of every film Jones ever made, even to the point of having his name included in the cast of performers. Since the star realized the extreme value of his horse, Buck had a few "doubles" for "Silver" whenever dangerous scenes were called for. After appearing with his master for the major part of his career, the equine star died in 1940 at a ripe old horse age.

In the years that followed, a long parade of cowboy heroes came to feature white horses as their pet mounts until it almost became a standard practice of hoss-operas. Among the most prominent were Jack Hoxie and his famous "Scout," Bill Cody and "King," Jack Perrin and "Starlight," Reb Russell and "Rebel," Buster Crabbe with "Falcon," Tex Ritter with "White Flash" and William (Hopalong Cassidy) Boyd and his famous "Topper."

Fred Thomson's "Silver King" was another example of how popular these horses became. Purchased by the star in New York, the animal was an Irish Gray Hunter originally dappled gray, but as time went by, his spots faded until he was almost completely white. When Thomson signed a contract to star in films for F.B.O., "Silver King" had been awarded his own contract stipulating that he should receive a weekly salary of two thousand dollars. Before the cameras, he was as much of an actor as the human performers, jumping high fences, hurdling stone walls and racing to the rescue of his master.

Not all cowboy stars chose to ride white horses however, for there were those who preferred the exact opposite. Among the most noted performers who featured equally handsome black steeds were Tim McCoy, who had started out with a white charger named "Starlight" (not the same horse as Jack Perrin's) but later exchanged him for a jet-black stallion called "Midnight," Lash LaRue and his "Rush," John Wayne and "Duke," Allan "Rocky" Lane and his handsome "Black Jack" and George O'Brien with "Mike." On the other hand, Western star Tom Tyler operated in exact reverse from Tim McCoy by beginning his career with a black steed called "Ace" and ending up riding a white horse named "Baron."

Probably the most famous black horse of them all was "Rex," billed as "King of the Wild Horses." During the 1920's and '30's, he received top billing above all other performers in a series of serials and features. Usually appearing riderless, "Rex" romped through some of the most exciting films of the silent and early sound eras, sometimes sharing the spotlight with dog star Rin-Tin-Tin, Jr.

Hoot Gibson and Ken Maynard were among the first Western stars to feature the golden Palomino as their favorite mounts. Gibson rode a beautiful stallion called "Goldie," which he used in most of his pictures and circus tours. Maynard's horse, "Tarzan," was almost white and had a bag of tricks that seemed endless. No matter where the star appeared, the fans always demanded to see "Tarzan" as well, for the horse and rider were considered inseparable. In the years that followed, the list of Palomino riders grew to include Johnny Mack Brown and his handsome horse, "Rebel," Jimmy Wakely and "Sunset," Rod Cameron with "Knight" and Leo Carrillo, who owned one of the most beautiful show horses in California. For years, Carrillo had taken great pride in riding his steed in the annual Pasadena Tournament of Roses parade on New Year's Day.

The most famous of all Palominos belonged to Roy Rogers and was known to the world as "Trigger." Billed as "The Smartest Horse in the Movies," the animal had been purchased by Rogers for a little under $300 and was featured in most of the cowboy star's pictures. Later,

1. *Tom Mix and "Tony"*
2. *Ken Maynard and "Tarzan"*
3. *Buck Jones and "Silver"*
4. *William Boyd and "Topper"*
5. *Gene Autry and "Champion"*
6. *Roy Rogers and "Trigger"*

1.

4.

2.

5.

3.

6.

Rogers reportedly turned down offers of $10,000 for "Trigger" at a time when Roy was known as the "King of the Cowboys." With the passing of time, the original "Trigger" grew too old and had to be retired. He later died at the ripe old horse age of twenty-eight. Meanwhile, Rogers had replaced him with another golden Palomino he called "Trigger Jr."

Not to be overlooked were the striking black and white Pintos among the Wonder Horses of the movies. Bob Baker rode a handsome steed called "Apache," Bill Elliott's favorite was named "Sonny," Roy Stewart owned a handsome horse known as "Ranger" and Duncan Renaldo rode "Diablo" in his popular Cisco Kid series.

In 1935, Gene Autry came to the screen riding his horse, "Champion." An intelligent chestnut Tennessee Walking Horse, the stallion resembled Tom Mix's "Tony" and was an instant hit with the public. When Autry was the leading cowboy hero of the movies, "Champion" shared top billing with his master, accompanying him in films, TV and rodeo tours. It was once reported that "Champ," as he was more familiarly known, became the first horse to fly cross-country by airplane. Like Roy Rogers' "Trigger," he too had to be retired because of old age and was replaced by another horse called "Little Champ."

Among the other well-known Wonder Horses of the screen, we must be sure to include such favorites as Bob Steele's "Brownie," Eddie Dean's "Copper," Rex Allen's "Ko-Ko," Monte Hale's "Pardner" and Tim Holt's "Lightning." Charles Starrett rode a handsome Arabian called "Raider" in his pictures which, by no means, should go without mentioning. All these and at least a dozen more constituted the roster of impressive Wonder Horses of the screen. During the early days of picture-making, horses had been badly abused due to the failure of taking precautions while filming dangerous action scenes. These animals had been considered more or less expendable. But with the arrival of cowboy stars who featured their mounts in roles of importance, the situation for horses greatly improved. Later, top-notch stunt directors like Yakima Canutt and watchful agents from the S.P.C.A. made the filming of action sequences a science with the use of special equipment and split-second timing. Directors finally came to realize that, with careful planning, no animal need suffer any risk of injury for the sake of making a picture.

In the days when Westerns were an important part of our lives, we were all accustomed to having a special favorite among the cowboy stars. When that particular favorite happened to have an exceptionally smart horse, we reserved a special fondness for the animal too. After awhile, it became inconceivable to picture one without the other. Thus, it is only fitting that we set aside this chapter in dedication to all those marvelous animal performers of yesteryear.

122

DENVER DIXON (1901-)

Victor Adamson was born in Auckland, New Zealand around 1901 and came to America while still a young lad. As a teenager, he worked as a trick rider for a Wild West Show until he had raised enough money to direct and star in a one-reel silent film which he used to advertise himself in Hollywood. A short time later, he was appearing in Westerns under the name of "Art James."

Known for his skill with a bullwhip, he made dozens of silent features under the name of Denver Dixon and, by 1920, was starring and directing in his own productions. In 1923, he organized his popular "Art Mix Productions," having adopted the name Art Mix in order to cash in on some of the phenomenal success of the current favorite, Tom Mix. As star-director-writer and producer, he turned a number of pictures into profits until he was finally forced to hire another actor called George Kesterson to play the "Art Mix" roles. As it turned out, Kesterson became more closely associated with the name than Dixon had ever been and, when another producer hired Kesterson to make Westerns under that name, the result was a mixture of court actions. Not to be outdone, Dixon found himself still another actor known as Bob Roberts to play in his Art Mix features. The confusion finally ended when the public lost interest and Kesterson and Roberts wound up playing third-rate villains.

In the 1930's, Dixon continued to produce, direct and star in talkies until he made his last appearance before the cameras in 1938, playing the lead in his own production *Mormon Conquest*. Married to his former leading lady, Dolores Booth, he has been content with occasional ventures as a producer-director for films like *Two Tickets to Terror* and *Halfway to Hell*.

FILMS: *Riders of Mystery Ranch. Ace of Cactus Range. The Old Oregon Trail. A Pair of Hellions. Desert Mesa. South of Santa Fe. Riders of Border Bay. West of the Rockies. Lightning Range. Mormon Conquest.*

WALLY WEST (1902-)

Theodore Wynn was born near Dallas, Texas around 1902 and became an expert horseman by the time he had reached the age of twelve. After working as a cowpuncher for the Mashed-O Ranch in Texas, he arrived in Hollywood in 1926 to play bit parts in silent films.

Although his acting assignments were rather scarce, he managed to appear with Buster Keaton in *The General* and doubled as a stuntman for various big name stars. Broke and discouraged, he returned to Texas to work as a bank clerk until he was ready to try Hollywood again in 1931. Hiring himself an agent, he changed his name to Wally West and achieved some success as a stuntman and supporting player opposite stars like Hoot Gibson, Ken Maynard, Bill Cody and Tim McCoy. By 1935, he was doubling for Gene Autry in Nat Levine's Mascot serial, *Phantom Empire*. It was due largely to his fine work in this chapter-play that he became employed at Republic Studios to appear in many films. In 1936, he again distinguished himself while performing the stunts for Bob Livingston in *The Vigilantes Are Coming*. This was followed by an association with Denver Dixon who was then producing the Art Mix Westerns. This time, Wally became known as Tom Wynn, star of the Dixon productions. Unfortunately, his career as a cowboy hero was short-lived and Wally resumed his stunt work, doubling for Tex Ritter. Since then he has been active as a villain, stuntman and doubled in many phases of Westerns for TV and movie features. Several years ago, Wally was performing as a double for actor Richard Egan on the "Empire" (later called "Redigo") TV series.

FILMS: *The General. Strawberry Roan. Desert Trail. Roaming Wild. Ambush Valley. Cowboy Counsellor. The Traitor. Phantom Empire. The Vigilantes Are Coming. Ride Tenderfoot Ride. Desert Mesa. Mormon Conquest. Starlight Over Texas. Law of the Lawless. Fighting Texan. Death Valley Rangers. Straight Shooter. Westbound Stage. Billy the Kid's Fighting Pals.*

NEWTON HOUSE (1913-)

Billed as "The Boy Wonder of Universal Westerns," Newton House rode through a series of cowboy thrillers from 1927 to 1932. His career was not unlike that of another young performer in Westerns, Buzz Barton, although House never quite attained the stature that Barton did.

Born in 1913, he won a dozen trophies for trick and fancy riding by the time he reached the age of fifteen. Spotted by a talent scout, he was immediately whisked off to stardom in a series of Universal Westerns in 1927, remaining active for over five years. Among his best-known roles, he co-starred with Louise Lorraine and Jay (Buffalo Bill, Jr.) Wilsey in Universal's hit serial of 1929, *The Final Reckoning*. Like so many other film players, the advent of sound pictures caused an interruption in his career. But he managed to overcome his difficulties without too much loss of popularity.

After 1932, his career as a cowboy hero came to an end and he was forced to undertake character parts. He fared surprisingly well in that capacity until his retirement in 1935.

Although never having attained major status, Newton had the physical ability and riding skill to match that of his competitors. His films at Universal had been well above average until they lost their originality. At the end of his career as a star, they became distinct disappointments, lacking any production value and very similar to each other. Nevertheless, he contributed his share toward the Western genre without any loss of dignity.

BUZZ BARTON (1914-)

Buzz Barton was one of the most promising newcomers in Westerns until the untimely arrival of talkies put an end to his career. Having all the skill and talent he needed for becoming a first-rate cowboy star, he unfortunately came upon the scene too late.

He was born in 1914 and raised on a ranch before making his first public appearance at a West Texas rodeo in 1924. His excellent riding and roping brought him cash awards and trophies from all over the country and he participated in rodeos of national importance. Having won the title of "Champion Trick and Fancy Rider," Buzz was spotted for the movies in 1926 when a talent scout for F.B.O. saw him perform at Cheyenne, Wyoming. The following year, he was starred in his first motion picture, *The Boy Rider*, and was hailed by film critics as a "combination of Tom Mix, Ken Maynard and Fred Thomson."

No sooner had Buzz started his career at F.B.O. Studios when the entire movie industry was thrown into chaos by the arrival of sound pictures. Actors who could not make the grade in talkies were released from their contracts, exhibition houses were rebuilt to show films with sound, Hollywood studios were being reorganized and movie-making involved entirely new methods of production. Among the companies affected, F.B.O. Studios were sold and emerged as part of a new organization called Radio-Keith-Orpheum (R-K-O).

Having survived the transition period, Buzz Barton was starred in a few talking Westerns at R-K-O. Unfortunately, he did not get the proper backing from studio bigwigs. His pictures had been good enough as far as action and excitement were concerned, but producers were reluctant to invest in any more cowboy stars at that particular time. Reduced to supporting roles, Buzz appeared with established performers like Tom Tyler, Tom Mix, Bob Steele, Fred Thomson and Rex Bell in many features that kept him actively employed until 1937. After that, he disappeared from the screen and was never heard of again. Such was the case in the careers of quite a few movie stars whose fame rose to meteoric heights. Having arrived at an inopportune time, their period of success was cut short by the sudden lack of interest. Had Buzz Barton entered movies a bit earlier, or later, he undoubtedly would have made the ranks of the more important stars in Westerns.

FILMS: *The Boy Rider. The Slingshot Kid. Wizard of the Saddle. Pioneer Scout. Jesse James. Freckled Rascal. The Lost Trail. The Little Savage. Arizona Streak. Born to Battle. Wild to Go. Lucky Larrigan. The Tonto Kid. Powdersmoke Range. The Pinto Kid. Little Buckaroo. Bantam Cowboy. The Young Whirlwind. The Fighting Redhead. Orphan of the Sage. Terror Mountain. Vagabond Cub. Rough Ridin' Red. Pals of the Prairie.*

LANE CHANDLER (1899-)

Lane Chandler was born Robert Lane Oakes in North Dakota on June 4, 1899. While he was still a child, his family went to live in Culbertson, Montana, where he attended school. He graduated from High School in Helena and entered the Montana Wesleyan College until he decided to take a job as a bus driver at Yellowstone National Park. In 1923, he went to Los Angeles, worked as a garage mechanic and met film director John Waters, who was then busy making a series of Zane Grey Westerns at Paramount. Changing his name to Lane Chandler, he talked Waters into giving him a chance in pictures and wound up as a bit player in a few horse-operas. By 1926, Paramount had him under contract and was starring him in B-Westerns while preparing him for better things alongside another newcomer named Gary Cooper.

For the next few years, the studio kept the two actors in close competition with one another until it was decided to promote Cooper to bigger and costlier productions. Meanwhile, Lane did fairly well for himself as a romantic lead opposite stars like Clara Bow, Esther Ralston and Greta Garbo. But, unfortunately, the arrival of talkies ended his promising career for awhile. Undaunted, Lane accepted a starring role in a Universal chapter-play entitled *Lightning Express*, which began his career anew in sound pictures. After that, he played leading roles in Westerns for the independent market such as Big Four and Willis Kent Productions.

One thing that Lane Chandler's movies never lacked was action. His tall, husky frame was visible evidence that he could handle him-

126

self in any sort of tight scrape and, like most of the old-timers in Westerns, he could perform his own stunts without too much trouble. His last important leading role was in Republic's hit serial of 1938, *The Lone Ranger,* in which he shared top honors with Lee Powell, Herman Brix, Hal Taliaferro and George (Montgomery) Letz. From then on Lane played character parts in many features for Republic, Warners and Paramount. He is still very active in films and TV.

FILMS: *Open Range. Love and Learn. Red Hair. The Big Killing. The First Kiss. The Single Standard. Rough Waters. Firebrand Jordan. Riders of the Rio. Outlaw Tamer. Under Texas Skies. Land of Fighting Men. Trouble Busters. Via Pony Express. Lightning Express. Battling Buckaroo. Cheyenne Cyclone. Hurricane Horseman. Lawless Valley. Reckless Rider. Guns For Hire. Texas Tornado. Wyoming Whirlwind. The Lone Bandit. Heroes of the Alamo. The Idaho Kid. Wolf of Wall Street. The Studio Murder Case. Forward Pass. Lawless Nineties. Return of Jimmy Valentine. Hearts of Bondage. Winds of the Wasteland. Stormy Trails. Sundown Jim. Virginia City. The Lone Ranger. Follow the Boys. Northwest Mounted Police. The Plainsman. Men on Her Mind. Saratoga Trunk. Casanova Brown. Great Mike. Laura. The Spider. Behind Green Lights. Pursued. Pride of the Yankees. Samson and Delilah. San Francisco Story. Reap the Wild Wind. Montana. Duel in the Sun. Take Me to Town. Thunder Over the Plains. Charge at Feather River. Border River. Return to Treasure Island. Shotgun. Tall Man Riding. Prince of Players. Creature With the Atom Brain. Quantrill's Raiders. Noose For a Gunman. Indian Fighter. Requiem For a Gun-fighter.*

WARNER BAXTER (1893-1951)

Because he was such a fine dramatic actor, few moviegoers realize the important part that Warner Baxter played in the advancement of the Western. Nevertheless, he was the first film star to portray O. Henry's famous fictional character, the Cisco Kid, on the screen and win audience acclaim for his characterizations of the roguish Mexican bandit. In 1929, Baxter was voted the best actor of the year because of his splendid performance in a film called *In Old Arizona,* the first sound feature ever to be photographed completely outdoors. Although he later became noted for serious dramas, Warner made numerous Westerns which stand among the greatest movies ever produced. In *Robin Hood of Eldorado,* he played the part of the notorious Joaquin Murietta. In

1. *Buzz Barton*
2. *Wally West*
3. *Lane Chandler*
4. *Warner Baxter*
5. *Newton House*
6. *Denver Dixon*

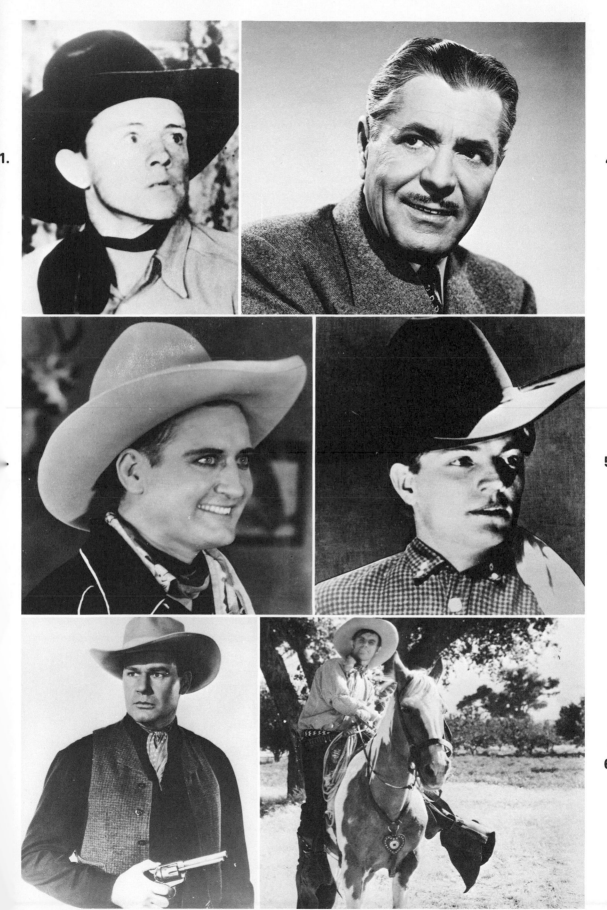

1.

4.

5.

6.

Ramona he was Alessandro and, in 1931, he starred in the first talking version of *The Squaw Man.*

Born in Columbus, Ohio on March 29, 1893, Warner Baxter was attending the University of Ohio when the death of his father interrupted his education and forced him to work as a machinery salesman. Later, deciding that he would like to be an actor, he joined a stock company to gather experience and made several appearances on the stage before entering motion pictures as a bit player in 1916. Finding little success in films, he returned to the stage by becoming a member of the Burbank Stock Company where he and a fellow actor named Richard Dix took turns in playing leads. Then came the chance to star on Broadway and Warner finally reached success in a play called "Lombardi Ltd." In 1924, he was called back to motion pictures when Paramount Studios hired him to star in a few features.

After completing his work at Paramount, Warner accepted a film contract with the Fox Studios and became one of their biggest stars. It was in 1929 that he won the Academy Award for his role in *In Old Arizona,* departing from his usual straight dramatic parts. The picture made screen history and Warner's popularity rose to great heights. Soon he was listed near the top of the twenty-five most important movie stars of the industry.

A versatile actor, Warner was particularly appealing to his fans when he played in Westerns. Having a special fondness for playing Mexican outlaws with hearts of gold, his Cisco Kid pictures were always big money-makers at the box-office. Throughout the 1930's, he made an impressive parade of screen hits which kept him among the most popular male stars. His keen sense of acting always kept him in demand, particularly when he made pictures like *The Cisco Kid, Under the Pampas Moon, Barricade, Prisoner of Shark Island* and *The Road to Glory.* As far as feminine fans were concerned, Warner's suave, debonair appearance made him a natural example of what the handsome, well-tailored movie idol should look like. But, contrary to the pattern of most male celebrities of the screen, his personality was backed by excellent talent. Not one to be a mere good-looking showpiece, Warner could act in any type of role, be it comedy or heavy drama.

With a long list of screen hits to his credit, Warner decided to retire from pictures after 1940 to concentrate on his successful real estate business and serve as mayor of Malibu. The arrival of World War II suddenly caused an important shortage of male stars and he was coaxed back into the movies when Columbia Studios offered him the lead in the new *Crime Doctor* series. He was active in these features until the time of his death from bronchial pneumonia on May 7, 1951. Divorced from Viola Caldwell, he was survived by his second wife, the former Winifred Bryson, whom he wed in 1920.

FILMS: *All Woman. Her Own Money. If I Were Queen. Alimony. The Runaway. Mannequin. Aloma of the South Seas. Great Gatsby. Miss Brewster's Millions. Mismates. Telephone Girl. The Coward. Drums of the Desert. Singed. A Woman's Way. Tragedy of Youth. Craig's Wife. Danger Street. West of Zanzibar. Three Sinners. In Old Arizona. Linda. The Far Call. Through Different Eyes. Behind the Curtain. Such Men Are Dangerous. Romance of the Rio Grande. The Arizona Kid. The Squaw Man. Daddy Long Legs. The Cisco Kid. Surrender. Under the Pampas Moon. Man About Town. 42nd Street. Stand Up and Cheer. Robin Hood of Eldorado. Wife, Doctor and Nurse. Wife, Husband and Friend. To Mary, With Love. Vogues of 1937. Broadway Bill. Ramona. Barricade. Renegades. Slave Ship. Kidnapped. Return of the Cisco Kid. Prisoner of Shark Island. White Hunter. The Road to Glory. I'll Give a Million. I Love You on Wednesday. Earthbound. Adam Had Four Sons. Lady in the Dark. Crime Doctor. Crime Doctor's Warning. Crime Doctor's Manhunt. Crime Doctor's Courage. State Penitentiary. Crime Doctor's Gamble. Crime Doctor's Diary. Gentleman From Nowhere. Devil's Henchman.*

BOB STEELE (1906-)

Bob Steele is another all-time favorite who earned himself a prominent place in the Western Hall of Fame. Having starred in over 150 pictures before he turned to character roles, Bob was among the most popular cowboy stars of the 1930's and early '40's. When it came to action, this range-buster ranked with the best and his films thrilled millions for many years.

He was born Robert North Bradbury, Jr., one of twin sons brought forth by Nita and Robert N. Bradbury on January 23, 1906 at Pendleton, Oregon. While the boys were still very young, their father took the family to live in Glendale, California where he was employed as a film director. Bob and his brother Bill got their first taste of acting when their dad decided to record their outdoor activities on a series of two-reel movies. These pictures were so good that Pathe Studios bought them and released them under the title of *The Adventures of Bob and Bill.*

Having had a sampling of show business, the twins then were booked for a series of vaudeville appearances with headliners like Fanchon and Marco in a comedy act that billed them as the Murdock Brothers. A while later, Pathe made an additional group of short pictures which featured the boys in a Western background. While squeezing in these juvenile acting jobs, Bob attended the Glendale High School, where one of his classmates was a fellow named Marion Morrison, a boy who later became famous as John Wayne.

In 1927, Bob Steele made his official debut in motion pictures when he played the lead in a film called *The Mojave Kid*. An instant hit, he was signed to a contract with F.B.O. and started a series of features that quickly brought him fame and success. By that time, F.B.O. had what was considered to be the biggest array of cowboy stars in the business with names like Tom Mix, Fred Thomson, Tom Tyler and Buzz Barton leading the parade. It was with these prominent names in Westerns that Bob joined the competition and, with his skill at riding and fighting, he was thoroughly capable of holding his own. After finishing his work with F.B.O., he came to the end of the silent picture era by doing a series for an independent outfit called Syndicate Pictures.

In 1930, Bob made his first talking Western, a film called *Near the Rainbow's End*. That was followed by a group of features for Tiffany-Stahl, Sono Art-World Wide, Monogram and Mascot. By 1934, he began his association with producer A. W. Hackle, for whom he starred in nearly three dozen Westerns. As if that weren't enough, Bob found time to appear in R-K-O's all-star feature of 1935, *Powdersmoke Range,* which had a cast that included Harry Carey, Hoot Gibson, Big Boy Williams and Tom Tyler in leading roles. Having risen to the list of top ten cowboys of the screen, he was constantly active in one film after another and completed the 1930's by starring in additional features for Republic and Metropolitan Pictures.

In 1939, Bob played one of his most unusual and important roles when he took the part of "Curley" in the Hal Roach production of John Steinbeck's famous novel, *Of Mice and Men*. Appearing with a cast that included such stellar performers as Burgess Meredith, Lon Chaney, Jr., Betty Field and Charles Bickford, he gave a performance that was hailed by critics and fans alike.

During the early 1940's, Bob was still one of the busiest actors in Westerns. He made a series of horse-operas for P.R.C. in which he played Billy the Kid and, in 1940, replaced Ray Corrigan in Republic's popular "Three Mesquiteers" Westerns. It was while appearing in the latter series that he again returned to the list of top ten cowboy stars from 1940 to 1943. When Republic ended the "Mesquiteers" features in 1943, Bob went to work for Monogram where he co-starred with Hoot Gibson and Ken Maynard in another group of "Trio Westerns" called "The Trail Blazers." His last starring roles came during 1945-1946 when he made some pictures for Lippert and P.R.C. which, unfortunately, were way below the usual standards of his films. After that, he turned to character parts, made a personal appearance tour with the Clyde Beatty Circus in 1955 and also included several guest shots at national rodeos. Still popular with his fans, he became a regular performer when he took the role of "Duffy" on the comedy Western series, "F Troop" for TV. He is still active in motion pictures, usually portraying outlaws in some of the major productions.

A perennial favorite of Western fans, Bob has contributed a major portion of talent and skill toward the advancement of the Western genre. Audiences who saw him in action were never short-changed when it came to thrills and excitement. Although unusually short in height for a cowboy hero, he proved himself quite capable of handling any rough stuff, whether it involved fistcuffs or stunt riding. He truly earned his title of "The Little Giant of Westerns."

FILMS: *The Mojave Kid. Laughing at Death. The Invaders. The Bandit's Son. Man in the Rough. Drifting Sands. Crooks Can't Win. Riding Renegade. Breed of the Sunsets. Captain Careless. Lightning Speed. Trial of Courage. Come and Get It. Amazing Vagabond. The Cowboy and the Outlaw. Near the Rainbow's End. Breezy Bill. Texas Cowboy. Man From Nowhere. Gallant Fool. The Fighting Champ. Trailing North. Mystery Squadron. Breed of the Border. The Navajo Kid. Young Blood. Big Calibre. Demon of Trouble. The Ranger's Code. Kid Courageous. Tombstone Terror. Smoky Smith. Galloping Romeo. Western Justice. Alias John Law. Red Rope. Sundown Saunders. Cavalry. Brand of Hate. Lightning Crandall. Powdersmoke Range. Arizona Gunfighter. Desert Patrol. Of Mice and Men. Lone Star Raiders. Westward Ho. Thundering Trails. Santa Fe Scouts. Pinto Canyon. Thunder in the Desert. Code of the Outlaw. Billy the Kid Outlawed. Billy the Kid's Revenge. The Great Train Robbery. Carson City Kid. Wildfire. Northwest Trail. The Big Sleep. Cheyenne. San Antone. Ride the Man Down. Exposed. Island in the Sky. The Enforcer. Killer McCoy. Once Upon a Horse. Fighting Chance. The Outcast. Drums Across the River. Requiem for a Gunfighter. Atomic Submarine. The Comancheros. Taggart. Bullet For a Badman. The Town Tamer. Cheyenne Autumn. Major Dundee. Steel Jungle. Shenandoah.*

RICHARD DIX (1895-1949)

One of the finest and best-loved actors that ever appeared on the motion picture screen was Richard Dix. With a rare ability of playing

1. *Gary Cooper*
2. *Randolph Scott*
3. *Bob Steele*
4. *Richard Dix*
5. *John Wayne*
6. *Rex Bell*

1.

4.

2.

5.

6.

all types of roles, he starred in everything from heavy melodramas to two-fisted action films and never failed to completely captivate his audiences. As a star in both the silent and sound eras of movies, he came to be known as "the Ideal He-Man of the screen" by projecting a sense of masculine virility and strength in every character he played. Tall and ruggedly handsome, Dix made some of the most successful films ever produced and was especially well-known in Westerns.

Born Ernest Carlton Brimmer at St. Paul, Minnesota on July 18, 1895, he entered Minnesota University after graduating from Central High School. Completing his education at Northwestern College, he undertook an acting career by appearing with a stock company in St. Paul, New York, Pittsburgh and Dallas before making his first big impression in a part opposite William Faversham in "The Hawk." With World War I raging in Europe, Dix took time out to serve in the U.S. Navy, until 1919, when he returned to the stage in association with producer Oliver Morosco.

In 1922, he made his film debut in *Not Guilty,* which drew him to the attention of Samuel Goldwyn. Dix was then chosen to play the lead in a Goldwyn production called *The Christian* which catapulted him to fame as a bright newcomer to the screen. A year later, director Cecil B. De Mille starred him in his spectacular epic *The Ten Commandments,* and Dix was placed under contract to Paramount as one of the studio's most important properties.

While at Paramount, Dix proved himself a versatile performer in dozens of top-notch films. He was particularly successful in 1925 when he made a Western called *The Vanishing American.* Cast in the role of an Indian, he gave an unusually sensitive portrayal and wound up in one of the biggest hits of the year. It was that picture that really started him on his way toward becoming a first-class action star. Every year thereafter, Dix was certain to appear in at least one saga of the West which was always a notch above the average. In 1931, his performance in the classic *Cimarron* earned him a nomination for an Academy Award and, although he did not win, the picture took the Oscar for "best film of the year." While working at Paramount, Dix starred in a series of outdoor adventures for producer Harry Sherman and, when Sherman moved to United Artists, he took the star along to continue turning out these excellent features.

During the years that followed, Dix appeared in films for M-G-M, Universal and R-K-O. He had just undertaken a new group of mystery dramas at Columbia, which were based on the popular radio series "The Whistler," when death overtook him on September 20, 1949. Divorced from Winifred Coe, he was survived by his second wife, the former Virginia Webster, and three children.

FILMS: *Not Guilty. The Glorious Fool. Dangerous Curves Ahead. Yellow Men and Gold. The Christian. The Ten Commandments. Manhattan. Too Many Kisses. The Shock Punch. Lucky Devil. Womanhandled. The Vanishing American. Let's Get Married. The Quarterback. Say It Again. Paradise For Two. Nothing But the Truth. Wheel of Life. Love Doctor. To the Last Man. Call of the Canyon. Icebound. Sin Flood. Redskin. A Man Must Live. Quicksands. Racing Hearts. Souls For Sale. Manpower. Fools First. Lovin' the Ladies. Public Defender. Shootin' Straight. Seven Keys to Baldpate. Lost Squadron. Cimarron. Roar of the Dragon. No Marriage Ties. Hell's Highway. The Great Jasper. The Conquerors. Day of Reckoning. Ace of Aces. Stingaree. His Greatest Gamble. The Arizonians. Special Investigator. Shanghai Bound. Yellow Dust. Devil's Playground. Sky Giant. Twelve Crowded Hours. Blind Alibi. Here I Am Stranger. Man of Conquest. Reno. Men Against the Sky. The Marines Fly High. The Roundup. The Town Too Tough to Die. Cherokee Strip. Tombstone. American Empire. Buckskin Frontier. The Kansan. Warming Up. Ghost Ship. Eyes of the Underworld. The Whistler. Mark of the Whistler. Power of the Whistler. Secret of the Whistler.*

GARY COOPER (1901-1961)

Only a few motion picture stars ever attained the stature of becoming a legend in their time, but one of the greatest was Gary Cooper. His tremendous popularity made him an immortal of the silver screen as far as film audiences were concerned. Who will ever forget his memorable performances in films like *Mr. Deeds Goes to Town, The Westerner, Pride of the Yankees, For Whom the Bell Tolls* and many other fine pictures? Gary was one of those rare actors who appealed to both male and female audiences. His rugged, down-to-earth roles were flavored with just the right amount of strong-but-shy type of he-man, while his drawing power at the box-office could only be equalled by a select few.

He was born Frank James Cooper on May 7, 1901 in Helena, Montana, the son of Alice and Supreme Court Justice Charles H. Cooper. While attending school at Bozeman, Montana, he proved to be an unruly student, forcing his parents to enroll him at a private academy in Dunstable, England. Instead of improving, he grew worse and before reaching the stage where he would be expelled, his father brought him back home and entered him at the Montana Wesleyan College. It was the same story all over again, with Gary carrying on his shenanigans, but he somehow managed to complete his education at Grinnell University in Iowa.

At eighteen, Gary was badly injured in an auto accident and was sent to recuperate on his father's ranch. It was then that he learned to ride a horse and acquainted himself with real cowboys and ranch life. In 1921, he took a job as a cartoonist for a Los Angeles newspaper, remaining there until his debut in motion pictures.

Without any previous acting experience, he was given the chance to play bit parts in some silent features during 1924-25, which decided him on an acting career. In 1926, Gary gave a surprising performance in a film called *The Winning of Barbara Worth,* which co-starred Ronald Colman and Vilma Banky. Paramount immediately signed him to a long-term contract, alternating him between romantic leads and cowboy roles until he had reached full-fledged stardom. It took the studio little time to discover just how big a star Gary was as he zoomed to the list of top ten money-making performers on the screen and remained there year after year.

In spite of the fact that Paramount gave him a wide variety of the choicest roles, Gary became known principally for his Westerns. His tall, lanky frame and natural manner completely captivated his audience, while his pictures ranked with the most successful productions of the times. Because of his strong, silent characterizations, he was branded as a man of few words until he became a favorite subject of many nightclub performers who did impersonations of him by merely uttering "Yep" and "Nope."

Although nominated for an Academy Award several times during his career, Gary won his first Oscar in 1941 for his role in *Sergeant York* and his second award in 1952 for *High Noon.* He reportedly earned an estimated $250,000,000 for Paramount before ending his association with the company in 1944. His first endeavor at producing his own films started with a successful feature called *Along Came Jones,* which turned out to be an amusing satire on Westerns.

After leaving Paramount, Gary operated his career on a free-lance basis. But, instead of working for a flat rate, he offered his services to producers at a minimum salary and a percentage of the gross profits of each film. He was one of the first four stars in Hollywood to work on such terms, the other three being James Stewart, Alan Ladd and John Wayne. Not too many actors were willing to risk such a transaction but Gary and his three colleagues proved it extremely profitable.

When the Academy Awards for 1960 were being presented on nationwide television in April, 1961, Gary's best friend, James Stewart, shocked the viewers with news that Gary Cooper was desperately ill. As he accepted a special award for Gary, Stewart made his sad and humble announcement to an astonished public. A month later, on May 13, 1961, Cooper died of incurable cancer at his home in Beverly Hills, marking the end of one of the greatest screen personalities of all time. Survived by his wife, the former Veronica Balfe, whom he had wed in 1933, and a grown daughter, Maria, Gary was buried at Our Lady of Lourdes Grotto in Holy Cross Cemetery in Hollywood. His last picture was *The Naked Edge*.

FILMS: *The Winning of Barbara Worth. Children of Divorce. It. Wings. Arizona Bound. Nevada. Beau Sabreur. Doomsday. Half a Bride. First Kiss. Shopworn Angel. Wolf Song. Lilac Time. Betrayal. The Virginian. City Streets. I Take This Woman. Fighting Caravan. Desire. The Spoilers. A Farewell to Arms. Operator 13. Today We Live. Devil and the Deep. His Woman. Design For Living. Alice in Wonderland. Now and Forever. Seven Days Leave. The Texan. Morocco. One Sunday Afternoon. Mr. Deeds Goes to Town. Bluebeard's Eighth Wife. Peter Ibbetson. The Plainsman. Lives of a Bengal Lancer. Beau Geste. The True Glory. The General Died at Dawn. Souls at Sea. Adventures of Marco Polo. The Cowboy and the Lady. The Westerner. Meet John Doe. Ball of Fire. Northwest Mounted Police. Sgt. York. Pride of the Yankees. Story of Dr. Wassell. For Whom the Bell Tolls. Saratoga Trunk. Casanova Brown. Good Sam. Along Came Jones. Cloak and Dagger. Bright Leaf. The Fountainhead. Dallas. Task Force. Unconquered. Distant Drums. High Noon. Springfield Rifle. Vera Cruz. Court Martial of Billy Mitchell. Return to Paradise. Friendly Persuasion. Love in the Afternoon. They Came to Cordura. 10 North Frederick. The Hanging Tree. The Wreck of the Mary Deare. The Naked Edge.*

JOHN WAYNE (1907-)

John Wayne is considered to be one of the all-time greats among motion picture stars, having earned an estimated $300,000,000 for his producers during a career that has lasted no less than forty years. Since 1949, he has been among the first ten money-makers in the industry and has appeared in numerous films that have kept him at the top of the list for nineteen consecutive years.

He was born Marion Michael Morrison in Winterset, Iowa on May 26, 1907 and brought up in California where he attended the Glendale High School. He entered the University of Southern California on

139

winning an athletic scholarship and distinguished himself as a star football player. Known to his friends as "Duke" Morrison, he was an outstanding tackle for the USC Trojans and played alongside a team-mate named Ward Bond. Years later, these two were to make dozens of movies together.

In 1927, producer-director John Ford went to the USC campus to film a football picture called *Salute* starring George O'Brien. Making use of the Trojan team, he hired Duke and the rest of the players to act a small part in the feature which started a long-time friendship between Ford and Wayne. When a leg injury forced him to quit football, Duke left college and found a job as a studio "grip" for the Fox Company, where he renewed his friendship with Ford. With the director's help, he met Raoul Walsh, who was in the process of making an epic Western called *The Big Trail*. Walsh had been searching for a young newcomer to play the lead in his picture and he gave Duke the part on Ford's recommendation. Released in 1930, *The Big Trail* was one of the major productions of the year and introduced John Wayne as a star.

After his initial success, Wayne was cast in a series of second-rate features which did little to improve his career. Not satisfied with his slow progress, he went to Columbia to make a string of pictures which were equally disappointing at the box-office. Then came a series of adventure-type films for Warners which improved his outlook toward the future. In 1932, Wayne joined Mascot Pictures and starred in a long list of Westerns known as Lone Star Productions. Between features and serials, he was one of the most active players in Westerns. It was during that period of his career that he portrayed the first singing cowboy hero on the screen. Getting the jump on Ken Maynard and Gene Autry by a couple of years, Wayne played the lead in the "Singing Sandy" series, which highlighted some scenes in each feature wherein the hero was supposed to vocalize. For these scenes, the producers dubbed in the singing voice of Smith Ballew while Wayne went through the actions.

When Monogram merged with Mascot, Consolidated and Lone Star to form the new Republic Studios in 1935, Wayne remained with the company for another year and then went to work for Universal and made a string of non-Western features. Around 1938, he returned to Republic to replace Bob Livingston in the "Three Mesquiteers" series and became one of the studio's most important stars.

Not yet having risen above starring in B-class horse-operas, Wayne received the biggest break of his career in 1939 when director John Ford selected him to play the lead in *Stagecoach*. Appearing with an excellent supporting cast that included Claire Trevor, Thomas Mitchell, George Bancroft and Andy Devine, he became a full-fledged star while the picture was hailed as the best Western ever made. From then on, Wayne appeared in nothing but top grade productions, many of which were directed by John Ford. By 1949, every major studio was applying for the new star's talents.

It would be difficult to pick out one picture as Wayne's best due to the fact that he made so many excellent films. He was nominated for an Academy Award as best actor of the year in 1949 when he played in *The Sands of Iwo Jima* and was also praised for his performances in *Shepherd of the Hills, Tall in the Saddle, Red River, The Quiet Man* and *The High and the Mighty*. During the 1950's, John organized his own Batjac Productions and, between making pictures for his company and other studios, he has remained one of the busiest actors on the screen.

When he is not making pictures, Wayne lives a rugged life similar to the one he portrays on the screen. Unlike most movie tough-guys, he is just as rough in real life. His nine-year marriage to Josephine Saenz ended in divorce in 1944. Two years later, he wed Esperanza Bauer, a union that lasted until 1953. He then married Pilar Pallette in 1954.

FILMS: *Salute. The Big Trail. Men Without Women. Words and Music. Three Girls Lost. Maker of Men. Arizona. Range Feud. Haunted Gold. Telegraph Trail. Hurricane Express. Shadow of the Eagle. Three Musketeers. Randy Rides Alone. Blue Steel. Riders of Destiny. Lucky Texan. Apache Trail. Dawn Rider. Texas Terrors. West of the Divide. Lawless Range. Westward Ho. Winds of the Wasteland. Lawless Nineties. King of the Pecos. Man From Monterey. Sea Spoilers. Idol of the Crowds. Adventure's End. I Cover the War. Pals of the Saddle. Santa Fe Stampede. Night Riders. Red River Range. Overland Stage Raiders. Wyoming Outlaw. Stagecoach. The Long Voyage Home. Dark Command. Shepherd of the Hills. Three Faces West. Lady For a Night. Seven Sinners. The Spoilers. Pittsburgh. Allegheny Uprising. Dakota. Flying Tigers. Fighting Seabees. Reap the Wild Wind. Reunion in France. The Lady Takes a Chance. War of the Wildcats. Flame of the Barbary Coast. Back to Bataan. Angel and the Badman. Tall in the Saddle. Tycoon. They Were Expendable. Wake of the Red Witch. The Fighting Kentuckian. Fort Apache. Red River. She Wore a Yellow Ribbon. Rio Grande. Three Godfathers. Sands of Iwo Jima. Operation Pacific. Flying Leathernecks. The Quiet Man. Big Jim McLain. Hondo. The High and the Mighty. Trouble Along the Way. The Conqueror. Blood Alley. The Sea Chase. Horse Soldiers. The Alamo. The Barbarian and the Geisha. The Man Who Shot Liberty Valance. Donovan's Reef. The Searchers. Wings of Eagles. Legend of the Lost. Rio Bravo. Hatari. How the West Was Won. The Comancheros. The Longest Day. McLintock. Eldorado. The Green Berets.*

141

RANDOLPH SCOTT (1903-)

Randolph Scott is another of those all-time favorites who enjoyed a long, successful career in motion pictures. Having gone through a phase where he was known as a romantic leading man, he favored more athletic roles in dozens of adventure-type features and came up with a reputation for being one of the outstanding Western heroes of the screen.

He was born Randolph Crane in Orange City, Virginia on January 23, 1903 and attended the universities of Virginia, Georgia Tech and North Carolina. While working as an administrative engineer, he was suddenly stricken ill and was advised by his doctor to go out West. Taking the advice, Scott went to California where he began an acting career by joining the Pasadena Community Playhouse and appearing in stage theatricals. It was during those lean years, while trying to get into movies, that he met another young hopeful named Archibald Leach. Sharing an apartment and living expenses together, Scott and his friend made the rounds of all the film studios until they were successful in getting their chances at fame and fortune. Years later, young Leach became famous as Cary Grant.

In 1929, Scott finally managed to make his screen debut in a Fox film called *The Far Call,* which proved to be his start to bigger and better things. After two years of playing minor roles, he made a hit in a picture entitled *Lone Cowboy* in 1931 and was awarded a contract with Paramount Studios. He was immediately given the chance to show what he could do in a series of Westerns based on the famous Zane Grey novels. These features had previously proved very successful when Jack Holt had made the silent versions back in the 1920's and the studio was hopeful that Scott could rise to stardom by appearing in the same stories with sound. As things turned out, a new star was born, for Scott proved himself quite capable of handling the action in these top-notch features.

Through the years that followed, Paramount gave Scott a wide variety of roles ranging from straight drama to light comedy. He even managed to survive a list of romantic features, often being loaned out to other companies for equally varied assignments. But it was in Westerns that he was at his best and his producers slowly came to realize this through experience. Besides his work at Paramount, Scott made some very good pictures for 20th Century Fox, Universal, Columbia and R-K-O, among which were two particularly fine action features, *The Spoilers* and *Pittsburgh.* Released by Universal, these films co-starred

Scott with John Wayne and Marlene Dietrich and the highlights of each production were two of the greatest knock-down drag-out fights between Scott and Wayne that had ever been staged.

In seeing Randolph Scott in a Western, one was reminded of watching the old silent favorite of the screen, William S. Hart. In many ways, both men resembled each other and played their roles somewhat identically. Each was the strong, silent type of hero. By 1950, the B-Westerns had started their descent to oblivion. When the final curtain was brought down on the horse-opera series after 1954, he was practically the sole surviving cowboy star on the screen. With a long and illustrious career behind him, he retired in 1965, choosing a life of leisure and only occasional guest appearances in films. As for his private life, after his divorce from Marianna Somerville DuPont, he wed his second wife, Patricia Stillman, in 1944.

FILMS: *The Far Call. Sky Bride. Under the Virginia Moon. To the Last Man. Heritage of the Desert. The Thundering Herd. The Last Roundup. Supernatural. Desert Gold. Nevada. Wild Horse Mesa. Wagon Wheels. Home on the Range. Hello Everybody. Village Tale. So Red the Rose. Last of the Mohicans. Follow the Fleet. Go West Young Man. Roberta. High, Wide and Handsome. Coast Guard. She. Island of Lost Souls. Sunset Pass. 20,000 Men a Year. Rocky Mountain Mystery. And Sudden Death. My Favorite Wife. Rebecca of Sunnybrook Farm. Western Union. Susannah of the Mounties. The Texans. Law of Vengeance. Jesse James. Captain Kidd. Belle Starr. To the Shores of Tripoli. Virginia City. Frontier Marshal. The Spoilers. Pittsburgh. Belle of the Yukon. China Sky. Bombardier. Corvette K225. Gung Ho. Badman's Territory. Abilene Town. Desperadoes. Home Sweet Homicide. Christmas Eve. Best of the Badmen. The Gunfighters. Canadian Pacific. Albuquerque. It's a Big Country. Walking Hills. Trail Street. Fighting Man of the Plains. Cariboo Trail. Santa Fe. Coroner's Creek. Tall Man Riding. Colt '45. Sugarfoot. Carson City. Thundercloud. The Nevadan. The Doolins of Oklahoma. Fort Worth. Hangman's Knot. Man Behind the Gun. Decision at Sundown. Bounty Hunter. Riding Shotgun. Ten Wanted Men. Man in the Saddle. Shootout at Medicine Bend. Comanche Station. Ride the High Country.*

REX BELL (1905-1962)

Rex Bell was born George Francis Beldam in Chicago, Illinois on October 16, 1905, the son of Daisy and George C. Beldam. He was educated at the University of Iowa, where he won recognition as an outstanding football player. In 1927, film director John Ford chose him along with a number of gridiron stars from all over the country to appear in a picture called *Salute,* starring George O'Brien. Without having had any previous acting experience, he made his debut under his real name with two other football athletes who later became famous as John Wayne and Ward Bond.

After getting his start as a bit player for Fox Studios, he took the name of Rex Bell and was featured in a few light comedies and collegiate pictures before getting his first chance to make a Western. As the lead in a movie entitled *From Broadway to Cheyenne,* Rex was an instant success and hailed as a bright newcomer. His youth and vitality blended well with his refreshing personality and movie fans took to him immediately. Although lacking the polish and grandeur of the larger-scale productions, his films were excellent little features made to accentuate the action and mild humor that appealed so much to his fans. As a cowboy star, Rex brought plenty of excitement to the screen without resorting to cruelty or unnecessary roughness. He made pictures mostly for the independents like Resolute and Monogram, but the over-all quality of these Westerns was well above average.

Because of his good looks and clean-cut appearance, Rex was regarded as one of the screen's handsomest cowboy heroes. He made the newspaper headlines across the country in 1931 by eloping to Yuma, Arizona with movie star Clara Bow after a whirlwind romance. The two of them had met previously while making a picture called *True to the Navy* and it became front-page news when the famous "It" girl married the cowboy star. Their marriage resulted in two sons and the family lived a peaceful life at Rex's spacious ranch in Searchlight, Nevada, away from the hullabaloo of Hollywood. Shortly after they were married, Clara Bow retired from the screen while Rex continued making Westerns. Throughout the 1930's, he was among the most active performers appearing in independent productions. But, when the singing cowboys arrived on the scene, his popularity faded slowly until he was almost completely inactive by 1938.

Rex played his last leading role in 1942 when he co-starred with Buck Jones in *Dawn on the Great Divide*. After that, he retired to his ranch and family in Nevada, operating a haberdashery shop in Las Vegas. In 1952, he made a brief appearance with Clark Gable in *Lone Star* and again in 1961 in *The Misfits*. By then, however, Rex had entered the field of politics and was elected lieutenant-governor of Nevada in 1954. As a public figure, he was extremely well-liked and held his office until the time of his death on July 4, 1962.

FILMS: *Salute. True to the Navy. Joy Street. Pleasure Crazed. Taking a Chance. They Had to See Paris. From Broadway to Cheyenne. West of Nevada. Battling With Buffalo Bill. The Man From Arizona. Too Much Beef. The Idaho Kid. Law and Lead. Stormy Trails. Lightnin'. Fighting Pioneers. Saddle Aces. Diamond Trail. Fighting Texans. The Fugitive. The Tonto Kid. Rainbow Ranch. Lucky Larrigan. Arms of the Law. Forgotten Women. Gunfire. Law of the Sea. Tombstone. Dawn on the Great Divide. Lone Star. The Misfits.*

TOM KEENE (1904-1963)

Very few Western stars could boast of a successful stage career before their entrance into the movies, but Tom Keene was one who had received acclaim by critics as well as the audience. He was born George Duryea at Smoky Hollow, near Rochester, New York on December 30, 1904. Orphaned at the age of six, he went to live with an aunt and uncle who saw to his upbringing. After attending Carnegie Tech, he graduated from Columbia University with a B.A. degree and decided to become an actor. He joined a stock company in Skowhegan, Maine and, within a short time, was appearing on the New York stage in hit plays like "White Cargo," "Madame X" and "Abie's Irish Rose." For over two years he starred in the role of "Abie" in the latter play on a tour that took him to Europe, New Zealand and Australia. On his return to America, he continued his success by playing the lead in another stage hit, "The Barber Had Two Sons."

In 1929, he entered motion pictures under his real name by appearing in C. B. De Mille's *The Godless Girl,* following that with a few films for Warners and the Wallace Reid Productions. In 1930, he began a long-term contract with R.K.O. Changing his name to Tom Keene, he was starred in a series of top-grade Westerns that brought him the fame and success he yearned for. Having risen to the ranks of upcoming cowboy stars, he was singled out for his performances in films like *Sunset Pass, Dude Wrangler* and *In Old California.* Aside from Westerns, Tom took time out to star in a few dramatic roles and, in 1934, was acclaimed for his acting in King Vidor's classic, *Our Daily Bread,* which was hailed as one of the best films about the Depression Years. However, it was through his cowboy roles that Tom achieved his purpose and he went on to make a long list of features for studios such as M-G-M and Pathe and a few Zane Grey Westerns for Paramount. In later years, after his popularity had subsided, he worked for independent producers under the banners of Crescent and Monogram, although none of these features could equal his earlier films at R-K-O.

1. *Charles Starrett*

2. *Johnny Mack Brown*

3. *Buster Crabbe*

4. *Joel McCrea seems to be in for a surprise as he confronts Michael Ansara in "The Tall Stranger"*

5. *Tom Keene*

6. *Jack Luden*

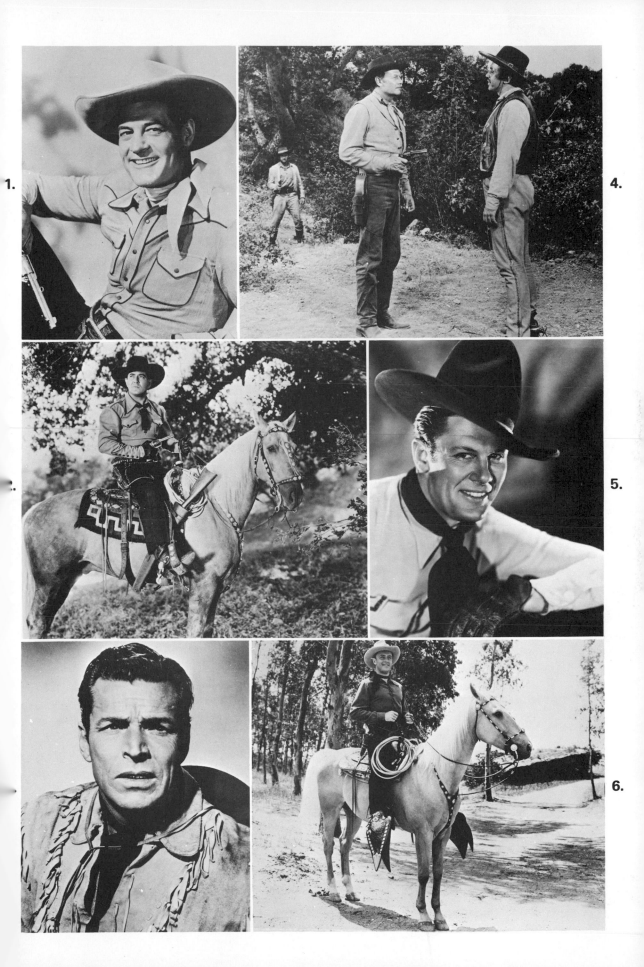

1.

4.

5.

6.

Tom was a star who helped mature the Western gradually but gracefully. He made certain that the plots of his pictures were believable and chose to characterize the hero as intelligent as well as a man of brute strength. He toned down the violence without taking away the sense of excitement. Having set the pattern, he introduced a hero who could think as well as fight and, in a short while, this pattern was adopted by William Boyd in the popular Hopalong Cassidy Westerns.

After completing his action series for Monogram, Tom took the name of Richard Powers and changed to character roles. He remained active as a supporting player up until the time of his death on August 6, 1963, when he died of cancer at Woodland Hills, California. He was married and divorced from actress Grace Stafford and was survived by his second wife, Florence, and a stepson, Robert.

FILMS: *The Godless Girl. Honky Tonk. Dude Wrangler. Strictly Business. Enchanted Cottage. In Old California. Sunset Pass. Tol'able David. Thunder. The Cheyenne Kid. Raw Timber. Pardon My Gun. Sunrise Trail. Gun Law. The Law Rides. Freighters of Destiny. Rebellion. Our Daily Bread. Scarlet River. Painted Trail. Tide of the Empire. Desert Gold. Saddle Buster. Renegades of the West. The Law Commands. Drift Fence. Hong Kong Nights. Glory Trail. Timothy's Quest. Western Mail. The Bad Man. Son of the Border. God's Country and the Man. Scarlet Trail. Arizona Roundup. Where Trails End. Battle of Greed. Dangerous Intruder. Indian Summer. Beyond the Rockies. Storm Over Wyoming. The Navy Way. Girls of the Big House. San Quentin. Crossfire. Race Street. Red Planet Mars. Trail of Robin Hood. Indian Agent. Brothers in the Saddle. Return of the Badmen. Blood on the Moon. Berlin Express. Dig That Uranium. Once Upon a Horse. Wetbacks.*

JOHNNY MACK BROWN (1904-)

Johnny Mack Brown was born in Dothan, Alabama on September 1, 1904, the son of Hattie Estelle and John H. Brown. He entered the University of Alabama in 1924 and won national recognition as an outstanding football player, performing as a halfback with one of the greatest teams in gridiron history. An excellent field runner and pass receiver, Johnny caught one of the longest completed passes on record during his first game against Georgia Tech. In a contest against Kentucky, he made a 100-yard dash to score the winning touchdown.

During the football season of 1925, Johnny received another record-breaking forward pass by team-mate Grant Gillis while playing against Washington University and ran the remaining twenty yards to a TD.

The following year, he caught a 65-yard pass by A. T. "Pooley" Hubert in the Rose Bowl classic that won Alabama the game. In the 1926 contest versus Georgia Tech, played on a muddy field, Johnny returned a kickoff by Doug Wyckoff, running fifty-five yards to make the only score of the game. Of all his spectacular feats on the gridiron, Johnny's greatest play was during the Rose Bowl classic of 1927 when he intercepted a pass and made the final touchdown with only seconds to play, helping his team to victory with a score of 20-19. Unbeaten in 1925 and 1926, Alabama ranked as one of the best teams in the country and Johnny Mack Brown became an All-American halfback. He was later elected to the Football Hall of Fame.

After finishing college, Johnny stayed on at Alabama U. as a coach. But Hollywood beckoned and he was led into making his movie debut in a 1927 M-G-M film called *The Bugle Call*. His immediate success earned him a contract with that studio and he was cast as a romantic lead opposite some of the biggest names in the business. Appearing with such popular feminine stars as Greta Garbo, Mary Pickford and Joan Crawford, Johnny quickly rose to the heights of fame and fortune through a long list of top-notch features.

In 1930, M-G-M released one of its greatest epics when it brought a picture entitled *Billy the Kid* to the screen. Filmed in a new 70 mm. wide-screen process, it starred Johnny Mack Brown as "Billy," with veteran character actor Wallace Beery and an excellent supporting cast. It was largely due to this picture that Johnny finally achieved stardom. By 1931, he was busy making a large number of features for M-G-M, First National and Paramount.

Although he had starred in at least a dozen fine melodramas, the lure of cowboy roles appealed most to Johnny, for it was in these action-type features that he felt most at home. Around 1933, he became associated with Universal Studios where he specialized in Westerns of exceptionally good quality, making a hit in a chain of thrilling serials and full-length features. From that time on, he was regarded as one of the most popular cowboy favorites in the movies. He had an extremely likeable personality and his handsome, clean-cut appearance blended well with his characterizations. Portraying the mild-tempered hero whose modesty concealed a strong, manly quality, Johnny was able to convey his fine sense of good sportsmanship to the thousands of fans that idolized him. Beginning in 1940, he was selected as one of the ten biggest money-making Western stars for eleven consecutive years. During his reign, he never gave a bad performance.

Upon completing his work at Universal, Johnny went to Republic and made a string of horse-operas for that company. Later, he starred in another series for Monogram, remaining there until the era of the B-Western series came to an end. Since then, he has made a few guest appearances in several pictures but has preferred to enjoy his retirement living quietly at his beautiful home on the outskirts of Beverly Hills. Johnny has been married to the former Cornelia Foster since 1926 and is the proud father of four children. A sports enthusiast, he enjoys playing golf, riding and hunting with his close pal, former cowboy star Charles Starrett.

FILMS: *The Bugle Call. Fair Co-ed. Our Dancing Daughters. Little Angel. The Great Meadow. A Woman of Affairs. Hurricane. Lady of Chance. Montana Moon. The Single Standard. Coquette. Undertow. Billy the Kid. Divine Woman. Female. St. Louis Woman. Malay Nights. 70,000 Witnesses. The Last Flight. Saturday's Millions. Annapolis. Belle of the Nineties. It Ain't No Sin. Flames. The Secret Six. Flaming Frontier. Born to the West. Vanishing Frontier. Fighting With Kit Carson. Riders of the Border. Ghost Guns. The Law Comes to Gunsight. Covered Wagon Trail. Hell Town. Desperate Trails. Bar Z Badmen. The Oregon Trail. Covered Wagon Days. Branded a Coward. Boothill Brigade. Gambling Terror. Lawless Hand. Wells Fargo. Undercover Man. Guns in the Dark. Arizona Cyclone. Cheyenne Roundup. Boss of Hangtown Mesa. Son of Roaring Dan. Little Joe the Wrangler. Lasca of the Rio Grande. Lone Star Trail. Drifting Along. Man From Sonora. West of Carson City. Crossed Trails. Back Trail. Canyon Ambush. Code of the Saddle. Flame of the West. Riders of Pasco Basin. Border Bandits. Colorado Ambush. Dead Man's Trail. Sheriff of Medicine Bow. Frontier Agent. Gun Talk. Gunning For Justice. Fighting Ranger. Man From Black Hills. Badman From Red Butte. Man From Whistling Hills. Bounty Killer. Requiem For a Gunfighter.*

CHARLES STARRETT (1904-)

Among the perennial cowboy favorites of the motion picture screen, Charles Starrett has had the distinct pleasure of being listed one of the top ten for no less than fifteen successful years. Also having once been voted "the handsomest Western star," he was the leading performer on Columbia Studios' roster of horse-opera heroes for many years throughout the 1940's.

He was born in Athol, Massachusetts on March 28, 1904, the son of Leroy S. Starrett, founder of the famous Starrett Precision Tool Company. After spending his childhood years in Maine, he became a student at Dartmouth University, where he won recognition as a football

150

athlete. His first taste of acting came when he took part in some college theatricals, and soon thereafter he had the chance to appear in his first movie. In 1925, he and some gridiron team-mates were selected to play minor roles in a Richard Dix picture called *The Quarterback* which was partly photographed on the Dartmouth campus. Convinced that he could do well in movies, Charles decided to become an actor.

After graduating from college with a B.S. degree, he pursued a career by landing a small part in a New York stage play that only lasted a week. Not to be discouraged, he took a job with Wanamaker's department store, acting in short presentations, until he had the opportunity to join the Stewart Warker Stock Company and tour the East. Three years later, he made a more impressive comeback to the New York stage in a play entitled "Claire Adams" and was spotted by a movie talent scout.

Arriving in Hollywood in 1930, he was placed under contract to Paramount Studios, where he was cast in a series of collegiate films as a young romantic lead. After three years, he finally won the notice of producers and movie audiences when he appeared with Boris Karloff in an adventure feature called *The Mask of Fu Manchu*. He then left Paramount to join Columbia Studios where he made numerous films that ranged from mysteries to dramas.

In 1936, Charles had the feeling that he could adapt himself to cowboy roles, so he talked his studio into letting him make Westerns. An immediate hit, he was voted to the list of top ten horse-opera heroes in 1937 and, except for an interruption in 1943, remained there for fifteen years.

Starrett's remarkable popularity was due largely to his wholesome appearance and the sense of good sportsmanship that he projected on the screen. In spite of the fact that his pictures became somewhat stereotyped because of the repetitious use of the same supporting players, the plots were usually good and the action was always exciting. At a time when singing cowboys were the rage, Starrett carried on in the old tradition by remaining a straight-action hero and when he began his popular "Durango Kid" series for Columbia, the added thrill of seeing him as a mysterious masked rider was another feature his fans enjoyed.

As the end of the B-Western came near, Charles Starrett was among the last well-known cowboy stars to go. After retiring in 1953, he chose to live a life of leisure and supervise his various business interests while residing at his beautiful home on the outskirts of Hollywood. He was married to the former Mary McKinnon in September, 1927 and became the proud father of twin sons in 1929. An avid sports enthusiast,

Charles and his pal, Johnny Mack Brown, take an active interest in golf, riding and hunting.

FILMS: *The Quarterback. Sweetheart of Sigma Chi. Murder on the Campus. Sons of Steel. So Red the Rose. Touchdown. Our Betters. The Mask of Fu Manchu. Make a Million. A Shot in the Dark. Jungle Bride. Along Came Love. Return of Casey Jones. Lightning Guns. Headin' West. Land Rush. Roaring Rangers. Blazing Six Shooters. Texas Stagecoach. Bullets For Rustlers. Lawless Empire. Desert Horseman. West of Tombstone. Cyclone Prairie Rangers. Buckaroos From Powder River. Both Barrels Blazing. Blazing a Western Trail. Fort Savage Raiders. Smoky Canyon. Overland to Deadwood. Laramie Mountain. Across the Badlands. The Blazing Trail. Bandits of El Dorado. Blazing Across the Pecos. Bonanza Town. Cyclone Fury. South of Death Valley. Challenge of the Range. Gunning For Vengeance. Cowboy From Lonesome River. Frontier Outpost. Cowboy Canteen. Galloping Thunder. The Fighting Frontiersman.*

LARRY "BUSTER" CRABBE (1909-)

Not too many movie enthusiasts would fail to recognize this famous hero of the screen. His popularity as a cowboy star and television idol was equally as great as the fame he received from appearing in serials. A renowned athlete, he had entered motion pictures after taking part in the Olympics and was also known for having played the role of "Tarzan of the Apes" on the screen.

He was born Clarence Linden Crabbe in Oakland, California on February 7, 1909. When he was two, his father took the family to live in Honolulu, Hawaii. While attending the Puna Hou High School, he developed a keen skill in athletics and won his letters each year in swimming, baseball, football and track. More familiarly known as Larry, he entered the University of Hawaii where he continued his activities in sports and won the light-heavyweight boxing title of the Hawaiian Islands.

In 1928, Larry was selected to represent the U.S.A. in the Olympic swimming contests in Los Angeles. Having returned to the continent, he enrolled at the University of Southern California to complete his education and was again chosen to be a member of the U.S. swimming team in the Olympics of 1932. That year, he won the 400-meter free-style event for America and, by the end of 1933, had broken five world's records, taken sixteen international titles and won thirty-five national championships in swimming. In all, he collected some seven hundred trophies and medals in athletic events all over the world.

In 1933, Paramount Studios grabbed Larry for the movies and gave him a role in *Island of Lost Souls* opposite Charles Laughton and Richard Arlen. By then, he became known to his friends as "Buster" due to his record-breaking reputation in the Olympics. His next part on the screen was the lead in a film called *King of the Jungle,* in which he played a character closely resembling Tarzan of the Apes. Realizing his great potential as an action star, Paramount gave him some good roles in the Zane Grey Westerns opposite Randolph Scott and Tom Keene. In order to take full advantage of his tremendous appeal, the studio also featured Buster in a series of collegiate films, but these did little to further his career. It was in action features that he had reached success and it was decided that he should remain as such.

During those early 1930's, Buster won himself a huge following after appearing in a serial entitled *Tarzan the Fearless.* Produced by Sol Lesser, the twelve-episode chapter-play had a good deal to do with establishing him as a star. In 1936, he was named one of the top ten cowboys of the screen at the same time that Paramount loaned him out to Universal. It was there that Buster made his indelible impression in movies by starring in a serial called *Flash Gordon.* He was so successful that Universal hired him for another chapter-play entitled *Red Barry* which was in turn followed by three more—*Flash Gordon's Trip to Mars, Buck Rogers* and *Flash Gordon Conquers the Universe.* By 1940, he was regarded as the "King of the Sound Serials."

Taking a short leave from movies, Buster found time to win the professional three-mile swimming meet at Los Angeles in 1940 and to appear as a featured performer at the New York and San Francisco World Fairs. When he returned to picture-making, he made a few films for Republic, Universal, Monogram and Columbia, until 1941, when P.R.C. signed him for a series of "Billy the Kid" Westerns. Appearing with him as his sidekick was veteran comedian Al "Fuzzy" St. John. Together, the pair made no less than forty-five features. It was unfortunate that the quality of these Westerns proved to be second-rate due to too much emphasis on comedy. In fact, some of the villains even took on the appearance of clowns rather than serving in their usual capacities. When Buster's role was changed to "Bill Carson," the series improved very little. Thus, in 1948, Monogram ceased production and he concluded his career with the studio.

Heeding the call of television, Buster entered the new medium during the early 1950's as host of a show that presented some of his old films. He then made a personal appearance tour with his own Wild

West Show. This only lasted a year after which he returned to TV as the host on a physical-fitness program. In 1953, he went to North Africa to film a new television series called "Captain Gallant of the Foreign Legion" which he also produced. In this series, Buster shared top honors with his son, Cullen, and comedian Fuzzy Knight.

Having since returned to feature movies, Buster is still an active performer on the screen. When he is not busy with pictures, he lives a comparatively quiet life with his wife, the former Virginia Held, whom he married in 1933, and their son and daughter. Among his many business interests, Buster is also active in promoting sales for his home-type swimming pools.

FILMS: *Island of Lost Souls. King of the Jungle. To the Last Man. Tarzan the Fearless. The Thundering Herd. Drift Fence. Sweetheart of Sigma Chi. Hold 'Em Yale. Rose Bowl. We're Rich Again. Murder Goes to College. Search For Beauty. Wanderer of the Wasteland. Nevada. Pigskin Parade. Desert Gold. Arizona Raiders. Forlorn River. Arizona Mahoney. Flash Gordon. Red Barry. Flash Gordon's Trip to Mars. Buck Rogers. Flash Gordon Conquers the Universe. Unmarried. Billy the Kid. Wanted. Billy the Kid's Roundup. Wild Horse Phantom. Overland Riders. Badge of Honor. Drums of Africa. The Contender. Jungle Siren. Nabonga. Jungle Man. Swamp Fire. Wildcat. Border Badmen. Fighting Bill Carson. Blazing Frontier. Ghost of Hidden Valley. Oil Raiders. Devil Riders. The Drifter. Rustler's Hideout. Western Cyclone. Renegade. Frontier Outlaws. Caged Fury. Valley of Vengeance. Fuzzy Settles Down. Pirates on the High Seas. Gun Brothers. Lawless Fifties. Badmen's Country. Gangster's Den. Gunfighters of Abilene.*

JOEL McCREA (1905-)

Joel McCrea is another all-time favorite among the super stars who became particularly famous for his cowboy roles. His success in Westerns was not just a matter of choosing the right pictures, but was due largely to his fine acting ability, his pleasing personality and a genuine fondness for that type of film.

He was born in Los Angeles, California on November 5, 1905, the son of Louise and Thomas P. McCrea, who were directly descended from pioneer settlers of California. Joel's first experience with motion pictures came to him when he was still a young lad, having been chosen to appear as an extra in a mob scene for an old Ruth Roland serial. After graduating from Hollywood High, he entered the University of Southern California and completed his education at Pomona College.

He embarked on an acting career by joining the Pasadena Community Playhouse, taking part in stage theatricals until 1929 when film director Sam Wood selected him to play in a picture called *The Jazz Age*.

As a new leading man, Joel became an immediate success through a number of features for F.B.O., M-G-M, and R-K-O, before Paramount signed him to a long-term contract. He managed to survive through the ordeal of being cast in a series of monotonous melodramas, rising to stardom after appearing in hits like *Bird of Paradise, Barbary Coast* and *Come and Get It*.

It was partly on the advice of old-time cowboy star William S. Hart that McCrea decided to try Westerns. In 1938, he starred in *Wells Fargo,* an A-class feature that also boasted of fine performers like Frances Dee, Bob Burns and Johnny Mack Brown. A year later, Joel made an exceptional hero in Cecil B. De Mille's *Union Pacific,* which became a classic among Westerns and once again featured the popular team of Joel McCrea and Barbara Stanwyck. From then on, McCrea was especially fond of appearing on the screen in tales of the Old West.

A versatile actor, he gave memorable performances in highly dramatic masterpieces such as *Dead End, Foreign Correspondent* and *Reaching For the Sun,* while displaying a flair for comedy in *Sullivan's Travels, Palm Beach Story* and *The More the Merrier*. But it was in Westerns like *Buffalo Bill, The Virginian* and *Ramrod* that Joel really had audiences in the palm of his hand.

Completing his long association with Paramount around 1949, McCrea undertook free-lancing for various studios and confining his activities to the type of pictures he enjoyed making best. The result was a string of top-notch Westerns for companies like Universal, M-G-M, Warner Bros. and United Artists. As the years passed, film fans were treated to seeing Joel in outstanding features like *Stars in My Crown, Four Faces West, Wichita, Trooper Hook* and others too numerous to mention. Throughout the 1950's, it seemed as if he was incapable of making a picture that was not a hit.

Not content with his success in movies alone, McCrea also did well in a radio series called "Tales of the Texas Rangers" and a television show entitled "Wichita Town." Since 1963, he has been in semi-retirement, choosing to make only occasional pictures now and then. A real cowboy off the screen as well as on, he has confined his time to his fabulous 2,500-acre ranch raising cattle and horses. When oil was recently discovered on his land, he held out from selling the drilling rights for fear that derricks would mar the scenery of his ranch. After receiving many offers, he finally consented to sell the oil rights for $13,000,000 with the stipulation that no drilling be done within sight of his home.

155

He has been happily married to actress Frances Dee since October 20, 1933, and he is the father of three children.

FILMS: *The Jazz Age. The Single Standard. Rockabye. Dynamite. The Silver Horde. Five O'Clock Girl. Girls About Town. Common Law. Born to Love. Kept Husbands. Lightnin'. Once a Sinner. Sports Parade. So This Is College. Lost Squadron. The Silver Cord. A Chance at Heaven. The Plutocrat. These Three. Bird of Paradise. Gambling Lady. Bed of Roses. The Richest Girl in the World. One Man's Journey. Barbary Coast. Come and Get It. Banjo on My Knee. Adventure in Manhattan. Interns Can't Take Money. Three Blind Mice. Youth Takes a Fling. Wells Fargo. Dead End. Union Pacific. Pioneer Women. They Shall Have Music. Primrose Path. He Married His Wife. Espionage Agent. Foreign Correspondent. Reaching For the Sun. Palm Beach Story. Sullivan's Travels. The Great Moment. The More the Merrier. The Great Man's Lady. The Unseen. Buffalo Bill. The Virginian. Ramrod. South of St. Louis. Frenchie. The Outriders. Four Faces West. Colorado Territory. Cattle Drive. Saddle Tramp. San Francisco Story. Stars in My Crown. They Passed This Way. Wichita. First Texan. The Oklahoman. Border River. Black Horse Canyon. Stranger on Horseback. Lone Hand. Shoot First. Cattle Empire. Fort Massacre. Trooper Hook. Gunsight Ridge. Gunfight at Dodge City. Ride the High Country. Guns in the Afternoon.*

JACK LUDEN (1902-)

This popular star of Westerns was born John Luden in Reading, Pennsylvania on February 6, 1902, the son of Anna and Jacob C. Luden, the famous manufacturer of cough drops. After attending the Cornwall-on-the-Hudson Military Academy and the Tome School at Ft. Deposit, Maryland, Jack studied for two years at the Johns Hopkins University. However, he decided he would rather act than become a doctor. In 1925, he was chosen among 30,000 applicants for a course at Paramount Pictures' Junior School of Acting in Long Island, New York and was given a chance to make his debut in a film called *Fascinating Youth* the following year.

In the Spring of 1926, Jack was transferred to Paramount's West Coast Studios, where he played his first leading role in *It's the Old Army Game.* After that he went on loan to F.B.O. to star in his first Western, *Shootin' Irons,* which led to a whole series of horse-operas. Having risen from featured player to leading parts, he was quite active during the

156

late years of the silent-picture era. But, the arrival of talkies ended his association with F.B.O. and Paramount.

While the movie industry underwent drastic changes in production methods, Jack learned that Columbia was organizing a new stable of cowboy stars with long-range plans of making money through all-talking Westerns. Having already signed such favorites as Buck Jones and Tim McCoy, Columbia added Jack to the growing list in 1931 and starred him in a series of action features that were well-received by cowboy fans.

By the mid-1930's, the screen was offering the biggest array of sagebrush heroes the movies had ever seen. With the B-Western at an all-time peak of production, the competition was extremely keen and many personalities were forced to either retire or accept minor roles. Such was the case with Jack Luden. After 1935, his career as a cowboy star was finished and he resorted to character parts. Up until the late 1940's, he appeared in many features for Republic, Monogram and P.R.C. in support of such heroes as Gene Autry, Don Barry, Eddie Dean and Jim Newill. Although his career had been relatively short in years, he had found adequate time to leave his permanent mark on the field of Westerns.

FILMS: *Fascinating Youth. It's the Old Army Game. The Jade Cup. Bill Grimm's Progress. Uneasy Payments. Shootin' Irons. The Last Outlaw. Yours to Command. Phantom Gold. City of Shadows. Tell It to Sweeney. Dangerous Curves. Two Flaming Youths. Partners in Crime. Woman From Moscow. Forgotten Faces. Sins of the Fathers. Why Bring That Up? Wild Party. Pioneer Trail. Stagecoach Days. Rolling Caravans. Brand of the Devil. Boss of Rawhide. Guadalcanal Diary. The Texas Rangers. Bordertown Trail. King of the Royal Mounted.*

REB RUSSELL (1905-)

During the years between 1930 and 1940, many of the cowboy stars on the screen had come from the ranks of football athletes. These rugged individuals were ideally suited for the fast-paced action that Westerns demanded. Stars like Johnny Mack Brown, Charles Starrett, John Wayne and Ward Bond had all been popular gridiron players before entering the movies. In the early 1930's, a former All-American named Reb Russell joined the ranks of Western favorites and enjoyed a short but impressive career in films.

Born Fay H. Russell on May 31, 1905, he grew up with a natural ability for sports. In 1929, he entered the Northwestern University where he excelled in football, baseball and wrestling. Having distinguished himself on the gridiron, he was chosen All-American fullback in 1930 and was elevated to the list of all-time greats. His exceptional performance on the field led him into motion pictures when, in 1932, he was hired along with a group of football players to appear in a Paramount film entitled *All-American*.

Following his debut, Russell was signed by producer Willis Kent to star in a series of independent Westerns. Riding a white horse he called "Rebel," the new cowboy hero whizzed through some of the fastest, thrill-packed adventures ever produced in the field of horse-operas. Although on a strict budget, these pictures were very good and contained plenty of action.

Russell remained a Western star until 1937, having made a score of films for the independent market. Had he been given the chance to star for the major companies, he would have surely reached greater heights.

FILMS: *Arizona Badman. Outlaw Rule. Man From Hell. Fighting Thru. Border Vengeance. Lightning Triggers. Rough and Tough.*

KERMIT MAYNARD (1902-   )

Kermit Maynard was born in Indiana on September 20, 1902, the son of Mr. and Mrs. William H. Maynard. While attending the Indiana University, where he studied engineering, he excelled in college sports and was a star halfback. After graduating, he worked as a claims agent for the Hormel Meat Packing Company until 1927, when he received a summons from his older brother, Ken, who was in Hollywood making movies. Answering the call, Kermit landed a job as a stuntman, doubling for his brother at First National Studios.

After almost two years of movie stunt work, he appeared as a supporting player under the name of Tex Maynard in a few features at F.B.O. which starred Lefty Flynn. By 1930, he had graduated to leading roles in a series of Westerns for the Rayart Company. While the movie industry was developing a voice, Kermit kept busy with stunt work and acting. In 1931, he drew some attention when he appeared in a featured role and as Tom Tyler's double in a Western serial called *Phantom of the West*. By that time, he was using his real name while gaining some prominence in horse-operas.

Between 1931 and 1933, Kermit starred in a group of fast-paced features for producer Maurice Conn and Ambassador Pictures. Although these films were released by the independent market, they contained plenty of fine action and gave Kermit lots of opportunity to show what he could do. In 1933, he took time out from movie-making to win the title of "World's Champion Trick and Fancy Rider" at a national rodeo competition in Salinas, California, an honor which greatly enhanced his value at the box-office. By the following year, he reached the zenith of his career in another series of Westerns loaded with action and excitement.

Among the many pictures Kermit made was a group of Canadian Mounted Police features which went over real big with his fans. They contained beautiful outdoor settings of the Northwest and were based on the stories of popular writers like James Oliver Curwood and Peter B. Kyne. Best of all was the presence of Kermit, himself. He always seemed to include scenes in which he was involved in a thrilling roof-top chase, hopping from building to building until he came to grips with the outlaws. An all-around athlete, he was more than capable of handling any action that came his way. Like all good Western stars, Kermit made sure to share the spotlight with his horse, "Rocky."

When the singing cowboys took over during the late 1930's, Kermit gradually turned to character parts and doubled for big-name stars in hazardous scenes. After 1941, he was playing mostly villains opposite stars like Gene Autry, Bob Livingston, Buster Crabbe and Johnny Mack Brown in Westerns for Republic, P.R.C., Monogram and Columbia. Due to his getting along in years, he gave up stunt work around 1958 to concentrate on character roles.

Although he never rose above the ranks of independent productions as a star, Kermit became extremely popular with cowboy fans as well as with his co-workers. For awhile, he served as a representative of the Screen Actors' Guild and was also responsible for several improvements in filming dangerous action sequences.

FILMS: *Ridin' Luck. Gun Hand Garrison. Wild Born. Prince of the Plains. Wanderer of the West. Drum Taps. The Fighting Trooper. Phantom of the West. Wilderness Mail. Outlaw Justice. Red Blood of Courage. Northern Frontier. Code of the Mounted. His Fighting Blood. Whistling Bullets. Trails of the Wild. Timber War. Wildcat Trooper. Song of the Trail. Fighting Texan. Galloping Dynamite. Wild Horse Roundup. Phantom Patrol. Valley of Terror. Rough Ridin' Rhythm. Stars Over Texas. Roaring Six Guns. Adventures of Wild Bill Hickock. Trail of Robin Hood. Gunsmoke Mesa. Fighting Terror. How the West Was Won.*

GENE AUTRY (1907-)

In all the annals of motion picture history, one of the greatest success stories is that of Gene Autry who started out as a railroad telegrapher and rose to become a multi-millionaire through movies, radio, recordings and television. Reputed to be worth in the neighborhood of fifty million dollars, Gene amassed his fortune through hard work and a number of enterprises that today include real estate, oil wells, radio stations, newspapers, theatres, recording firms and a variety of other interests.

Born in Tioga, Texas on September 29, 1907, the son of Delbert and Nora Autry, he left high school in 1925 to work for the San Francisco Railroad as a telegraph operator. After serving as a station telegrapher in Ravia and Sapulpa, Oklahoma, he became a dispatcher for the depot at Chelsea, Oklahoma, where he first met Will Rogers. Having had the occasion to hear Gene sing, Rogers advised him to get into show business. In 1928, Autry got his chance to vocalize for a radio station in nearby Tulsa. Two years later, he was being featured on NBC's popular "National Barn Dance" program over station WLS in Tulsa. This led to a series of recordings and personal appearances.

In 1934, Gene and his radio pal, Smiley Burnette, were called upon to sing in a couple of short musical scenes for two Ken Maynard Westerns. A year later, producer Nat Levine, who was in the process of organizing the new Republic Pictures Corporation, gave Gene and Smiley their first leads in a chapter-play called *Phantom Empire* which led to a feature film entitled *Tumblin' Tumbleweeds*. The pair was so successful that Levine signed them to a long-term contract and starred them in a long list of Westerns. By 1937, Gene had managed to dislodge the formidable Buck Jones from his lofty pedestal as "King of the Cowboys" and became the new leader of sagebrush heroes.

With each successive picture, Gene's singing was spotlighted in bigger and costlier productions. It was something entirely new in Westerns to have the hero deliberately take time out from chasing outlaws to sing a song, but movie fans took to the cowboy vocalist immediately. Among the stars that played in non-musical horse-operas, the arrival of the singing cowboy was considered an insult to the tradition of Westerns and, although several predicted that these guitar-strumming heroes were a fad and wouldn't last, Gene Autry became one of the biggest hits in movie history.

For six years Gene was Republic's top money-maker, riding his horse, "Champion," through one successful film after another and vocal-

160

izing his songs until the public voted him one of the top ten box-office favorites. The popularity of his films soon brought a parade of singing cowboys to the screen until Westerns were swamped with music and it seemed like the horse-opera was doomed to die amidst a flurry of guitars and yodeling. In 1942, Gene entered the U.S. Air Corps, serving with the Air Transport Command during World War II. When he left Republic, the studio wasted no time in replacing him with another singing cowboy named Roy Rogers, who took over as King in 1943.

When Autry returned to pictures after the war, he found that his place had been taken at Republic. Undaunted, he went over to Columbia Studios where he started making a new series of Westerns billed as "Public Cowboy No. 1" and quickly resumed his successful career. By that time, musical cowboys had lost some of their flavor and Gene selected to tone down his singing numbers in favor of more action. The result was an even better quality of horse-operas insofar as the singing no longer interfered with the plots of his pictures.

Having already returned to radio on his old program for the Wrigley Chewing Gum Corporation, Autry also resumed his tours with the "Gene Autry Rodeo" which appeared throughout the country annually. Noted for his shrewd business know-how, he organized his Gene Autry Enterprises into a multi-million dollar empire and became the first cowboy star to make a series of films exclusively for television when he appeared on his "Gene Autry Show" in 1950. It was at that time that he brought suit against Republic for releasing his old pictures to TV, and when he failed to get satisfaction, he went into TV production himself and competed with his own films. As owner of the Flying A Productions, he was responsible for such noted television shows as "The Gene Autry Show," "The Range Rider," "Annie Oakley," "Young Buffalo Bill," "Cavalcade of America," "Death Valley Days" and "The Adventures of Champion."

Since 1960, Gene has been content with leaving motion pictures to other hopeful players in preference to managing his wide business interests and appearing on TV. He ceased production on his television series a few years ago to retire to his spacious "Melody Ranch" in California, where he lives with his wife, the former Ina Mae Spivey, whom he married in 1932. A talented composer of cowboy ballads, Gene has several of the tunes he helped to make popular bearing his name and many of his recordings have sold over the million mark. In 1961, he became part owner of a major league baseball club, the Los Angeles Angels, and has had the honor of having the town of Berwyn, Oklahoma change its name to "Autry."

1. *Tex Ritter*
2. *Kermit Maynard*
3. *Gene Autry*
4. *Fred Scott*
5. *Smiley Burnette and Virginia Grey have quite an audience in "Idaho," a Republic Picture*
6. *Reb Russell*

1.

4.

2.

5.

6.

FILMS: *Mystery Mountain. In Old Santa Fe. Phantom Empire. Tumblin' Tumbleweeds. Comin' 'Round the Mountain. Git Along Little Dogies. The Old Corral. Melody Trail. Sagebrush Troubadour. The Singing Cowboy. El Rancho Grande. Down Mexico Way. Melody Ranch. My Little Buckaroo. South of the Border. Ride Tenderfoot Ride. The Singing Hills. The Last Roundup. Guns and Guitars. Radio Ranch. Song of Old Wyoming. Gaucho Serenade. Ride Ranger Ride. Gold Mine in the Sky. Western Jamboree. Man of the Frontier. Star Eyes of the Sage. Yodelin' Kid From Pine Ridge. Colorado Sunset. Red River Valley. Carolina Moon. Blue Montana Skies. Shooting High. Back in the Saddle. Bells of Capistrano. Call of the Canyon. Cowboy Serenade. Gay Ranchero. Man From Music Mountain. Sierra Sue. Mexicali Rose. Big Broadcast of 1937. Singing Vagabond. Roundup Time in Texas. Public Cowboy No. 1. Rootin' Tootin' Rhythm. Springtime in the Rockies. Rhythm of the Range. Prairie Moon. Home on the Prairie. In Old Monterey. Oh Susanna. Mountain Rhythm. Under Fiesta Stars. Riding on a Rainbow. Empty Saddles. Stardust on the Sage. Home in Wyoming. Heart of the Rio Grande. Boots and Saddle. Silver on the Sage. Sioux City Sue. Saddle Pals. Robin Hood of Texas. Blazing Sun. Blue Canadian Skies. Big Sombrero. Barbed Wire. Apache Country. Little Champ. Indian Territory. Ghost Riders in the Sky. Mule Train. The Cowboy and the Indians. On Top of Old Smoky. Saginaw Trail. Last of the Pony Riders. Gold Town Ghost Raiders. Winning of the West. Cow Town. Gene Autry and the Boy Scouts. Sons of New Mexico. Rim of the Canyon. Loaded Pistols. Riders of the Whistling Pines. Strawberry Roan.*

SMILEY BURNETTE (1911-1968)

Lester Burnette was born in Summum, Illinois on March 18, 1911 and attended Astoria high school before entering show business. While appearing in vaudeville, he amazed his audiences with his ability to play a wide variety of musical instruments as he presented his one-man show on the stage. Within a short time, he was featured on a radio program emanating from Tusceola, Oklahoma, where he first met singing cowboy Gene Autry. The two entertainers became close friends and appeared together on the "National Barn Dance" radio show in Tulsa for four years. The program eventually brought them nation-wide fame, leading them into motion pictures in 1934, when they performed in a Ken Maynard serial called *Mystery Mountain*. That same year, Smiley and Gene made another appearance with Maynard in a feature film

164

entitled *In Old Santa Fe,* which enabled them to make a lasting impression on film fans.

In 1935, producer Nat Levine was in the process of merging his Mascot Productions with several other companies to form an outfit called Republic Studios when he decided to feature Autry and Burnette in a serial entitled *Phantom Empire.* The film was such a smash hit that Levine wasted no time in starring them in a full-length feature called *Tumblin' Tumbleweeds,* which led to a long-term contract with the new company. It was the first of over fifty pictures that Smiley made with Gene for Republic between 1935 and 1942. Playing a character known as "Frog Millhouse," he provided the comedy along with his own brand of musical versatility and became a favorite among Western fans up to the point where he was listed as one of the top ten cowboy stars in 1940, a place in which he remained for twelve consecutive years. In a way, Smiley established a new precedent when he made the roster of the top ten because, technically, he was playing Gene Autry's sidekick and was not really a full-fledged star. Until he appeared on the list, the first ten cowboy favorites had been restricted to the leading players in Westerns, but Smiley changed all that when he became the first "sidekick" to be included with the heroes of horse-operas. In the years that followed, other popular sidekicks like Gabby Hayes, Andy Devine and Fuzzy Knight were to receive this same honor.

When Gene Autry left Republic in 1942 to enter the Armed Forces, Smiley stayed on at the studio to complete a series of Westerns with Allan "Rocky" Lane and another with Sunset Carson. In 1944, he left the organization to join Columbia Studios where he was featured with Charles Starrett in another long string of pictures that lasted until the early 1950's.

After 1953, Smiley retired from the movies to live a quiet life with his wife, the former Dallas MacDonald, and concentrate his efforts towards song-writing. He came out of retirement in 1964 to appear as a featured player with his old pal, Rufe Davis, in a popular TV series called "Petticoat Junction" until his death in 1968.

FILMS: *Mystery Mountain. In Old Santa Fe. Phantom Empire. Tumblin' Tumbleweeds. Comin' 'Round the Mountain. Git Along Little Dogies. The Old Corral. Melody Trail. Sagebrush Troubadour. The Singing Cowboy. El Rancho Grande. Down Mexico Way. Melody Ranch. My Little Buckaroo. South of the Border. Ride Tenderfoot Ride. The Singing Hills. The Last Roundup. Guns and Guitars. Radio Ranch. Song of Old Wyoming. Gaucho Serenade. Ride Ranger Ride. Gold Mine in the Sky. Western Jamboree. Man of the Frontier. Star*

Eyes of the Sage. Yodelin' Kid From Pine Ridge. Colorado Sunset. Red River Valley. Carolina Moon. Blue Montana Skies. Shooting High. Back in the Saddle. Bells of Capistrano. Call of the Canyon. Cowboy Serenade. Gay Ranchero. Man From Music Mountain. Sierra Sue. Mexicali Rose. Bordertown Trail. Code of the Prairie. Gunning For Vengeance. Galloping Thunder. Headin' West. Terror Trail. Blazing Six Shooters. Smoky Canyon. Gold Town Ghost Riders. 'Neath Western Skies. Across the Badlands. Challenge of the Range. Buckaroo of Powder River. Blazing Across the Pecos. Bandits of Eldorado. Desert Horseman. Cyclone Fury. Fort Savage Raiders. Bonanza Town. Fighting Frontiersman.

TEX RITTER (1907-)

When Gene Autry became an overnight sensation with his musical Westerns for Republic Studios, the first singing cowboy that appeared to give him real competition was Tex Ritter. Shortly afterwards, there came a host of cowboy vocalists—Dick Foran, Bob Baker, Fred Scott and George Houston—but it was Ritter who took up the challenge before any others.

He was born Woodward Maurice Nederland Ritter in Murvaul, Texas on January 12, 1907. Graduating from Beaumont High, he attended the University of Texas, where he earned his B.A. degree, and then studied law at the Northwestern University. After a year of practicing as an attorney, he decided he would rather be in show business, so be bought himself a guitar and landed a job singing on radio. Two years later, he was being featured in stage productions like "Green Grow the Lilacs," "The Roundup" and "Mother Lode."

Returning to radio, Tex managed to include several successful recordings to his name which brought him to the attention of film producer Edward Finney. When Gene Autry struck it rich at Republic Studios in 1935, Finney hastened to star Tex in a group of musical Westerns released under Grand National in 1936. The success of his first feature, *Song of the Gringo,* made him one of the top ten cowboy stars in 1937, where he remained until 1941. In 1944 and 1945, he was again elected to the list of favorite sagebrush heroes, thus giving him a total of seven years as a leading performer in Westerns.

With his series for Grand National completed in 1938, Tex moved to Monogram Studios where he starred in another string of features. Possessing one of the most original singing voices, he warbled his way to fame and fortune through motion pictures, radio and recordings. Besides his vocalizing ability, he could handle action well and the fans en-

166

joyed seeing him astride his wonder horse, "White Flash," as he romped through one screen adventure after another.

In 1942, Tex became a part of the roster of cowboys working for Columbia, where he stayed until 1944. After that, he accepted an offer to co-star with Johnny Mack Brown in the "Frontier Marshals" series at Universal and his popularity reached new heights in these fast-paced action features. During the late 1940's, Tex made his last regular series of pictures for P.R.C. when he appeared with Dave O'Brien in the "Texas Rangers" Westerns. Since then, he has concentrated on radio and television and has made only occasional films. On television, he has played host on shows like "Western Ranch Party" and "Cowboy Jamboree," while his long list of recordings have made him one of the leading personalities in the field of Country and Western music.

Although he wasn't seen on the screen, Tex was selected to sing the musical themes on the sound tracks of notable films like *High Noon* and *Trooper Hook* and he has been an active player in several recent pictures. A noted recording artist for Capitol Records, he has also composed many successful ballads. He and his wife Dorothy (his former leading lady) and their two sons live a comparatively quiet life at their beautiful California ranch home.

FILMS: *Song of the Gringo. Golden Trail. Starlight Over Texas. Rhythm of the Rio Grande. Frontier Town. Riders of the Rockies. Rolling Plains. Utah Trail. Trouble in Texas. Lone Star Trail. Tex Rides With the Boy Scouts. Cheyenne Roundup. Whispering Skull. Little Joe the Wrangler. Riders of Pasco Basin. West of Carson City. Return of the Rangers. Dead or Alive. Three in the Saddle. Sun on the Prairie. Where the Buffalo Roam. Arizona Frontier. Marked For Murder. Enemy of the Law. Apache Ambush. Flaming Bullets. Frontier Fugitives. Guns of the Law. Gangsters of the Frontier.*

FRED SCOTT (1902-)

Fred Scott was born in Fresno, California on February 14, 1902 and received his education in the local schools. He first learned to ride a horse while vacationing at his grandfather's ranch, but had little notion then that he would ever become a cowboy star. After studying music at a conservatory, Fred entered show business as a singer in vaudeville in 1919. The following year, he met actor-producer J. Stuart Blackton who gave him a part in a motion picture called *The American* starring Charles Ray. For Fred Scott, that marked the beginning of his career in movies.

167

Fred's next move was to play minor roles in a series of Keystone Comedies for Mack Sennett. It was the era of slapstick comedians like Fatty Arbuckle and Al St. John, who were then among the leaders of Sennett's stable of stars. After a few years, Fred abandoned the movies for the legitimate stage and appeared in concerts, musical revues and Broadway productions. By 1928, he had also included a few radio shows to his experience.

In 1929, every major film studio was busy producing at least one musical. The arrival of talking motion pictures had set Hollywood in an uproar. Metro-Goldwyn-Mayer was presenting *Broadway Melody*. Warner Brothers made *Show of Shows*. Paramount came up with *The Love Parade,* while Universal produced *Showboat*. Meanwhile, Radio Pictures refused to be outdone and entered the competition with a film entitled *Rio Rita,* based on the popular stage show and novel of Edna Ferber. The stars of *Rio Rita* were John Boles and Bebe Daniels and one of the featured players was none other than Fred Scott.

Having finally reached success in talking pictures, Fred was given a number of good roles after playing his first lead in Pathe's *The Grand Parade* in 1930. He was cast in several fine musicals, lending his pleasing voice to the quality of his films. While working at Pathe Studios, he became friendly with Tom Keene and William Boyd, who were then active in Westerns, and it was at that time that Fred first expressed his desire to appear in cowboy features. But, as it turned out, he left the movies once again in 1932 to star with the San Francisco Opera Company, appearing with the famous Maria Jeritza.

Four years passed before Fred realized his ambition of being a cowboy star. In 1936, the producing team of Jed Buell and George Callahan offered him the chance to make a series of singing Westerns for the Spectrum Corporation in hopes that he would provide suitable competition for the horde of new singing sagebrush heroes. His first feature was *Romance Rides the Range* and, after its initial success, he made a whole series which billed him as "The Silvery-Voiced Buckaroo" of Westerns. Ironically, Al St. John, whom Fred had supported in earlier silent films, was now featured as the comedy relief opposite the new cowboy vocalist. In 1938, the team of Scott and St. John started another string of horse-operas for Atlas Productions. Lasting until 1942, these were the last pictures Fred made before he went on a nation-wide tour of personal appearances with his wife in 1943.

During the late 1940's, Fred worked as a singer and manager of Nils T. Granlund's "Florentine Gardens Revues," before establishing himself in the real estate business. Except for a short period when he was employed by M-G-M sound recording department, he has been in the real estate business ever since.

FILMS: *The American. Mack Sennett Comedies. Rio Rita. The Grand Parade. Swing High. Night Work. Beyond Victory. Romance Rides the Range. Singing Buckaroo. Melody of the Plains. Fighting Deputy. The Last Outlaw. Moonlight on the Range. Roaming Cowboy. Ranger's Roundup. Knight of the Plains. Songs and Bullets. Code of the Fearless. In Old Montana. Song of the Prairie. Rodeo Rhythm.*

BOB ALLEN (1906-)

Bob was born Irving Theodore Baer at Mt. Vernon, New York on March 28, 1906. After graduating from the N. Y. Military Academy, he entered Dartmouth University as a special student and completed his education by attending the universities of Columbia and Virginia. For a short time, he labored as a truck driver and then became a clerk for the National City Bank of New York. Discontented with his work, Bob decided to try his hand at being a professional artist. But, instead, he wound up as a pilot for the Curtis Flying Service.

Recalling his old school days at Dartmouth back in 1926, Bob remembered how he had been hired as an extra in a Richard Dix movie called *The Quarterback*, filmed on the college campus. In 1931, he went to Hollywood and managed to get signed by Warner Brothers for a few drawing-room dramas. After completing those, he made some minor appearances on the Los Angeles stage, finally drawing attention in "A Few Wild Oats" and "The Greeks Had a Word for It." Soon thereafter Bob was called to New York, where he starred in several Broadway shows—"Society Girl," "There's Always Juliet," "The Church Mouse" and "Holiday." Continuing with his career on the stage, he was hailed for his performances in "Criminal at Large," "The Late Christopher Bean," "The Second Mrs. Tangueray" and "Mona Vana."

While in New York, Harry Cohn, president of Columbia Pictures, met Bob and offered him a contract to return to Hollywood in 1934. Ever since his days at Warners, his name had been changed to Robert Allen, and it was under that name that he went back to movies. At Columbia, however, he was given slightly better roles and kept more active by appearing in several mystery dramas. In a short time, he found himself back where he had started, as a leading man in drawing-room dramas. Nevertheless, he did manage to win the box-office Blue Ribbon Award in 1935 for his role opposite Grace Moore in *Love Me Forever*. That same year, Bob had been an interested spectator on the sets where cowboy star Tim McCoy was busy making Columbia Westerns. He managed to talk the director into letting him make a few features with McCoy and surprised the studio heads with his excellent horsemanship.

In 1936, he started a series of his own for Columbia and emerged as a popular new cowboy hero. With a true talent for dramatics and the ability to handle action, Bob's good looks completed the blend that was necessary for a successful Western star.

Even though his career as a cowboy hero lasted only a short time, Allen's "Texas Ranger" series for Columbia allowed him to make an impression in the field of horse-operas. He left all that behind when he accepted an offer to join 20th Century Fox Studios in the latter part of 1937, being featured in a group of melodramas. Completing his activities in motion pictures in 1939 with Republic and producer Walter Wanger, while on loan-out from Fox, he then returned to the Broadway stage.

His first appearance back in the legitimate theatre was with Rozalind Russell in "Auntie Mame," a play that became a huge success. That was followed by parts in "Kiss Them for Me," "I Killed the Count," "Janie," "Junior Miss," and a revival of "Showboat." These were only a few of the stage hits that kept Bob active in later years. Recently, he has been busy with television, appearing in shows such as "Naked City," "Kraft Theatre," "Armstrong Theatre," "The Web," "The Philco Show" and "Suspense." His work has also led him into making pictures produced on the East Coast which do not interfere with his stage roles. Married to the former Evelyn Pierce, Bob remains one of the most active performers in various branches of the entertainment world.

FILMS: *The Quarterback. Big Business Girl. Party Husband. Reckless Hour. Night Nurse. Menace. White Lies. Death Flies East. Jealousy. Crime and Punishment. Love Me Forever. Party Wire. Guard That Girl. The Black Room. Lady of Secrets. Craig's Wife. The Awful Truth. Pride of the Marines. Perils of Pauline. Revenge Rider. Law Beyond the Range. Fighting Shadows. Holiday. The Unknown Ranger. Ranger Courage. Rio Grande Ranger. Law of the Range. Reckless Ranger. The Rangers Step In. Social Register. Race Track. The Captain Hates the Sea. Air Fury. Fighting Squadron. Bodyguard. Air Hawks. I'll Love You Always. Meet the Girls. Keep Smiling. Up the River. City of Chance. Everybody's Baby. Fighting Thoroughbreds. Winner Take All. Winter Carnival. Fire Away, the Story of a Trotter.*

SMITH BALLEW (1912-)

Smith Ballew was born in Palestine, Texas around 1912 and was a student at the Texas University before entering show business by way of radio. Beginning his career as a singer, he performed with his own orchestra in radio and vaudeville until 1931, when he wound up making his debut in motion pictures. His first job in movies came when he was called upon to sing in some two-reel musical short-subjects which gave him an opportunity to find out how films were made.

In 1933-34, Smith was hired to dub his voice in for John Wayne's during some singing scenes for a series of Westerns in which Wayne was supposed to vocalize. Known as the "Singin' Sandy" series, these features were put out by Lone Star Productions and were technically the first Westerns that contained a singing cowboy hero. It was not until 1935 that Gene Autry came upon the scene to introduce his musical horse-operas to the world. Meanwhile, Smith Ballew's voice was the one that audiences heard while watching John Wayne go through the synchronized lip movements.

In 1935, Paramount Studios finally gave Smith his chance to act before the cameras by featuring him in a movie called *Palm Springs*. He then made a few appearances in several other films without achieving much in the way of success. By 1936, Gene Autry, Tex Ritter and Dick Foran were only a few of the growing list of singing cowboys on the screen and Paramount decided to star Smith in his own group of musical Westerns. After several pictures, he became associated with producer Sol Lesser who hired him to make an additional string of Westerns for 20th Century Fox release and, by 1938, Smith was one of the ten biggest money-making cowboys in movies. Among his better films was a feature called *Rawhide*, which also spotlighted the famous Yankee baseball player, Lou Gehrig, in a leading role.

As in many other cases, Smith Ballew's career was cut short unnecessarily due to the avalanche of singing cowboys that appeared in pictures. Although his vocalizing was good and his personality was pleasing, he failed to register with Western fans for some vague reason. After five years as a cowboy star, he descended to supporting roles and was active until the late 1950's.

FILMS: *Palm Springs. Racing Lady. Roll Along Cowboy. Western Gold. Hawaiian Buckaroo. Panamint's Badman. Rawhide. Driftin' Along. Gaucho Serenade. Under Arizona Skies. The Man Who Walked Alone. I Killed Geronimo.*

DICK FORAN (1911-)

Dick Foran was born John Nicholas Foran in Flemington, New Jersey on June 18, 1911, the son of Senator Arthur F. Foran. After receiving his education at the Hunn School and then Princeton University, he worked as a seaman on a freighter and later became a special investigator for the Pennsylvania Railroad.

In 1934, Dick entered motion pictures by way of summer stock and the musical stage, first appearing under the name of Nick Foran in a film called *Gentleman Are Born*. When a producer discovered that he could sing, Dick was given an important part in *Stand Up and Cheer* starring Warner Baxter. It was that picture which first gave a little girl named Shirley Temple her big break in movies. Having changed his name to Dick Foran, the handsome young singer was placed under contract to Warner Brothers and featured in many small roles. He played his first important part opposite Humphrey Bogart in *The Black Legion*. Released in 1935, the film was a highly dramatic type and gave Dick a real opportunity to show what he could do.

The following year, his studio was desperately searching for a likely prospect to star in a group of musical Westerns in order to compete with the phenomenal success of Republic's Gene Autry. After some coaxing, Dick managed to convince his employers to give him a chance and, in a short time, he became Warners' Number One Cowboy star. The first year of his debut in horse-operas, 1936, Dick rose to the list of the top ten in Westerns, climbing as high as fourth place in 1937. A year later, he moved from Warners to Universal and was again voted one of the first ten. Although the screen had become saturated with singing cowboys, Dick was one of the better vocalists and his acting was well above average. He could handle action without any difficulty, having been a football athlete at college, and his good looks went well in cowboy costumes. At Universal, he was starred in a number of particularly entertaining features and serials, his best being an all-star chapter-play called *Riders of Death Valley*, which Universal boasted as a million dollar serial. Containing a cast that included Buck Jones, Charles Bickford, Leo Carrillo, Big Boy Williams and Noah Beery, Jr., the cliff-hanger was crammed with action and ranks as one of the most thrilling Western serials of all time.

When his cycle of cowboy pictures had thinned out, Dick gradually abandoned Westerns to star in a group of large scale productions for both Universal and Warners. Then came a series of various adventure films for other studios. By then, he was no longer singing in movies but was concentrating strictly on dramatics. During the 1950's, Dick went into television, playing straight roles in shows like "Playhouse 90," "Kraft Theatre," and many more. Since then, he has aimed his efforts towards the two mediums of entertainment—movies and TV. In spite of this, his

172

fans will always remember him best for the exciting Westerns he made at Warners and Universal.

In private life, Dick was divorced from Ruth Hollingsworth in 1940 and married to Carole Gallagher in 1945. An avid sportsman, he is deeply interested in all sorts of athletic events when enjoying leisure time.

FILMS: *Gentlemen Are Born. Stand Up and Cheer. Change of Heart. One More Spring. Lottery Lover. Shipmates Forever. The Big Noise. Accent on Youth. The Black Legion. Petrified Forest. The Perfect Specimen. Moonlight on the Prairie. Song of the Saddle. Trailin' West. Land Beyond the Law. Guns of the Pecos. Treachery Rides the Range. Ride 'Em Cowboy. Prairie Thunder. Blazing Sixes. Cherokee Strip. Devil's Saddle Legion. Empty Holsters. Wagon Mail. Cowboy From Brooklyn. Boy Meets Girl. Over the Wall. She Loved a Fireman. Private Detective No. 1. Four Daughters. Inside Information. Fighting 69th. Daughters Courageous. Four Wives. House of Seven Gables. Horror Island. My Little Chickadee. The Kid From Kansas. Mob Town. Riders of Death Valley. Golden Arrow. The Mummy's Hand. South of Karanga. The Mummy's Tomb. Road Agent. Unfinished Business. Guest Wife. Private Buckaroo. Winners of the West. Hi Bud. Easy Come Easy Go. Al Jennings of Oklahoma. Fort Apache. Please Murder Me. Treasure of Ruby Hills. The Doolins of Oklahoma. The Fearmakers. Atomic Submarine. The Big Night. Taggart.*

LEO CARRILLO (1880-1961)

Leo Carrillo was born in Los Angeles, California on August 6, 1880, a descendant of the Spanish Dons of early California. His great-grandfather was the first provincial governor of the territory. After receiving his education at the University of St. Vincent of Loyola, Leo worked as a cartoonist for the *Los Angeles Examiner* and "Variety" publications. His first impression on the stage was made in 1905, when he appeared in a show sponsored by the San Francisco Press Club. As a dialect comedian, he performed in vaudeville for several years until his entrance into the legitimate theatre. He had roles in "Twin Beds," "Fads and Fancies," "Gypsy Jim" and "The Brigand." His next role was in "Lombardi Ltd." with Warner Baxter and this brought him the leading role in another stage hit called "Mister Antonio."

In 1927, Hollywood beckoned to Leo to play in the screen version of "Mister Antonio," and he remained in pictures thereafter. He was featured in movies for Paramount, M-G-M, Warners, Columbia, Fox and Universal, delighting audiences with his original brand of light humor. While portraying a wide variety of lovable characters, he became an accomplished scene-stealer and was familiar to fans the world over. Although he was versatile, Leo specialized in playing Latin-types that permitted him to use his comical dialects and rapid chatter. He was particularly popular in Westerns as a roguish Mexican bandit, completely dominating each scene he appeared in. Occasionally, he would take a straight dramatic role and prove that he was equally capable of wringing tears from the audience, but comedy was his forte and he always kept it at a high level without resorting to the ridiculous.

Leo made too many good pictures to pick out only one as his best. He was especially appealing in *The Gay Desperado, Twenty Mule Team, Riders of Death Valley* and *The Daring Caballero,* but his greatest fame came from playing the part of "Pancho" in the popular "Cisco Kid" Westerns. During the late 1940's, United Artists had started a new series of features about O. Henry's famous character, casting Duncan Renaldo as "Cisco" and giving the part of his side-kick to Carrillo. Together, the team made a number of films with great success until the studio ceased production on the series. In 1950, the two stars were reunited for a weekly television show of half-hour films about the adventures of "Cisco Kid," once again enjoying success on an even larger scale.

On September 10, 1961, Leo Carrillo died of cancer at his home in Santa Monica, California at the age of eighty-one. Buried in Woodlawn Cemetery near Hollywood, he was survived by a daughter and two brothers. One of filmdom's best-loved performers, he had been known for his personal appearances in parades, having made many in the annual Tournament of Roses pageants while riding his beautiful Palomino horse.

FILMS: *Mister Antonio. Deception. Manhattan Melodrama. In Old Caliente. The Dove. Viva Villa. Girl of the Golden West. Broken Wing. Girl of the Rio. The Winning Ticket. Barnacle Bill. Men Are Such Fools. The Gay Desperado. History Is Made at Night. Moonlight and Pretzels. The Band Played On. If You Could Only Cook. Blockade. Moonlight Murder. Society Lawyer. Twenty Mule Team. Lillian Russell. Fisherman's Wharf. Sin Town. Captain Caution. Gypsy Wildcat. Under Western Stars. Phantom of the Opera. Bowery to Broadway. Crime Inc. Too Hot to Handle. The Fugitive. Moonlight and Cactus. Arizona Wildcat. Escape From Hong Kong. Horror Island. Kid From Kansas. Riders of Death Valley. Timber. Ghost Catchers. Mexicana. Girl From San Lorenzo. Wyoming. The Daring Caballero. Rio. South of the Rio Grande.*

WILLIAM BOYD (1898-)

When William Boyd first took the role of "Hopalong Cassidy" on the screen in 1935, little did he realize that he would become so closely connected with the character that audiences would readily identify him as "Hoppy" for the remainder of his career. Having been popular as a star of silent films, he lost his appeal because of a cruel quirk of fate during the early 1930's but his undying spirit helped him achieve one of the most successful screen comebacks of film history.

William Lawrence Boyd was born in Hendrysburg, Ohio on June 5, 1898. His father was killed in an accident shortly after moving the family to Tulsa, Oklahoma, where young Bill was forced to quit school to work in the oil fields. Before he was twenty, he struck out on his own and labored at odd jobs such as grocery clerk, miner, auto salesman, lumberjack and truck driver before ending up in Akron, Ohio, working in a rubber factory. When World War I broke out, he tried to enlist in the Army but was rejected because of an injury he had sustained as a lumberjack. Wandering aimlessly to Arizona, Bill took a job as a hotel manager and met and married an heiress named Ruth Miller. Divorced a short time later, he then traveled on to California where he found work as a movie extra in 1919. Making his film debut in a silent flick called *Why Change Your Wife?* he became acquainted with producer-director C. B. De Mille at Paramount Studios and began a long and financially successful friendship which carried him to stardom in De Mille productions.

In 1926, Bill made his first important picture, *The Volga Boatman,* which established him among the leading screen performers of that period. That same year, he married his leading lady, Elinor Fair, a union that again lasted only a short time. In the meantime, his career reached new heights as he appeared in a series of first-grade productions such as *Jim the Conqueror, Yankee Clipper* and *The Leatherneck.* As one of Paramount's hottest properties, he was given his choice of roles and was earning a salary that permitted him to live in luxury. When soundless pictures ended, he adapted himself to the talkies without any hardships.

In 1931, Bill suddenly found himself involved in a major Hollywood scandal when another actor named Bill Boyd was arrested for taking part in a shocking beach party which made headlines all over America. Unknowingly, the movie-going public began to stay away from the innocent Boyd's pictures and, as a result, Bill's career suffered badly. Although it was no small task to educate the fans into believing that an

1. *Dick Foran*
2. *Smith Ballew*
3. *Bob Allen*
4. *William Boyd*
5. *Leo Carrillo*
6. *James Ellison*

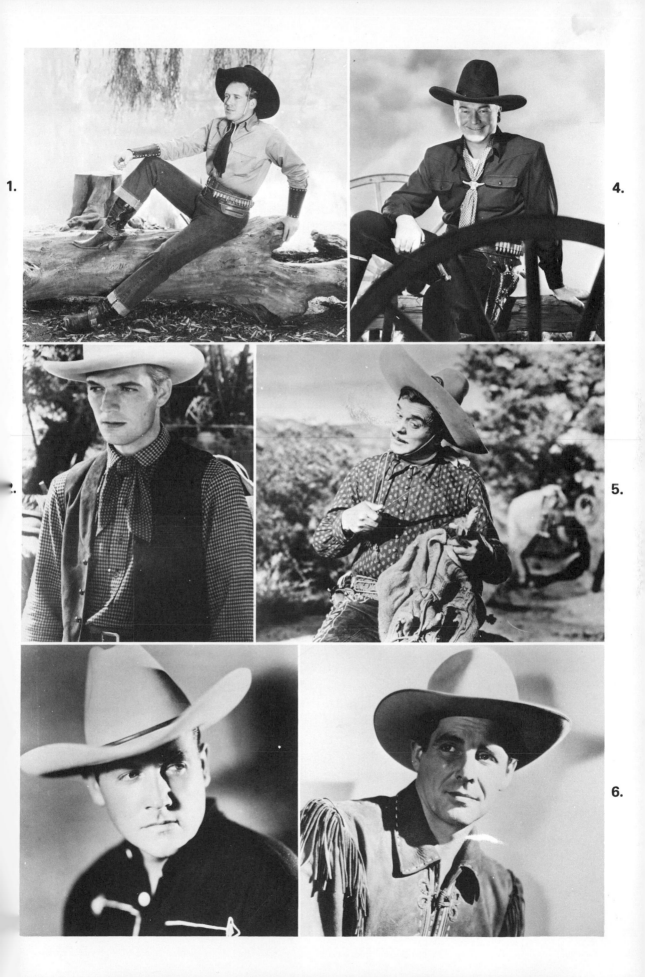

1.

4.

2.

5.

6.

injustice had been done, he finally managed to make a comeback after nearly four years off the screen. Since that incident, actors have tried to avoid using the same name, but it was unfortunate that an example had to occur before the lesson was learned. With most of his fortune gone and his hair having turned prematurely white, Bill was finally able to persuade some film producers into giving him a chance to win back the favor of the public. He made a few features which, although fairly-well received, fell short of re-establishing him to his former status as a star.

When producer Harry Sherman of Paramount decided to begin a new series of Westerns based on the stories of Clarence E. Mulford, he selected Bill for the lead role of "Hopalong Cassidy." At first, the actor had entertained some doubts about the part, fearing that his future looked dim. As it turned out, the first feature, *Hopalong Cassidy Enters* became a huge hit and started Bill Boyd on a whole new career in 1935. Focusing attention on three principal characters rather than the usual lone hero, the "Cassidy" series opened new possibilities in the field by introducing the "Trio Westerns" to the genre. Soon afterward, the trend picked up momentum as Republic and Monogram Studios followed suit.

With renewed success, Bill became an important film figure once again and was named to the list of top ten money-makers in Westerns of 1936. He remained in that lofty position for ten consecutive years until Harry Sherman decided to abandon production on the series in 1945. With amazing foresight, the cowboy star decided that "Hopalong" was still good for a few years and proceeded to buy the rights to the features. This involved going into hock for everything he had, plus the fact that he had to borrow substantial amounts in order to continue production. However, Bill finally managed to gain complete control of the exhibition rights to his old series and, in 1946, was able to resume his activities as "Hopalong Cassidy" on the screen. As a result, he also made a comeback to the list of top ten cowboy favorites, a position he maintained for another six years.

After starring in no less than sixty-six "Hoppy" features, Bill finally came to the end of his career on the screen in 1951 when he admitted that public interest had switched from feature movies to TV. Suddenly, he discovered a new market for his features when television bought the rights to show his old pictures on the home screens. Within a year, he was riding the crest of a new wave of popularity, even more profitable than the first. The ravenous appetite of TV caused him to increase his supply of "Cassidy" Westerns by returning to production and turning out an entirely new series of films exclusively for home viewing. Emerging as a national idol, Bill reaped a fortune from TV and a group of fifty enthusiastic manufacturers willing to pay him for using the name of "Hopalong Cassidy" on their products. By 1954, the cycle of success was complete and Bill went on a nation-wide personal appearance tour with the Cole Bros. Circus before retiring.

In portraying "Hopalong Cassidy," Bill had introduced a cowboy hero who could think as well as fight. A more mature and gentlemanly type, he resorted to violence only when all else failed. In spite of this unusual philosophy for Westerns, his pictures never lacked interest and the action was sufficient to satisfy his millions of fans. Riding his wonder horse, "Topper," Bill resembled the fictional black knight on the white charger. With success once more in his grasp, he forgot the extravagant days of his silent picture career and the unpleasant experience of being a forgotten man. In June of 1937, he married an actress named Grace Bradley, with whom he finally found happiness and a more optimistic outlook. His phenomenal success enabled him to retire with the dignity and security he so richly deserved.

FILMS: *Why Change Your Wife? Bobbed Hair. Forty Winks. New Lives For Old. Feet of Clay. Triumph. The Golden Bed. Road to Yesterday. Her Man o' War. Midshipman Sterling. The Volga Boatman. Eve's Leaves. Steel Preferred. The Last Frontier. Wolves of the Air. Jim the Conqueror. Beyond Victory. King of Kings. Thumbs Down. Yankee Clipper. Two Arabian Knights. Dress Parade. The Cop. Night Flyer. Skyscraper. The Leatherneck. Power. Crashing Through. High Voltage. Flying Fool. The Painted Desert. Gun Smoke. The Big Gamble. State's Attorney. Men of America. The Chief. Port of Lost Dreams. The Young Rajah. The Locked Door. Carnival Boat. Hopalong Cassidy Enters. Eagle's Brood. The Bar 20 Rides Again. Call of the Prairie. Three on the Trail. Hopalong Cassidy Returns. Trail Dust. Borderland. Texas Trail. Hills of Old Wyoming. Partners of the Plains. Bar 20 Justice. The Frontiersman. Sunset Trail. Silver on the Sage. Range War. Hidden Gold. Pirates on Horseback. Outlaws of the Desert. Riders of the Timberline. Hoppy Serves a Writ. False Colors. Lumberjack. Forty Thieves. Fool's Playground. Hoppy's Holiday. The Marauders. Sinister Journey. Strange Gamble.*

JAMES ELLISON (1910-)

Jim Ellison was born with the name of James Smith at Guthrie Center, Iowa, in 1910, and raised on a ranch in Valier, Montana, where he became an accomplished rider as a young lad. It was not until his family moved to Los Angeles, that he decided he would like to be an

179

actor, so he joined a stock company and traveled eastward giving stage performances. Winding up on the New York circuit, Jim appeared with the Moscow Art Theatre group for awhile, then returned to California, where he acted with the Beverly Hills Little Theatre Company. Spotted by a talent scout for the movies, he was given his first chance to perform in pictures when Warner Brothers cast him in *Play Girl* in 1934. That led to a few more minor parts which had him playing romantic leads.

In 1935, Jim was selected to portray "Johnny Nelson" in a new series of Westerns which producer Harry Sherman was making at Paramount Studios. These features starred William Boyd as a character called "Hopalong Cassidy" and also had Al St. John to provide the comedy relief. Actually, this was the first cowboy series which had three important players and it marked the beginning of the "trio Westerns." Needless to say, these pictures were a smash hit and brought success to all concerned. As Johnny Nelson, Jim provided the romantic interest in the series.

After being featured in the first eight films of the "Cassidy" Westerns, Jim Ellison decided to try for other things. In 1937, he landed an important part portraying Buffalo Bill Cody in Cecil B. De Mille's epic, *The Plainsman* starring Gary Cooper and Jean Arthur. After that, he made a variety of features ranging from comedies to straight dramas which had him cast as a romantic lead once again. Having starred in films for every major studio in Hollywood, Jim decided that he had enjoyed making Westerns best of all and returned to cowboy roles during the mid 1940's. He teamed up with Russell Hayden, who had been his replacement in the Hopalong Cassidy films, and started a new series of action features about the adventures of two cowboys called "Shamrock" and "Lucky." It was in this series that Hayden also served as co-producer and played the role of "Lucky." Although lacking production value, the pictures contained plenty of thrills and excitement and were released under the banner of Robert L. Lippert Productions.

When his series with Hayden ended around 1949, Jim went to work for Monogram where he co-starred with Johnny Mack Brown in another string of Westerns. These lasted until the early 1950's, after which Jim retired from the screen.

FILMS: *Play Girl. Death on the Diamond. Reckless. Hopalong Cassidy Enters. Eagle's Brood. The Bar 20 Rides Again. Call of the Prairie. Three on the Trail. Heart of the West. Hopalong Cassidy Returns. Trail Dust. The Plainsman. Annapolis Salute. The Winning Ticket. Vivacious Lady. 5th Avenue Girl. Mother Carey's Chickens. Hitch Hike Lady. Charley's Aunt. Ice Capades. Lady, Let's Dance. The Undying Monster.*

Army Surgeon. Dixie Dugan. The Gang's All Here. Hollywood and Vine.
23½ Hours Leave. Johnny Doesn't Live Here Anymore. Sorority House.
Anne of Windy Poplars. They Met in Argentina. You Can't Fool Your
Wife. The Ghost Goes Wild. Calendar Girl. Last of the Wild Horses.
The Texan Meets Calamity Jane. G.I. War Brides. I Killed Geronimo.
Kentucky Jubilee. Crooked River. Lone Star Lawman. The Man From
Whistling Hills. And So They Were Married. Ghost Town. Desert Hawk.
The Man From Black Hills. Fast on the Draw. Colorado Ranger. Hostile
Country. Dead Man's Trail. When the Girls Take Over.

THE TRIO WESTERNS

It was something entirely new when the "Hopalong Cassidy" Westerns introduced the first trio of leading characters in a regular series of feature pictures. Until then, it had been customary to have only a single hero in a horse-opera, unless, of course, he was accompanied by a sidekick who usually provided bits of comedy to interrupt the steady flow of action. Except for an occasional film which really called for three main figures, a trio of easily-identifiable characters sharing the spotlight in a series of pictures was unknown. There had been early attempts at grouping a number of famous names together in "all-star" features, but these were never successfully extended into a regular series. In 1935, R-K-O had released a picture entitled *Powdersmoke Range* which boasted of not one, but five principal characters, teaming Harry Carey, Bob Steele, Hoot Gibson, "Big Boy" Williams and Tom Tyler together with a supporting cast that read like a "Who's Who" of Westerns. Along with a few notable serials and features of the silent era, this film stood out as an individual example of combining several popular stars in one package.

It was also in 1935 that producer Harry Sherman brought out the first of the "Hopalong Cassidy" Westerns, starring William Boyd in the title role, accompanied by James Ellison (as Johnny Nelson) and comic Al St. John (as Windy Holliday). Following the initial feature, *Hopalong Cassidy Enters*, George "Gabby" Hayes replaced St. John and the series continued with phenomenal success. During the years that passed, Boyd remained in his role until he became consistently identified as "Hoppy" while the other two characters were played by a variety of actors. When Ellison left for greener pastures, his role was taken over by Russell Hayden (who portrayed Lucky Jenkins) and Hayes vacated his part to old-time comedian Andy Clyde. As the series went on its successful way, the fans became attached to the trio of range riders without

181

tiring of them until no less than sixty-six features had been released over a period of thirteen years.

In 1936, Republic Pictures came up with what turned out to be the most popular cowboy trio of them all when they introduced "The Three Mesquiteers" to the screen. Adapted from the novels of William Colt MacDonald, the series started out with Bob Livingston (as Stony Brooke), Ray Corrigan (as Tucson Smith) and Sid Saylor (as Lullaby Joslin). After the first picture, Saylor was replaced by Max Terhune and the new combination was unbeatable. Along with good stories, fine directing and three popular players, the high production value of these features made them extremely successful. During the eight years they existed on the screen, the "Mesquiteers" appeared in fifty-one features and were continuously listed among the top ten money-making Western stars. Similar to the "Hopalong Cassidy" series, the lead roles were played by various performers at different times, the part of "Stony Brooke" having been successively taken by John Wayne and Tom Tyler. "Tucson Smith" was portrayed by Corrigan's successor, Bob Steele and "Lullaby Joslin" was played by Rufe Davis and Jimmie Dodd. For a single film, Ralph (Dick Tracy) Byrd replaced Bob Livingston when the latter was injured during an action scene, and for a spell between 1939-1940, the three main characters had been completely revamped with Livingston sharing the spotlight with Duncan Renaldo and Ray Hatton. In all, the "Mesquiteers" had involved a total of twelve actors for the duration of the series before it came to an end in 1943.

The next series of "Trio Westerns" to come upon the scene was Monogram's "Range Busters," starring Ray Corrigan (who had left Republic's Mesquiteers), John "Dusty" King and Max Terhune. Between 1940 and 1944, they turned out twenty-four pictures that were slightly below the fine standards of the previously-mentioned series. Alternately, the leading roles vacated by Corrigan and King near the end of the series were taken over by Dave Sharpe and Dennis Moore.

By 1940, Monogram decided to enter its second series of "Trio Westerns" into the competition when Buck Jones, Tim McCoy and Raymond Hatton were teamed up for "The Rough Riders." Surprisingly enough, these old-timers did fairly well against the younger competitors and managed to bring their pictures well up to standards. Unfortunately, Jones died in 1942 and McCoy entered the Army, thus leaving Monogram no choice but to cancel production. A short time later, the studio organized another trio known as "The Trail Blazers" with veteran stars Hoot Gibson, Ken Maynard and Bob Baker in the leading roles. After the first feature, Bob Steele replaced Baker for the remainder of the series, while Maynard's retirement in mid-season left his role to be played successively by Chief Thundercloud and Rex Lease.

The 1940's saw several other groups of Westerns that featured a trio of heroes. Although somewhat less prominent, they all held a brief and mildly successful existence during the years when "Trio Westerns" were the style. Among the better known were "The Frontier Marshals" with Johnny Mack Brown, Bob Baker and Raymond Hatton; "The Texas Rangers" with James Newill, Dave O'Brien and Guy Wilkerson (Newill was later succeeded by Tex Ritter); "The Border Rangers" co-starring Johnny Mack Brown, Tex Ritter and Fuzzy Knight; "The Trigger Pals" with Lee Powell, Al St. John and Art Jarrett (which later changed to Lee Powell, Art Davis and Bill (not Hopalong) Boyd, and, finally, "The Border G-Men" with Russell Hayden, James Ellison and Jackie Coogan. Basically, these were all imitations of the original, but the trend managed to survive at least ten years before it died. Surprisingly, it was revived briefly on television for another eager generation to see.

These were the horse-operas that placed the emphasis on three heroes, each possessing his own individual talent and skills. It was a treat to the audience to see their excellent teamwork, providing us with three times as many thrills. In times of danger, their "one-for-all, all-for-one" attitude gave us the message that true friendship was a valuable asset in life, a lesson that too many people in the world tend to forget.

RUSSELL HAYDEN (1912-)

Russell Hayden was born in Chico, California on June 12, 1912 and was christened Pate Lucid. Getting his start in the film industry at the very bottom, he first worked as a studio "grip" at Universal, then became a member of the sound recording department for Paramount. Learning the technical points of movie production, he graduated to the position of film cutter, was promoted to assistant cameraman, and eventually wound up as a business agent before making his actual debut as an actor in 1934. Few motion picture players ever learned as much as Russ did about the intricate business of making movies.

After spending a year of playing minor parts, Russ got his big break when producer Harry Sherman chose him to succeed Jim Ellison in the popular "Hopalong Cassidy" Westerns. Beginning in 1937, he played "Lucky Jenkins" for the next five years, sharing honors with William Boyd and George "Gabby" Hayes. These features, released by Paramount, were among the best straight-action Westerns ever made.

183

1. *Rufe Davis, Bob Steele and Tom Tyler as "The Three Mesquiteers"*

2. *Andy Clyde, William (Hopalong Cassidy) Boyd and Russell Hayden*

3. *Buck Jones, Tim McCoy and Raymond Hatton as "The Rough Riders"*

4. *Ken Maynard, Bob Steele and Hoot Gibson as "The Trail Blazers"*

5. *Max Terhune, Ray Corrigan and John King as "The Range Busters"*

6. *Dave O'Brien, Tex Ritter and Guy Wilkerson as "The Texas Rangers"*

1.

4.

5.

6.

They had good plots, fine supporting casts and sufficient production value to rate them a notch above the ordinary B-class horse-operas.

When Russ vacated the series around 1941, he stayed on at Paramount to star in a few more Westerns of his own. After that, he joined Columbia Studios, made an additional number of outdoor films and was named among the top ten cowboy stars of 1943 and 1944. He then entered the U.S. Army, serving his country until his release in 1946. The following year, he returned to motion pictures by co-starring with his old pal, Jim Ellison, in a new group of Westerns which he co-produced. At the end of that series, he began a second group of features known as the *Border G-Men* with veteran actor Jackie Coogan.

As the B-Westerns went out of existence in 1954, Russ undertook a career in television by becoming executive producer and vice-president of the Quintet Film Production Company, an organization employed to make movies for TV. In recent years, he has been associated with M-H TV Productions as a director and producer. In private life, he was divorced from Lillian Porter and married to actress Jane Clayton. When not busy making pictures, Russ is a devoted sports enthusiast.

FILMS: *Hills of Old Wyoming. Borderland. North of the Rio Grande. Rustler's Valley. Hopalong Cassidy Rides Again. Texas Trail. Pride of the West. Cassidy of the Bar 20. Partners of the Plains. Heart of Arizona. Bar 20 Justice. In Old Mexico. Sunset Trail. The Frontiersman. Silver on the Sage. Range War. Renegade Trail. Law of the Pampas. The Showdown. Santa Fe Marshal. Hidden Gold. Three Men From Texas. Stagecoach War. Doomed Caravan. Pirates on Horseback. Knights of the Range. Rolling Home. Gambler's Choice. Saddles and Sagebrush. 'Neath Canadian Skies. Trail of the Mounted. Where the West Begins. Minesweeper. Two in a Taxi. Silver City Raiders. The Last Horseman. Badmen of Nevada. Colorado Ranger. Crooked River. Sons of Adventure. Fast on the Draw. Hostile Country. Man From the Rio Grande. Brothers Apart. West of the Brazos. Wyoming Hurricane. Albuquerque. The Vigilantes Ride. Border G-Men. Marshal of Gunsmoke. Apache Chief.*

BOB LIVINGSTON (1908-)

Bob Livingston was born Robert Randall in Quincy, Illinois on December 9, 1908, the son of newspaper editor Edgar Randall and writer Clarena Myers Randall. When he was twelve, his family moved to Glendale, California, where Bob completed his education. Later, he worked at a variety of jobs that included cowpuncher, seamen, lumberjack and construction laborer before finally landing with the *Los Angeles Daily News* as a reporter. While writing an article about the Pasadena Community Playhouse, he became interested in acting and decided to join the school of dramatics.

In 1929, Bob entered motion pictures as a bit player in Universal's series of collegiate films. Graduating to featured parts, he made a few pictures for Tiffany Productions and then became a contract player at M-G-M in 1933. The studio planned to give him a big build-up as a romantic lead, but Bob decided his progress was too slow when acting assignments grew farther apart.

After three years at M-G-M, he obtained a release from his contract and accepted an offer from the newly formed Republic Studios to play the lead in a serial called *The Vigilantes Are Coming*. Released in 1936, the chapter-play was a smashing success and Bob was catapulted to fame as the masked hero known as "The Eagle." It marked the real beginning of his career for, in later years, he was to play a wide variety of masked men in Westerns, probably more so than any other actor in motion pictures. Realizing his drawing power at the box-office, Republic wasted no time in starring Bob in the studio's first color feature, *The Bold Caballero*. In that picture, he played the popular masked hero of old California, "Zorro." In earlier years, Douglas Fairbanks had immortalized the character in silent films, but it remained for Bob to recreate the role for talking pictures.

The year 1936 proved a fruitful one for Livingston as he achieved stardom. Besides scoring two big hits with his first serial and feature with Republic, the studio gave him the principal role of "Stony Brooke" in "The Three Mesquiteers," a new series of Westerns which had three main characters. Although producer Harry Sherman had actually started the fad of using three leading characters the year before by introducing the popular "Hopalong Cassidy" series, it was the "Mesquiteers" that brought the "trio Westerns" to a peak of popularity. During the eight years that Republic produced these features, the "Mesquiteers" were consistently part of the top ten list of cowboy stars. In the initial film of the series, Ray "Crash" Corrigan played "Tucson Smith" and comedian Sid Saylor was "Lullaby Joslin." For the second film, the producers decided to replace Saylor with a ventriloquist named Max Terhune, who seemed to fill the bill a bit better. Together, Livingston, Corrigan and Terhune made fourteen pictures which were highly entertaining and classified among the best B-Westerns ever made. Having exceptional production value, the stories were well above average and each of the three main characters had his own unique talent and personality.

187

In 1938, Bob Livingston stepped out of the "Mesquiteers" to star in another Republic serial entitled *The Lone Ranger Rides Again*. This was a sequel to an original serial the studio had made the year before with Lee Powell. The desire to play different roles led Bob to pursue leading parts in a series of different pictures for awhile, but, in the latter part of 1939, he returned to his original role of "Stony Brooke" and made another fourteen features with the "Mesquiteers." In 1941, he vacated the series and left Republic Studios to star in a group of "Lone Rider" Westerns for P.R.C.

By 1946, Bob had completed his cycle as a film star and turned to character roles. As a villain, he took part in several features for Republic, Universal and Columbia before finally leaving the screen around 1950. Living in semi-retirement, he concentrated his efforts toward writing screenplays. His best-known works were done in collaboration for films such as *Enlighten Thy Daughter* and *The Girl Said No*. Happily married, Bob lives just outside Hollywood with his wife and their son, Addison, named after Bob's older brother who was famous in cowboy pictures as Jack Randall.

FILMS: *Borrowed Wives. Sunny Skies. Public Enemy No. 2. The Band Plays on. Baby Face Harrington. Mutiny on the Bounty. West Point of the Air. Absolute Quiet. The Vigilantes Are Coming. Bold Caballero. The Three Mesquiteers. Ghost Town Gold. Roarin' Lead. Riders of Whistling Skull. Hit the Saddle. Gunsmoke Ranch. Come on Cowboys. Range Defenders. Heart of the Rockies. Wild Horse Rodeo. Purple Vigilantes. Call the Mesquiteers. Outlaws of Sonora. Riders of the Black Hills. Heroes of the Hills. Kansas Terrors. Cowboys From Texas. Heroes of the Saddle. Pioneers of the West. Covered Wagon Days. The Lone Ranger Rides Again. Rocky Mountain Rangers. Oklahoma Renegades. Under Texas Skies. Trail Blazers. Lone Star Raiders. Night Hawk. Arson Racket Squad. Larceny on the Air. Ladies in Distress. Pals of the Pecos. Saddlemates. Gangs of Sonora. Federal Manhunt. Prairie Pioneers. Overland Stagecoach. Wolves of the Range. Raiders of Red Gap. Wild Horse Rustlers. Law of the Saddle. Laramie Trail. Big Bonanza. Undercover Woman. Goodnight Sweetheart. Pistol Packin' Mama. Lake Placid Serenade. Dakota. Tell It to a Star. Don't Fence Me In. Valley of the Zombies. Mule Train. Daredevils of the Clouds. Night Stage to Galveston. Steppin' in Society. Winning of the West. Once Upon a Horse.*

NOAH BEERY, Jr. (1916-)

With a famous father and an uncle in motion pictures, it was only natural for Noah Beery, Jr. to seek an acting career in the movies. He was born in California in 1916 and educated at Hollywood High and the Urban and Harvard military schools. At the tender age of four, he got his first taste of acting when he appeared with his dad and Douglas Fairbanks, Sr. in *The Mark of Zorro*.

Noah gained his experience by joining a stock company and taking part in stage theatricals until given the chance to make his official screen debut in 1929. Playing a small role opposite his father and Jack Holt in *Father and Son,* he followed through with a series of features at Universal Studios where he became a contract actor. For the next few years, he ably supported stars like Tom Mix and Johnny Mack Brown in Westerns of unusually high calibre. Although most of his work was done in horse-operas, he managed to squeeze in a few parts in several first-class productions that ranged from comedy to straight melodrama.

During the early 1930's, Noah was finally given some leading roles in B-grade features, but his specialty was still portraying the secondary parts of the hero's pal in most of his films. It was that type of character which made him especially popular in serials like *Ace Drummond* and *Fighting With Kit Carson*. To many fans, he was known as a shy, soft-spoken countryboy who could always be depended on in case things got tough. In 1939, Noah played one of his best roles opposite his famous uncle, Wallace Beery, in *Twenty Mule Team* which led him into a series of class-A features for various major studios like M-G-M, Columbia, R-K-O and Paramount. It was at that time that he starred in *The Mighty Treve,* a small, cheaply made B-feature which surprisingly turned out to be an excellent film.

In 1940, Noah married Maxine Jones, the daughter of cowboy star Buck Jones, with whom he had appeared in many Westerns. The early 1940's saw him co-starring with Jimmy Rogers, son of Will Rogers, in a series of comedy features for producer Hal Roach. After that, he returned to his home base, Universal, to make at least a dozen more pictures. Since then, he has been constantly active in movies and television, his most prominent TV work being that of a star in the "Circus Boy" series of the late 1950's and as host of his own "Noah Beery, Jr. Show."

When he is not busy acting, Noah produces travel documentaries for TV. He is the proud father of three children and, to thousands of movie fans, his presence has enhanced many motion pictures and his performances never lacked honesty or talent.

FILMS: *The Mark of Zorro. Father and Son. Rustler's Roundup. Stormy. Parole. Heroes of the West. The Trail Beyond. Tailspin Tommy. The Road Back. Ace Drummond. Fighting With Kit Carson. Overland Mail. Forbidden Valley. Only Angels Have Wings. All American Co-ed. Of Mice and Men. Twenty Mule Team. Bad Lands. Passport to Alcatraz. The Mighty Treve. Tanks a Million. Dudes Are Pretty People. Prairie Chickens. Calaboose. Gung Ho. Corvette K225. Weekend Pass. Slick Chick. Follow the Boys. Top Man. Hi Beautiful. Under Western Skies. Frontier Badmen. The Daltons Ride Again. We've Never Been Licked. Allergic to Love. The Beautiful Cheat. The Crimson Canary. Sergeant York. The Savage Horde. The Texas Rangers. Red River. Davy Crockett, Indian Scout. The Doolins of Oklahoma. Indian Agent. Two Flags West. Last Outpost. The Story of Will Rogers. The Cimarron Kid. White Feather. Rocket Ship XM. Spirit of St. Louis. Inherit the Wind. Yellow Tomahawk. Jubal. War Arrow. Wings of the Hawk. Black Dakotas. The Fastest Gun Alive.*

DAVE (TEX) O'BRIEN (1912-)

Dave O'Brien was born at Big Springs, Texas on May 13, 1912. After completing his education, he worked at a variety of jobs before making his screen debut as a bit player in Paramount's *Jenny Gerhart* in 1933. Then came a series of small roles, such as in *The Little Colonel* with Shirley Temple, until Dave started realizing that his career was sadly lacking picture assignments. Turning to stunt work, he doubled for big-name stars in dangerous action scenes and managed to get a featured part opposite Ralph Graves in a serial called *The Black Coin* in 1936. For the next few years, he earned his living by working as an actor, writer, stuntman and photographers' model until 1941, when he appeared with Jim Newill in Monogram's *Renfrew of the Mounted* series. These adventure features, based on a popular radio program, were loaded with action and suspense and furnished Dave with the chance he had been looking for.

It was in 1943 that M-G-M decided to star Dave in a series of short two-reel comedies called *The Pete Smith Specialties*. At first, these films had been made strictly as "program fillers," but the huge success they had with movie fans made them an award-winning drawing card at the box-office. The plot of each film in the series was to show

190

the audience how an "ordinary" citizen, played by O'Brien, could get involved in all sorts of tight scrapes while performing ordinary everyday tasks. As a skilled stuntman, Dave took some of the most difficult tumbles and pratfalls ever filmed for the sake of comedy. Realizing the popularity of the series, M-G-M continued making the *Pete Smith Specialties* throughout the 1940's.

Meanwhile, O'Brien was still active in action features and found time to co-star with Jim Newill in *The Texas Rangers* series for P.R.C. By that time, several studios were producing "trio Westerns" which contained not one, but three principal characters. Republic was going strong with the "Three Mesquiteers." Monogram had the "Rough Riders" and the "Range Busters." Paramount was still active with the "Hopalong Cassidy" series. In the beginning, Dave and Jim Newill had been the only main characters in "The Texas Rangers," but after two pictures, the producers decided to add Guy Wilkerson for comedy relief, thus bringing another "trio Western" to the screen. Besides acting, Dave and Jim also collaborated in writing original songs and stories for this series, until Newill retired in 1946 and was replaced by Tex Ritter.

In 1948, Dave played one of his most exciting roles when he starred in a chapter-play entitled *Captain Midnight*. This, too, had been brought to the screen after repeated success on the airwaves and the part gave Dave plenty of opportunity to show off his bag of tricks. During the early 1950's, he entered the field of television as a writer and star of a show called "Meet the O'Briens," which was very similar to his Pete Smith comedies. After that, Dave became associated with Red Skelton as a writer for the comedian's TV show and has been active in that capacity ever since.

FILMS: *Jenny Gerhart. The Little Colonel. Welcome Home. The Black Coin. East Side Kids. Boys of the City. Captain Caution. That Gang of Mine. Son of the Navy. Tahiti Nights. Renfrew of the Mounted. Yukon Flight. Renfrew and the Stolen Treasure. Sky Bandits. Danger Ahead. Murder in the Yukon. On the Great White Trail. Border Buckaroo. The Man Who Walked Alone. Devil Bat. Captain Midnight. Texas Rangers. The Rangers Take Over. Spook Town. Boss of Rawhide. Badmen of Thunder Gap. Return of the Rangers. Pinto Bandit. Crashin' Thru. Three in the Saddle. Fighting Valley. West of Texas. Dead or Alive. Cowboy Reckoning. Enemy of the Law. Outlaw Roundup. The Spider Returns. Gangsters of the Frontier. Flaming Bullets. Brand of the Devil. Gunsmoke Mesa. Frontier Fugitives. Guns of the Law. Kiss Me Kate. Pete Smith Specialties. Tennessee Champ.*

1. *Russell Hayden*
2. *Bob Livingston*
3. *Noah Beery, Jr.*
4. *Lee Powell (at left) with Al "Fuzzy" St. John (center) and Art Jarrett in "Trigger Pals"*
5. *Dave "Tex" O'Brien*
6. *Cesar Romero*

1.

4.

5.

6.

LEE POWELL (1909-1944)

In August of 1944, a newspaper article announced the death of "the famous Lone Ranger of the movies" when an actor named Lee Powell was reported to have been killed in action while fighting with the U.S. Marines during World War II. This was an example of the widespread fame that Powell had received from playing the popular masked hero of radio and comic-strips. Although he had only portrayed "The Lone Ranger" once in the original movie serial, it was for that role that he became famous.

Powell was born in 1909 and decided on becoming an actor after completing his education. His first experience came from amateur theatricals, after which he joined a stock company and toured the midwest. In 1936, he entered motion pictures as an extra, playing bit parts without too much success until the following year, when he learned that Republic Pictures had been searching for talent to appear in a new serial. Based on a famous radio series, the chapter-play introduced the popular masked rider to the movies. The main gimmick of the serial was to keep the audience guessing until the very last episode as to which one of five Texas Rangers was the principal hero of the film's title. With a sudden change of luck in his career, Lee Powell was selected to play the part of the Ranger that survived until the last chapter. Along with him were Lane Chandler, Hal (Wally Wales) Taliaferro, George Letz (who later made a name for himself as George Montgomery) and Herman (Bruce Bennett) Brix, all playing the remaining Texas Rangers. The part of the faithful Indian, Tonto, was brought to the screen by veteran character actor, Chief Thundercloud.

When *The Lone Ranger* was released in 1938, it was a smashing success and, today, ranks with the best serials ever made. Having finally reached stardom, Lee Powell was immediately cast in another Republic chapter-play called *The Fighting Devil Dogs* in which he again co-starred with Herman Brix. After that, Powell decided that the studio was not giving him enough opportunity to really show what he could do so he left Republic to go on tour with the Wallace Bros. Circus, billed as the "original Lone Ranger." Shortly afterward, a court action by the owners of the "Lone Ranger Inc." sought to restrain him from cashing in on the title. Final judgement came in 1942, when the courts ruled in favor of the corporation.

Having brought his circus tour to an end in 1940, Powell started a new series of features for Grand National, sharing the spotlight with

Al (Fuzzy) St. John and Art Jarrett. Unfortunately, these Westerns had little production value and were poorly made. The company went broke shortly afterward and Powell went to work for P.R.C. (Producers' Releasing Corporation), where he made another group of horse-operas with Art Davis and Bill (Cowboy Rambler) Boyd. At the end of the series, he made a minor appearance in a picture called *The Adventures of Mark Twain*, and then decided to enter the armed forces.

Entering the U.S. Marine Corps in the summer of 1942, Powell underwent his training at San Diego Marine Barracks and was assigned to the Second Marine Division. A short time later, he saw action against the Japanese at Tarawa and Saipan. Finally, on August 30, 1944, the U.S. Navy Department officially announced that Sergeant Lee Powell (USMC) had been killed in action at Tinian on July 20, 1944.

Although his screen career had only been mildly successful and relatively short, Lee Powell left an indelible mark in the cowboy Hall of Fame. His biggest contribution to motion pictures was that he had been the first actor to play the "Lone Ranger" on the screen.

FILMS: *The Lone Ranger. The Fighting Devil Dogs. The Lone Rider Rides On. Prairie Pals. Fighting Leathernecks. Texas Manhunt. Trigger Pals. Raiders of the West. Rolling Down the Great Divide. Tumbleweed Trail. Along the Sundown Trail. The Adventures of Mark Twain.*

AL "FUZZY" ST. JOHN (1892-1963)

Alfred St. John was born in Santa Ana, California on September 10, 1892. While still a child, he made his debut on the vaudeville stage with his parents and was literally raised in show business. After touring the country in a family act for four years, he struck out on his own and became a headliner from coast-to-coast.

It was in 1914 that movie producer-director Mack Sennett lured Al into motion pictures by hiring him to play one of his original "Keystone Cops." In the years that followed, he helped to make film history by appearing in a series of two-reel comedies that became the rage of the entertainment world. Unparalleled in the annals of screen comedy, the Sennett pictures made stars of men like Charlie Chaplin, Fatty Arbuckle, Buster Keaton and Al St. John.

After leaving Sennett, Al appeared with his old colleague, Fatty Arbuckle, in a series of comedies for the Arbuckle Production Company. Next, he starred in films for the Triangle Studios. By 1920, he had taken his place among the immortal funny-men of the screen, his superb pantomime adding greatly to an era that produced the greatest comedians the world has ever known.

Just before the arrival of talking pictures in 1927, Al was starring in short comedies for Paramount known as the "Speed" series. When sound came, he began making his first talkies by appearing in two-reelers for Educational Pictures. Unfortunately, his type of slapstick humor was better paced for silent movies, so he left the screen around 1933 to play in a stage comedy called "Bambina."

In 1935, Al made a comeback to films when he accepted an offer to appear with "Big Boy" Williams in a Western entitled *Law of the '45's*. That same year, he played William Boyd's sidekick, "Windy Holliday" in a new Hopalong Cassidy Western at Paramount. Having finally found success once again in horse-operas, Al made a series of features with singing cowboy, Fred Scott, in which he created his role of "Fuzzy Q. Jones." After that, he appeared in countless Westerns with stars like Lee Powell, Jack Randall, Bob Steele, Buster Crabbe, George Houston and Lash LaRue. Unfortunately, some producers placed too much emphasis on Al's slapstick comedy and his laugh-making dominated the action. In fact, some of his pictures for Monogram and P.R.C. were downright comedies instead of Westerns, but the younger element that made up the major part of the audience was greatly impressed by Al's antics on the screen. After all, the purpose of the hero's sidekick was to provide comedy relief and Al St. John did this very well.

On January 21, 1963, Al died of a heart attack at the age of seventy while making a personal appearance tour in Vidalia, Georgia. He was survived by his wife, the former Flo-Bell Moore.

FILMS: *Mack Sennett Comedies. The Alarm. Dance of Life. Western Knights. Fatty and Mabel Adrift. He Did and He Didn't. Bright Lights. She Goes to War. Casey Jones. His Wife's Mistake. The Butcher Boy. Reckless Romeo. Rough House. The Moonshiners. His Wedding Night. Hell Harbor. Fresh Eggs. Speed. Wanderer of the Wasteland. High Sign. Law of the '45's. Hopalong Cassidy. Fugitive of the Plains. Songs and Bullets. Melody of the Plains. Gunsmoke Trail. Return of the Lone Rider. Border Roundup. Frontier Scout. Lawless Town. Caravan Trail. Ghost of Hidden Valley. Billy the Kid Rides Again. Billy the Kid's Roundup. Border Badmen. Fighting Bill Carson. Western Cyclone. Valley of Vengeance. Fuzzy Settles Down. Cheyenne Takes Over. Lash of the West. Return of the Lash. King of the Bullwhip. Law of the Lash. Dead Man's Gold.*

CESAR ROMERO (1907-)

Few people of the last generation can recall that Cesar Romero was once known as a Western star, but most film fans over the age of thirty will remember him as one of the most popular "Cisco Kid" actors of the screen. He was born in New York City on February 15, 1907 of Cuban parentage and attended the Collegiate and Riverdale Country Schools. After working briefly as a bank messenger and clerk, he entered show business as a professional ballroom dancer, appearing in vaudeville and nightclubs all over New York. In 1927, he made his initial bow on the Broadway stage in a play called "Lady Do," followed by some successful appearances in "Strictly Dishonorable," "Stella Brady," "Cobra" and "Dinner at Eight."

Cesar made his movie debut in 1934 as a bit player in *The Thin Man* opposite William Powell and Myrna Loy. Within a short time, he had climbed the ladder to stardom after playing minor roles in a number of assorted pictures for Warners, Paramount and M-G-M. Having survived a period in which he had been typed as a slick-haired gangster, he went under contract to 20th Century Fox, playing suave leading men opposite stars like Alice Faye, Sonja Henie and Betty Grable.

It was in 1939 that he first became associated with the fabulous character, "The Cisco Kid." In a film entitled *Return of the Cisco Kid,* he played a supporting role while Warner Baxter portrayed the famous "Robin Hood of the West." In less than a year, he succeeded Baxter as "Cisco" when Fox gave him the part in a new series of pictures starting with *The Cisco Kid and the Lady.* For the next few years, Cesar starred in an impressive list of excellent outdoor adventures that made him extremely popular in his new type of role. He added his suave, devil-may-care attitude to the part and was completely convincing as the dashing Mexican caballero.

The Second World War suddenly interrupted Cesar's career in films, as he served with the U.S. Coast Guard. On his return to movie-making, he achieved even greater success by appearing in large-scaled productions ranging from musical extravaganzas to serious melodramas. He completed his association with Fox, then starred for various companies as a free-lance player.

Ever since first entering pictures, Cesar has been regarded as a smooth, debonair playboy of the film colony and considered one of Hollywood's most eligible bachelors. In spite of this, he is looked upon by his co-workers as a fine, upstanding actor whose versatile talent has allowed him to remain one of the screen's most popular stars for many years. In recent times, he has been equally active in motion pictures and television.

FILMS: *The Thin Man. British Agent. Strange Wives. Cheating Cheaters. Clive of India. Cardinal Richelieu. The Devil Is a Woman. Hold 'Em Yale. 15 Maiden Lane. Show Them No Mercy. Dangerously Yours. The Little Princess. My Lucky Star. Wee Willie Winkie. Wintertime. Happy Landing. Return of the Cisco Kid. The Cisco Kid and the Lady. Romance of the Rio Grande. Lucky Cisco Kid. The Gay Caballero. Viva Cisco Kid. Frontier Marshal. Tall, Dark and Handsome. Once a Thief. Dance Hall. A Gentleman at Heart. Coney Island. The Lady in Ermine. Springtime in the Rockies. Deep Waters. The Beautiful Blonde From Bashful Bend. Love That Brute. Captain From Castile. Happy Go Lovely. He Married His Wife. The Jungle. Lost Continent. F.B.I. Girl. Scotland Yard Investigator. Shadow Man. Prisoners of the Casbah. The Americano. Around the World in 80 Days. Vera Cruz. Donovan's Reef. If a Man Answers. We Shall Return. Leather Saint. The Racers. Panic Button. Valley of the Swords. A House Is Not a Home. Two on a Guillotine.*

RAYMOND HATTON (1887-)

This notable performer of the screen was born in Red Oak, Iowa on July 7, 1887 and was raised in Des Moines where he attended grammar school. At the age of twelve, he made his debut on the vaudeville stage and then toured the midwest as an actor with a stock company until he found himself in New York almost penniless. As a desperate move, he decided to try getting into moving pictures as early as 1912 and succeeded in landing a few film assignments at the old Kalem Studio. From there, he went to work for the Biograph Company, making silent flickers by the dozen.

In 1914, Ray became associated with Mack Sennett who gave him a chance at slapstick comedy in the old Keystone one-reelers. Within two years, he was regarded as one of the screen's foremost character actors. During that period of his career, Ray was noted for playing villains opposite some of the brightest celebrities in pictures. His expert knowledge in the use of make-up helped him create a wide array of unusual characters and he was constantly in demand at every studio.

Having made his move to the West Coast, Ray was signed to a contract at Paramount Pictures in 1918 and appeared in an endless number of feature films throughout the 1920's. His big step to stardom came in 1925 when he shared top billing with Wallace Beery in a series of first-rate comedies for Paramount. Opposite the huge bulk of Beery, Ray looked like a dwarf and the screen antics of these two veteran performers was enough to convulse any audience.

Although he had played an important part in Paramount's early Zane Grey Westerns during the 1920's, Raymond Hatton did not really become a regular in cowboy features until the early 1930's. Beginning around 1932, he started his twenty-year cycle as one of the most popular Western sidekicks in screen history. His familiar characterizations as a rip-snorting, tobacco-chewing sourdough made him a favorite among Western performers year after year and fans were delighted to see him in any number of films, particularly when he was riding alongside his old pal, Johnny Mack Brown. These two made no less than forty-four pictures together for Universal and Monogram, including a half dozen top-notch serials, and their combination was one of the most successful in the history of Westerns.

In 1939, Ray went to work at Republic Studios where he became a member of the "Three Mesquiteers" series. Having replaced Max Terhune, he appeared in nine features before moving on to Monogram in 1940. For the next two years, he was co-starred with Buck Jones and Tim McCoy in Monogram's series of "Rough Riders" Westerns, after which he returned to playing Johnny Mack Brown's saddle partner.

Since 1960, Ray has been in semi-retirement but can still be seen in an occasional picture on television. His long career in films is conclusive evidence of his fine ability as an actor and it seems unlikely that he will ever be forgotten.

FILMS: *Joan the Woman. Oliver Twist. The Woman God Forgot. One More American. Firefly of France. Less Than Kin. The Source. Cruise of the Make Believe. We Can't Have Everything. Whispering Chorus. Johnny Get Your Gun. Arizona. Trent's Last Case. The Mighty. Office Scandal. Rip Snorter. The Thundering Herd. Horse Sense. Three Wise Fools. Bunty Pulls the Strings. Hunchback of Notre Dame. Honorable Friend. Circus Man. Affairs of Anatole. Polly of the Circus. Hell's Heroes. Behind the Front. We're in the Navy Now. Silence. Forlorn River. Born to the West. Wife Savers. Fireman Save My Child. Now We're in the Air. Murder on the Roof. Border Bandits. Hidden Gold. The 4th Horseman. Big Cage. Driftin' Along. Alice in Wonderland. Strangers in Town. The Big Killing. Terror Trail. Hi Yo Silver. Under the Tonto Rim. Wyoming Outlaw. The Texans. New Frontier. Kansas Terrors. Cowboys From Texas. Covered Wagon Days. Oregon Trail. Rocky Mountain Rangers. Oklahoma Renegades. The*

*Rough Riders. Ghost Town Law. Gun Trouble. Riders of the West.
Arizona Bound. Fighting With Kit Carson. Gunman From Bodie. Code
of the Saddle. West of the Rio Grande. Flame of the West. Fighting
Ranger. Sheriff of Medicine Bow. Gunning For Justice. Frontier Feud.
Crossed Trails. Treasure of Ruby Hills. Twinkle in God's Eye. Dig That
Uranium. The Quick Gun.*

GEORGE HOUSTON (1898-1945)

George Houston was born at Hampton, New Jersey in 1898, the
son of a blind evangelist. He received his education at Rutgers University and studied vocal training at the Julliard Institute of Music. At
the age of nineteen, he entered the U.S. Navy, serving overseas in France
with the French Ambulance Corps during the First World War. When
he returned to America, he took a job as a bank messenger in New York,
but decided that music was his chief interest. He then opened a small
studio and taught singing lessons until he was forced to give it up because
of the lack of pupils. A short while later, George became a member of
the American Opera Company of New York and was once privileged
to perform before President Calvin Coolidge in a presentation of
"Faust." As time went by, he discovered that opera offered him little
in the way of success so he left the world of classical music in favor of
the Broadway stage. Among his better-known musical hits were "Shooting Star," "New Moon," "Chee Chee," "Casanova," "Fioretta,"
"Thumbs Up," "The O'Flynn" and "Melody."

In 1934, George answered the call to Hollywood when he was
offered the chance to make his film debut in a picture called *The
Melody Lingers On*. Possessing a natural flair for acting after his
experience on the operatic stage, he continued to work in movies and
made a series of features which accentuated his fine singing talent.

By 1943, musical Westerns were at the height of their popularity
with singing cowboys like Gene Autry, Roy Rogers and Tex Ritter
reaping in big profits at the box-office. When George learned that the
Producers' Releasing Corporation (P.R.C.) was on the verge of scrap-
ping its "Lone Rider" series after Bob Livingston vacated the role, he
was able to convince the studio heads to give him a chance to play the
part. By persuading the producers that the series would probably do
better with a singing cowboy hero, George started a whole new group
of features, introducing the "Lone Rider" as the leading character in
musical Westerns. Riding alongside Houston in these pictures was the
ever popular Al (Fuzzy) St. John, who provided the comedy-relief.

Even though the singing cowboys were a dime-a-dozen at the time, the series did surprisingly well and lasted for a little over two years.

George Houston was making Westerns when death brought his career to an end in November, 1945.

FILMS: *The Melody Lingers On. Wallaby Jim of the Islands. Captain Calamity. The Great Waltz. Let's Sing Again. Return of the Lone Rider. Border Roundup. The Lone Rider Rides Again. Outlaws of Boulder Pass. Riders of the Plains. Lawless Town. Frontier Scout.*

GILBERT ROLAND (1905-)

Gilbert Roland was born Luis Antonio Damasco Alonso in Chihuahua, Mexico on December 11, 1905. Since both his father and grandfather were famous bullfighters, it was only natural for young Luis to want to be a matador. He was still attending private school in Mexico when Pancho Villa and his revolutionists were terrorizing the country. Forced to leave their village, the Alonsos moved to El Paso, Texas where the boy completed his education.

In 1925, young Luis met film producer B. P. Schulberg who helped him get his first part in a motion picture called *The Plastic Age*. Changing his name to Gilbert Roland, he started in movies at an opportune time since every studio was searching for Latin-type actors to compete with the idol of the silent screen, Rudolph Valentino. Stardom did not come easy however, because it took a few films as a bit player before Gilbert graduated to major roles. His big break came in 1927, when he appeared opposite Norma Talmadge in *Camille*. After that, he became one of the classic leading men of the screen, co-starring with names like Bebe Daniels, Billie Dove, Clara Bow and Mae West.

Gilbert was one of the few stars that successfully made the change from silent to sound pictures. But, by 1934, the "Latin Lover" craze was well on its way out. His popularity declining, he was forced to play a series of supporting roles and for awhile it seemed like he was doomed to act the part of a slick gangster in every picture he made. Around 1942, the end of his career was postponed when he became the third actor to portray the famous "Cisco Kid" in a series of Westerns for Monogram. Having originally started with Warner Baxter as the dashing "Robin Hood of the West," the role had been taken over by Cesar Romero in 1939 for a string of features by 20th Century Fox. When Monogram decided to produce an entirely new series about O. Henry's fabulous character, Gilbert eagerly accepted the part. It was

1. *Gilbert Roland*

2. *John "Dusty" King is having a hard time with villain Glenn Strange*

3. *Ray "Crash" Corrigan*

4. *Raymond Hatton with Johnny Mack Brown*

5. *Bob Baker*

6. *George Houston being held up by badman Kenne Duncan*

1.

4.

5.

6.

interesting to note that each individual portrayed the "Cisco Kid" in entirely different moods. While maintaining a high standard in his films, Gilbert contributed a strict sense of seriousness to his role in comparison to Cesar Romero's gay, devil-may-care portrayals.

In 1943, his movie career was cut short while he entered the Armed Forces, serving with the Air Corps until the end of World War II. When he returned to movie-making, he was given only a few acting jobs which barely kept him going and, by 1947, Gilbert Roland had practically vanished from the screen. Two years later, he staged one of filmdom's greatest comebacks with his memorable performance in *We Were Strangers* starring John Garfield and Jennifer Jones. Since then, Roland has been constantly active in movies and TV, particularly in Westerns. His long career has seen him star in pictures for First National, United Artists, Paramount, Warners, P.R.C., Monogram, Fox, Universal, M-G-M and R-K-O. Having once been selected as "the most virile actor in movies," Gilbert has managed to keep his looks and fine physique despite the fact that he has entered his sixties. His three-year marriage to actress Constance Bennett ended in divorce in 1944. Shortly afterward, he wed Guillermina Cantu.

FILMS: *The Plastic Age. Campus Flirt. The Blonde Saint. Rose of the Golden West. Camille. The Dove. The Love Mart. A Woman Disputed. Call Her Savage. After Tonight. Woman in Room 13. Ladies Love Danger. She Done Him Wrong. Mystery Woman. Juarez. Last Train From Madrid. Gambling on the High Seas. Rangers of Fortune. Angels With Broken Wings. Captain Kidd. Beauty and the Bandit. Pirates of Monterey. Cisco Kid and the Angel. South of Monterey. Romance of the Rancho. Gay Cavalier. Robin Hood of Monterey. Riding the California Trail. Mark of the Renegade. High Conquest. The Dude Goes West. Sea Hawk. Malaya. The Torch. The Crisis. We Were Strangers. The Bullfighter and the Lady. Thunder Bay. Miracle of Fatima. Beneath the 12 Mile Reef. French Line. The Furies. Diamond Queen. My Six Convicts. Ten Tall Men. The Bad and the Beautiful. The Racers. Guns of the Timberland. Apache War Smoke. Underworld. Glory Alley. Underwater. Treasure of Pancho Villa. The Big Circus. Last of the Fast Guns. The Wild and the Innocent. Three Violent People. Samar. Eyes of Father Thomasino. Cheyenne Autumn. The Reward. Harlow.*

RAY "CRASH" CORRIGAN (1907-)

Not many Western fans of the 1930's and '40's will ever forget this two-fisted action hero of the screen. Having gone from bit player to stuntman, then to stardom, Ray "Crash" Corrigan was a favorite among cowboy stars for many years and when his pictures were exhibited, fans were sure to get a treat.

Ray was born Raymond Bernard in Milwaukee, Wisconsin on February 14, 1907 and was brought up and educated in Denver, Colorado, where he studied electronics. He tried to go into business for himself by opening an electrical shop but soon went broke. Having excelled in athletics, he started a school of physical culture and also modeled for sculptors and artists. He won several awards for "possessing the manliest physique" and then took a job in Hollywood instructing movie stars how to keep in good physical shape. When a friend told him he should try getting into pictures, Ray joined a stock company of actors and this gave him a chance to make his film debut in 1934.

For a year, Ray appeared in nothing but small unimportant roles in various features. Finally in 1935, Republic Pictures gave him a good featured part in a chapter-play called *The Leathernecks Have Landed,* which brought him to the attention of movie fans. The following year, Ray played his first starring role in a serial called *Undersea Kingdom,* which zoomed him to new heights as one of the screen's favorite adventure stars. With his success in films, Ray earned himself the nickname of "Crash" because of his daredevil stunts and unusual strength and stamina.

The same year that Ray achieved stardom at Republic, the studio decided to inaugurate a new series of Westerns which would have three leading characters instead of only one. That was the beginning of the "Three Mesquiteers" and the trio of actors chosen for the principal parts were Ray Corrigan, Bob Livingston and Sid Saylor. After the first picture in the series, Saylor was replaced by Max Terhune and the rest is movie history. Together, Corrigan, Livingston and Terhune became the most successful trio of performers ever to appear in motion pictures. They were selected to the list of top ten cowboys and appeared in some of the best horse-operas ever produced by any studio. While co-starring in this series, Corrigan played the part of "Tucson Smith," a character that soon won over millions of fans. Besides working in these features, he found time to make another hit serial, *The Painted Stallion* in 1937, which ranks as one of the best Western chapter-plays of all time.

After making twenty-four pictures with the "Mesquiteers," Ray gave up his role to join Monogram Studios where he co-produced another series of "trio Westerns" called "The Range Busters." This time, he shared top billing with John "Dusty" King and his old pal, Max Terhune, who had left the "Mesquiteers" just previous to Ray's departure. Once again, a new trio of cowboy stars took to the screen, bringing with them an immeasurable number of thrills that constantly delighted the audience. During the four years that the "Range Busters" lasted on the screen, Ray played the leader of the group in another string of twenty-four Westerns until production ceased in 1944. After that, he retired from the screen to manage his many business ventures, including a soft drink company, real estate, a swimming pool firm and his authentic Western town, Corriganville, which has been used as a filming location for countless movies.

The proud holder of twenty-one patents for electrical and electronic equipment, Ray is married to the former Elaine DuPont and, except for a few recent appearances in pictures, has been content with seeing his old features on television while living a life of leisure.

FILMS: *Mystery Ranch. Singing Vagabond. Dante's Inferno. Night Life of the Gods. Mutiny on the Bounty. Romance in the Rain. She. Undersea Kingdom. Country Gentleman. The Three Mesquiteers. Ghost Town Gold. Roarin' Lead. Gunsmoke Ranch. Hit the Saddle. Riders of Whistling Skull. Come on Cowboys. Purple Vigilantes. Trigger Trio. Call the Mesquiteers. Range Defenders. Heart of the Rockies. Outlaws of Sonora. Wild Horse Rodeo. Riders of the Black Hills. Heroes of the Hills. Night Riders. Overland Stage Raiders. Red River Range. Three Texas Steers. Pals in the Saddle. Santa Fe Stampede. Wyoming Outlaw. New Frontier. The Painted Stallion. The Range Busters. The Kid's Last Ride. Trailing Double Trouble. West of Pinto Basin. Arizona Stagecoach. Rock River Renegades. Saddle Mountain Roundup. Fugitive Valley. Tumbledown Ranch in Arizona. Boothill Bandits. Trail of the Silver Spurs. Texas to Bataan. Bullets and Saddles. Underground Rustlers. Haunted Ranch. Black Market Rustlers. Wranglers' Roost. Cowboy Commandos. Tonto Basin Outlaws. Trail of Robin Hood. Zamba. It. The Terror From Outer Space.*

JOHN KING (1909-)

John King was born Miller MacLeod Everson in Cincinnati, Ohio on July 11, 1909, the son of Ernest and Ruth Bromfield Everson. After graduating from high school, he entered the University of Cincinnati and then worked at odd jobs such as selling furniture, bookkeeping, meat checker and grain elevator stoker. In 1932, he landed a position as a radio announcer for station WCKY, where he had a chance to make occasional use of his excellent singing voice. A year later, he played host on a variety program on station WKRC and also filled in as a featured vocalist. That led to a job singing with Ben Bernie's orchestra and an appearance in a short musical film in Hollywood.

In 1934, John made his acting debut as a featured player in a chapter-play called *The Adventures of Frank Merriwell* which starred Don Briggs. This resulted in a contract with Universal Studios and the leading roles in several melodramas. Having established himself as a rising newcomer, he made his first big impression on movie audiences in 1936, while starring in an exciting serial entitled *Ace Drummond*. Adapted from a popular radio series, the film was based on the thrilling adventures of a character created by Captain Eddie Rickenbacker, flying ace of World War I, and became one of the top action serials of that period.

Throughout the remainder of the 1930's, John appeared in a wide variety of features for Universal ranging from musicals to straight melodramas. In 1940, he left that organization to join Monogram Pictures where he became exclusively associated with Westerns. That year, Monogram decided to compete with the phenomenal success of Republic's "Three Mesquiteers" by introducing "The Range Busters" to the screen. Following the pattern set by the "Hopalong Cassidy" features and the "Mesquiteers," Monogram brought John King, Ray Corrigan and Max Terhune together for a brand new series of "trio Westerns" which, although not quite as successful as its predecessors, did very well on its own.

As a member of the "Range Busters," John reached the peak of his career and his role of "Dusty" offered him ample opportunity to display his talent as a singer. On the other hand, he proved to be a formidable hero when it came to action scenes and he did his share of pulling his two comrades out of many-a-tight scrape.

When "The Range Busters" started losing ground and it seemed like Monogram was about to discontinue the series, John vacated his role in 1943 in favor of playing in other types of features. He made a few appearances in several straight dramas before retiring from the screen around 1946.

FILMS: *The Adventures of Frank Merriwell. Fighting Youth. State Police. Masked Trouble. The Phantom Trio. Mystery of Rio. Ace Drummond. Terror of the Range. Secret of Devil's Gorge. Wandering Justice. Whistling Phantom. Love Before Breakfast. On the Town. Showboat. Crash Donovan. Three Smart Girls. Postal Inspector. The Road Back. Three Smart Girls Grow Up. Nobody's a Fool. Midnight Limited. The Range Busters. Trail of the Silver Spurs. Arizona Stage-*

coach. Rock River Renegades. Fugitive Valley. Boothill Bandits. Texas Trouble Shooters. The Kid's Last Ride. Saddle Mountain Roundup. Trailing Double Trouble. Tumbledown Ranch in Arizona. West of Pinto Basin.

BOB BAKER (1914-)

Immediately following the success of Gene Autry's Westerns at Republic Studios in 1935, Hollywood producers began a frantic search for likely talent in order to compete in the field of musical horse-operas. As many of them later discovered, only a handful of performers chosen had the necessary qualifications. Some could hardly sit astride a horse, much less ride or rope. Among the few that had an authentic Western background was Bob Baker, a young, good-looking cowboy from Colorado.

Born Leland Weed in Forest City, Iowa on November 8, 1914, he was raised and educated in Arizona and Colorado, where he spent his younger years learning all about ranch life. His first job came when he was still in his teens, riding herd on a cattle ranch in southern Colorado. There he picked up the nickname of "Tumble" Weed. A short time later, he worked as a dude ranch guide, scoutmaster, National Guardsman and rodeo performer before winding up as a singer of cowboy ballads on radio. Before long, he was a featured vocalist on the famous "National Barn Dance" radio program originating from Tulsa, Oklahoma, a show that was noted for its fine Country and Western Musical talent. A few years earlier, the program had been chiefly responsible for bringing Gene Autry and his sidekick, Smiley Burnette, into the spotlight.

During the latter part of 1936, Leland's mother learned that the Universal Studios were searching for a new singing cowboy star and she decided to send in her son's photograph as a possible candidate. A short time later, an audition was arranged and a screen test made at Universal headquarters in California. Luckily, Leland had met an old friend, cowboy star Max Terhune, who had given him a few lessons prior to the test and the result was that he was selected among dozens of performers to make a picture called *Courage of the West*. Under the name of Bob Baker, the newcomer made his debut in 1937 and became an overnight success.

Placed under contract to Universal, Baker appeared on the list of top ten cowboy stars of 1939, starring in a series of features that were extremely well-received by the fans. An able performer, he had a pleasing personality, good looks and a fine singing voice. In addition to his personal appeal, he rode a beautiful Pinto pony called "Apache" and was accompanied by veteran screen comedian Fuzzy Knight. With the competition at its peak, Universal took no chances with the Bob Baker Westerns and real effort was made to give these fine B-grade pictures the proper support. After his original series was completed, Baker started another group of films for Universal, this time, teamed with Johnny Mack Brown and Fuzzy Knight. Known as "The Frontier Marshals," these features were snappy little Westerns that made full use of their three principal performers. Contrary to the usual pattern of singing cowboys of that era, Baker never dominated the action content with his vocalizing. His musical scenes were injected with care at intervals that seemed to please his fans.

After leaving Universal in 1941, Baker went to work for Monogram and co-starred with Hoot Gibson and Ken Maynard in a few features in the "Trail Blazers" series. Unfortunately, these lacked the special polish of his earlier pictures and, after completing his last film, *Wild Horse Stampede* in 1943, he retired from the screen.

FILMS: *Courage of the West. Border Wolves. The Last Stand. The Singing Outlaw. Western Trails. Outlaw Express. The Black Bandit. Ghost Town Riders. Honor of the West. Guilty Trails. Prairie Justice. The Phantom Stage. West of Carson City. Badman From Red Butte. Riders of Pasco Basin. Wild Horse Stampede.*

JACK RANDALL (1906-1945)

The average movie fan fails to realize the danger that some actors undergo in order to make motion pictures. When it comes to filming a Western, the hazards are particularly numerous due to the high action content of these features. In the old days of picture-making, stars were often called upon to perform stunts that endangered life and limb, for it was not until later that professional stuntmen were hired to double for them. On the other hand, some big-name personalities simply refused to use a double unless a scene involved an extremely perilous trick that only a stuntman could do. The names of those that became known for doing their own action sequences were many, including such stars as Tom Mix, Buck Jones, Hoot Gibson, George O'Brien, Bill Duncan, Yakima Canutt, Bob Steele and Tom Tyler. On July 16, 1945, a popular cowboy named Jack Randall died from injuries sustained from a fall off his horse while filming a movie, after having performed dozens of

209

dangerous stunts. With the loss of Randall, Western fans had been deprived of one of the most beloved cowboy entertainers in motion pictures.

Jack was born Addison Randall in San Fernando, California, on May 12, 1906, the son of editor Edgar Randall and writer Clarena Myers Randall. After leaving college, he undertook a career in show business by entering vaudeville as a singer, gradually rising to musical stage productions which kept him active until he made his debut in movies. In 1934, he started out as a bit player taking minor roles in various films, until 1937, when Monogram Studios hired him to make Westerns. After his initial appearance as a singing cowboy hero in *Riders of the Dawn,* Jack became a hit with Western fans. He starred in a long list of features aided by comedian Al St. John and was among the favorite cowboy vocalists of the early 1940's. Shunning the use of any unnecessary violence, he portrayed a gentlemanly-type of hero whose sense of fair play stood out above all his other qualities. He had a good singing voice and his ability to handle action was excellent.

On June 7, 1941, Jack married actress Barbara Bennett, daughter of the famous actor Richard Bennett. In the meantime, he was busy turning out some of the best features Monogram ever produced. However, when the Second World War gained momentum in 1942, Jack found time to make a tour of training camps entertaining troops and selling war bonds. A little while later, he entered the U.S. Air Corps, serving until 1945 when he was discharged with the rank of captain.

He had just signed a new contract with Universal Studios and was in the process of filming a serial entitled *The Royal Mounted Rides Again* when he took a bad spill from his horse. The fall proved fatal and the whole world mourned the loss of a brilliant personality who had helped make Westerns a little bit better. After a funeral that was attended by many close friends and relatives, Jack was laid to rest at the Garden of Memories in the Forest Lawn Cemetery, Hollywood, California. During the span of his career as a cowboy star, he made twenty-two pictures and was the brother of Western favorite Bob Livingston.

FILMS: *The Family Tree. Another Face. Two in the Dark. Love on a Bet. Follow the Fleet. Navy Born. Don't Turn Me Loose. Flying Hostess. Riders of the Dawn. Gun Packer. Land of Fighting Men. Gunsmoke Trail. Man's Country. The Mexicali Kid. Danger Valley. Where the West Begins. Wild Horse Canyon. Oklahoma Terror. Westbound Stage. Across the Plains. Stars Over Arizona. Trigger Smith. Down the Wyoming Trail. Land of Six Guns. Overland Mail. Rolling Westward. The Kid From Santa Fe. Covered Wagon Trail.*

ROY ROGERS (1912-)

The last movie star to hold the title of "King of the Cowboys" was Roy Rogers. He was born in Cincinnati, Ohio, on November 5, 1912 and christened Leonard Slye. After leaving high school, he worked in a shoe factory in Ohio, then wound up as a truck driver and fruit picker in California in 1929. Having learned to play a guitar as a boy, he teamed up with a cousin, Stanley Slye, and formed a singing duet. In 1934, he changed his name to Dick Weston and organized a musical cowboy group with Bob Nolan called "The Sons of the Pioneers," which included Tim Spencer and Hugh Farr. When the quartet finally reached public notice over radio station KFWB in Los Angeles, another member, Pat Brady, was added to the group.

In 1937, almost every film studio was frantically searching for likely candidates to compete with Republic's new singing sensation, Gene Autry. Learning that Universal was auditioning musical talent, young Weston made an attempt to get into pictures but lost out to a singer named Bob Baker. Without being discouraged, he took a few small roles in a string of Westerns before finally landing a contract with Republic. Taking the name of Roy Rogers, he played his first starring role in a picture entitled *Under the Western Stars* in 1938. Republic soon learned that it had another successful star on its payroll and decided to give Rogers a big build-up. In that way, should the studio lose Autry, Rogers could be his successor. In the meantime, Roy made a series of pictures that zoomed him into third place on the list of top ten cowboy stars of 1939, 1940 and 1941. The following year, he climbed into second place and was busy making eight pictures per year.

At the end of 1942, Gene Autry entered the U.S. Air Corps and Roy became the new "King of the Cowboys," just as the producers at Republic had anticipated. From 1943 on, he kept the title, even after the regular series Westerns had ceased production. Republic was a studio that took great pride in its large array of cowboy stars because Westerns and serials were the company's chief sources of income. Realizing that Rogers was their hottest property, the studio heads backed him all the way and increased the production value of his films.

The first of two outstanding features of Roy's pictures was the presence of his loyal sidekick, Gabby Hayes, a veteran scene-stealer who shared in the adventures of forty-seven features with Rogers. Then came Roy's popular Palomino stallion, "Trigger," billed as "the smartest horse in the movies."

When the B-series Westerns ceased to exist after 1954, Rogers retired from the screen to form his own enterprises. This included a television series along with dozens of other financial interests, such as real estate, radio stations and a rodeo. In private life, the star patterned his way of living in a clean fashion modeled after the image he projected on the screen. After ten years of marriage, his first wife, Arlene Wilkins, died in 1946. A year later, Roy married his leading lady, Dale Evans, with whom he has raised nine children, most of them adopted from foundling homes. Their joint efforts in teaching a true love of God and fighting prejudice have made them one of Hollywood's most respected couples. When Roy and Dale are not busy with television appearances or rodeo tours, they enjoy life with their family on their beautiful 138-acre ranch at Chatsworth, California.

FILMS:*Wild Horse Rodeo. The Old Corral. Under Western Stars. The Old Barn Dance. Billy the Kid Returns. Come on Rangers. Rough Rider's Roundup. The Frontier. Pony Express. The Dark Command. Southward Ho. In Old Caliente. Wall Street Cowboy. Arizona Kid. Saga of Death Valley. Young Buffalo Bill. Carson City Kid. Man From Cheyenne. Nevada City. Young Bill Hickock. Badmen of Deadwood. Red River Valley. Jesse James at Bay. Sons of the Pioneers. South of Santa Fe. Sunset Serenade. Idaho. Roll on Texas Moon. Song of Nevada. Silver Spurs. Brazil. Bells of Rosarita. Heart of the Rockies. Hollywood Canteen. My Pal Trigger. Lake Placid Serenade. Springtime in the Rockies. Don't Fence Me In. Hands Across the Border. Melody Time. Utah. Susanna Pass. Bells of Coronado. Trail of Robin Hood. Along the Navajo Trail. Gay Ranchero. Apache Rose. Bells of San Angelo. The Far Frontier. Hellorado. Golden Stallion. Spoilers of the Plains. Yellow Rose of Texas. Down Dakota Way. The Cowboy and the Senorita.*

"WILD BILL" ELLIOTT (1903-1965)

Beginning with the year 1940, Bill Elliott was a consistent member of the list of top ten cowboy stars for fourteen consecutive years. Movie critics unanimously agreed that he came the closest to duplicating the style of old-time Western star William S. Hart. Having adopted the format of portraying the "good Badman," Elliott became a familiar figure with his characterizations of grim, poker-faced gunmen, usually starting out on the wrong side of the law, but redeeming himself by becoming a hero at the end of the last reel.

Born Gordon Elliott in Pattonsburg, Missouri in 1903, he was raised and educated in Kansas City, where his father was an agent for the stockyards. It was there that he became acquainted with genuine cowboys from the West and learned to ride a horse like an expert. By the time he reached the age of sixteen, he had competed in a few rodeo contests and won his first trophy. Years later, Elliott went to California, where he studied dramatics and took part in theatricals at the Pasadena Community Playhouse. Making his entrance in motion pictures in 1928, he appeared under his real name in several minor roles. It was not until 1934 that he was able to gain any recognition. In that year, he made an impression when he played a featured part in a film called *Wonder Bar*. Then came a period of struggling to achieve stardom while he worked as a supporting actor, playing mostly villains in Westerns.

In 1938, Gordon changed his name to William and received the big break of his career when he was chosen to play the title role in a Columbia serial called *The Adventures of Wild Bill Hickock*. He proved to be such a success that the studio quickly starred him in another chapter-play entitled *Overland With Kit Carson* before the year was over. However, it was his role of Wild Bill Hickock that caused the fans to stick the term "Wild Bill" to his name. For nearly five years after that, he remained with Columbia Studios as a star of Western features that finally brought him success and fame.

In 1943, Bill went to work for Republic Pictures where he succeeded Don Barry as the star of the popular "Red Ryder" Westerns. After appearing in a string of these popular features, he vacated the series in 1945 in order to produce and star in his own films. It was then that he portrayed characters fashioned after the type made famous by William S. Hart. Doing away with the spectacular action of the ordinary B-Westerns, Bill Elliott concentrated more on realism and grown-up plots. At a time when cowboy features were being over-run by singing heroes, he remained one of the few straight action stars, playing his roles with unusual zest and sincerity.

Completing almost twenty years as a cowboy star, Elliott retired from the screen in 1957 after making his last picture, *Footsteps in the Night*. He left a trail of over seventy films in which he had displayed his fine horsemanship and a knack for handling action. One of his features which fans liked was the way he wore his guns in a reversed-holster fashion and he was generally regarded as the fastest man on the draw since the days of old-time cowboy star Tim McCoy.

Although the B-Westerns had gone out of production after 1954, Elliott remained active by touring with a circus and hosting a TV show which re-ran his old pictures. Unlike most of the new breed of cowboy stars, he was a conscientious rancher in real life and owned a sizeable

1. *Jack Randall*
2. *Wild Bill Elliott*
3. *Allan Lane*
4. *Roy Rogers*
5. *Dave Sharpe*
6. *Don Barry*

1.

4.

5.

6.

spread near Calabasas, California, raising cattle and horses at a profit. As far as hobbies, Bill was an avid student of geology and collected Western souvenirs. While busy making a picture, he resided at his home in Westwood nearer Hollywood. But, after his retirement, he lived at his ranch near Las Vegas, Nevada. It was there that Bill died of cancer after a long illness on November 26, 1965. His marriage to his first wife, Helen, had ended in divorce after thirty-four years. He was survived by his second wife, the former Dolly Moore, and a daughter, Barbara.

FILMS: *Restless Youth. The Great Divide. Broadway Scandals. Wonder Bar. Roll Along Cowboy. The Law Comes to Texas. The Adventures of Wild Bill Hickock. Overland With Kit Carson. King of Dodge City. The Return of Wild Bill. Frontiers of '49. Across the Sierras. The Return of Daniel Boone. In Early Arizona. Lone Star Pioneers. Prairie Schooners. Rebel City. Wildcat of Tucson. Taming the West. Cheyenne Wildcat. Colorado Pioneers. California Gold Rush. Conquest of Cheyenne. The Plainsman and the Lady. Wyoming. Old Los Angeles. Gallant Legion. The Fabulous Texan. Hellfire. The Last Bandit. Showdown. The Savage Horde. Bitter Creek. The Longhorn. Waco. Vengeance Trail. Kansas Territory. Fargo. The Forty Niners. Topeka. Calling Homicide. Vigilante Terror. Dial Red O. Chain of Evidence. Sudden Danger. Footsteps in the Night.*

DAVE SHARPE (1911-)

For years it has been common knowledge that stuntmen constitute a minority group of unsung heroes in the movie industry. These reckless daredevils continuously risk life and limb each time they are hired to double for big-name stars during the filming of dangerous action scenes. Many of them earned their fame and fortune through Westerns and one of the best of these was Dave Sharpe.

Born in St. Louis, Missouri in 1911, David Sharpe made his first screen appearance at the age of seven when he played in an old Douglas Fairbanks, Sr. film called *Thief of Bagdad*. While he was attending military school in Los Angeles, he managed to take part in an occasional movie as a juvenile actor. Having been impressed by the great Fairbanks' acrobatics, he took up athletics and was later chosen to represent the Los Angeles Sports Club in amateur competitions. Before Dave had reached the age of twenty, he won the National Tumbling Championship.

In 1928, Dave entered motion pictures as a bit player. He had his first good role the following year in *Masked Emotions,* which led to a series of short comedies for Fox, Paramount and Hal Roach Studios. By 1933, he was playing leads in the *Young Friends* series for Ajax Productions. Throughout the 1930's he acted in a variety of roles which ranged from heroes to villains in a score of Westerns for various companies. Among the best work he did on the screen was when he co-starred with Herman (Bruce Bennett) Brix and Charles Quigley in a Republic serial called *Daredevils of the Red Circle* in 1939. The part gave him an opportunity to show what he really could do when it came to action.

Dave began his long association with Republic as a stuntman and actor and, in many cases, found himself working hand-in-hand with the King of Stuntmen, Yakima Canutt. His specialty being fist fights and bar-room brawls, Dave soon became known as the "Crown Prince of Daredevils" and many a cowboy star was only too happy to see him handle the rough-and-tumble action in their place. Besides his work for Republic, Dave also handled perilous scenes for stars at Universal, Columbia and Monogram. It was during 1942-43 that he stepped in to replace John King in Monogram's popular "Range Busters" series which co-starred Ray Corrigan and Max Terhune.

In the latter part of 1943, Dave entered the U.S. Army and served until the end of the Second World War. Returning to Hollywood, he resumed his career as a stuntman, eventually rising to the position of action director. He handled sequences for dozens of films including *The Exile,* in which he worked with Douglas Fairbanks, Jr., *Desert Legion, Mark of the Renegade, Cimarron Kid* and *Colorado Serenade.* Also active in television, Dave performed stunts for the "Wild Bill Hickock" and "Zorro" series.

FILMS: *Thief of Bagdad. Scaramouche. A Social Error. I'll Tell One. Front Money. Hollywood Love. Adventurous Knights. Roaring Roads. Masked Emotions. Mind Your Own Business. Melody of the Plains. Drums of Destiny. Dick Tracy. Perils of Nyoka. King of the Mounties. Silver Stallion. Haunted Ranch. From Texas to Bataan. Two Fisted Justice. Trail Riders. Covered Wagon Trails. Colorado Serenade.*

DONALD "RED" BARRY (1912-)

Don was born Donald Barry de Acosta in Houston, Texas on January 11, 1912. He became a football athlete during his days in high school and was elected to the roster of Texas All-Stars in 1929. Entering the Texas School of Mines, he furthered his reputation on the gridiron before leaving college to work as an advertising agent in California. Don then decided to become an actor and joined a stock company. He was part of a troupe that presented "Tobacco Road" on tour before he made his debut in motion pictures in 1936 as a bit player in *Night Waitress*.

Stardom came slowly to Don as he appeared in a string of minor roles at various studios. He finally won recognition in 1939 when he played the villain in one of Republic's popular "Three Mesquiteers" Westerns, *Wyoming Outlaw*. The following year, the studio gave him his first starring role in a serial entitled *The Adventures of Red Ryder,* a cowboy hero made famous by Fred Harmon in comic strips. Needless to say, the chapter-play was a big hit and Don emerged as a new Western star. By that time, Republic was known as the "Home of the Westerns" because of its large array of cowboy personalities. The studio was turning out horse-operas and serials by the batch and the producers decided to add another new series of features about "Red Ryder" with Don Barry playing the lead. Aided by young Tommy Cook, who portrayed his little Indian friend, "Little Beaver," Don made a score of these fast-action thrillers for nearly four years. After that, he felt that he was ready for other things and vacated the series in 1943.

The following months saw Don making several pictures of a different variety. In his spare time, he helped to entertain troops at training camps all over the country and sold War Bonds. Meanwhile, he succeeded in being voted one of the top ten cowboy stars from 1942 to 1945. Shortly afterwards, Don concluded his association with Republic Studios in order to produce and star in his own productions. After a series of straight dramas for the Robert L. Lippert Company which failed to keep up with his previous films, he made an attempt to return to Westerns. Unfortunately, these too, met with failure largely because of poor stories and too little production value.

Having made his sizeable contribution to Westerns while he starred as "Red Ryder," Don turned character actor. In this capacity, he has managed to appear in major films at various studios and in television. Once in a while, he can even be seen as a supporting player in a feature Western.

In private life, Don was divorced from his first wife, the former Helen Talbot, and married to actress Peggy Stewart in 1944.

FILMS: *Night Waitress. The Woman I Love. Only Angels Have Wings. The Crowd Roars. Sinners in Paradise. Wyoming Outlaw. The Adventures of Red Ryder. Red Headed Justice. Death Valley Outlaws. Carson City Cyclone. Black Hills Express. Outlaws of Santa Fe. Fugitive From Sonora. Remember Pearl Harbor. The Traitor Within. West Side Kid. My Buddy. The Purple Heart. Ringside. The Last Crooked Mile. The*

Chicago Kid. Jesse James Jr. I Shot Billy the Kid. The Prizefighter.
Man From the Rio Grande. Gunfire. That's My Girl. Madonna of the
Desert. The Dalton Gang. China Doll. Jesse James' Women. Border
Rangers. Warlock. I'll Cry Tomorrow. Frankenstein 1970. Walk on the
Wild Side. Twilight of Honor.

ALLAN (ROCKY) LANE (1904-)

Allan was born Harold Albershart near Mishawaka, Indiana on September 22, 1904. While attending Notre Dame University, he became proficient in sports and earned himself an offer to play professional football after college. In off-season periods, he worked as a photographic illustrator, learning the techniques of camera work and reproduction. One day, a friend suggested that he should try acting as a career and arranged for Allan to join a stock company of performers. After a short while, he took part in several stage theatricals, until 1929, when he entered motion pictures as a bit player.

Beginning at Fox Studios, Allan appeared in minor roles and rose gradually to more important parts. His work was extended to include several films for Paramount and Columbia, usually playing secondary leading men in pictures of relatively little importance. Finally, after ten years of getting nowhere, he was given the chance to star in a serial for Republic entitled *The King of the Royal Mounted* in 1939. The role gave his career the necessary shot in the arm that it needed and Allan was on his way. He made a number of exciting features and chapter-plays for Republic which brought his name into prominence as one of the screen's top action stars. When Bill Elliott vacated the popular "Red Ryder" Westerns in 1945, Allan was given the opportunity to show what he could do in the role. In an entirely new series, he brought revitalized interest from fans who had finally grown weary of the "Red Ryder" character. Having first been brought to the screen by Don Barry in 1941 and extended into another series with Bill Elliott, the cowboy character had grown monotonous and was in bad need of new blood.

For over three years, Allan became closely identified with the "Red Ryder" series, starring in no less than twenty-one features until he grew tired of the role. In 1948, he began a new string of Westerns for Republic and succeeded in being named to the list of top ten cowboy stars of 1951 and 1953. Sharing the spotlight with him were his wonder horse, "Blackjack" and veteran character actor Eddy Waller. As a whole, these features were well done and had plenty of action, but the rising costs of production and the arrival of television were to take their toll on all

219

B-Westerns. After 1954, Republic Pictures ceased to make any more series like those that had made the company famous. Allan Lane found himself to be one of the last remaining cowboy stars to appear in the type of features which had been the backbone of the Western genre.

With the ending of his contract at Republic, Allan undertook some personal appearance tours with rodeos and a circus before finally retiring in 1956. He left the screen contented that he had achieved at least seventeen years as a prominent cowboy star and had made over 125 films. With that in mind, he was certainly deserving of the dignified exit he made at the closing of a chapter in moving picture history. Like most cowboy stars of the screen, his private life had been comparatively uneventful except that he had been divorced from his first wife, the former Gladys Leslie, and later married to actress Sheilah Ryan.

FILMS: *Not Quite Decent. Forward Pass. Glove in the Rough. Madame Satan. Miss Pinkerton. Stowaway. Big Business. The Duke Comes Back. Night Spot. This Marriage Business. Crime Ring. Pacific Liner. Grand 'Ole Opry. The Maid's Night Out. They Made Her a Spy. King of the Royal Mounted. Perils of the Darkest Jungles. King of the Mounties. Call of the South Seas. Yukon Patrol. Tournament Tempo. Panama Lady. Night Train to Memphis. Daredevils of the West. The Tenderfoot. Tiger Woman. Stagecoach to Denver. Sheriff of Sundown. Silver City Kid. Vigilante Hideout. Gunmen of Abilene. Rustlers on Horseback. Powder River Rustlers. Trail of Robin Hood. Bold Frontiersman. Bandit King of Texas. Carson City Raiders. The Denver Kid. Desperadoes of Dodge City. Navajo Trail Raiders. Bandits of Dark Canyon. Death Valley Gunfighters. Night Riders of Monterey. Fort Dodge Stampede. Black Hills Ambush. Code of the Silver Sage. Covered Wagon Raids. Desert of Lost Men. Frontier Investigator. Bandits of the West. El Paso Stampede. The Saga of Hemp Brown.*

SUNSET CARSON (1921-)

Sunset Carson was born in Plainview, Texas, about 1921, the son and grandson of former rodeo performers. By the time he reached the age of twelve he had already competed in forty rodeo competitions and won a dozen trophies for bronc-riding and calf roping. When cowboy star Tom Mix first saw him, he gave the boy his first job as a circus performer. After touring the country and making a few motion picture appearances as a bit player, he traveled to South America where he won the title of Champion All-around Cowboy at Buenos Aires in 1941 and 1942. On his return to the U.S.A., he made his official screen debut in a film called *Stage Door Canteen* in 1943 under the name of Michael Harrison. That same year, Republic Studios awarded him a contract to star in a new series of Westerns in which he would be known as Sunset Carson. By 1946, he ranked eighth on the list of top ten cowboy stars.

Riding his white horse through one exciting screen adventure after another, Carson brought his enemies to justice by using his fists, his guns and his skill with a bullwhip. He was an ideal hero for action features because he possessed the tall, husky physique of an athlete and was extremely good looking. Republic kept him active in Westerns for several years until the advent of television put an end to the standard hoss-operas. After starring in a few films for some independent outfits like Astor Pictures, Carson retired from motion pictures in 1952. His efforts to get his own television series never panned out so he accepted an offer to tour with the Clyde Beatty Circus for a couple of seasons. Since that time, he made only a few public appearances and quickly faded into obscurity. His is a tragic case for he seems to have gotten his start at a time when Western stars were too numerous and the demand was too little. He showed great possibilities of becoming a big star, but some say that he acquired drinking habits which helped finish his career. No matter what happened, Sunset Carson certainly left his brand on the Westerns.

FILMS: *Stage Door Canteen. County Fair. Indian Territory. El Paso Kid. The Big Sleep. Alias Billy the Kid. In the Days of Buffalo Bill. Red River Renegades. Santa Fe Saddlemaster. Rio Grande Raiders. Call of the Rockies. Bordertown Trail. Code of the Prairie. Firebrands of Arizona. Sheriff of Cimarron. Bandits of the Badlands. The Cherokee Flash.*

WARD BOND (1905-1960)

Ward Bond was born in Denver, Colorado, on April 9, 1905. After attending the Colorado School of Mines, he became a student at the University of Southern California where he played tackle on the college football team alongside a tall, lanky fellow called "Duke" Morrison. Years later, Morrison was to become famous in movies as John Wayne.

In 1927, director John Ford went to the USC campus to film scenes for a George O'Brien movie entitled *Salute* and Ward Bond and his gridiron team-mates were hired to take part in the picture. Graduating with a B.S. degree, Ward decided to try the movies as a career and landed a job as a stuntman. Within a short time, he was playing villains opposite stars like Buck Jones, Ken Maynard and Tim McCoy. When his old school chum John Wayne started making Westerns for Lone Star

Productions, Ward was seen as a "heavy" in many films of the series. It was the beginning of a long and close association with Wayne in pictures.

All through the 1930's, Bond was one of Hollywood's busiest performers making dozens of appearances in features that usually had him cast as a tough bully. For awhile, it seemed as if he would be eternally doomed to play that type of role until his old friend John Ford gave him a chance to show what he could really do in pictures such as *Drums Along the Mohawk* and *The Long Voyage Home*. With the help of his genuine talent, and director Ford, Bond finally broke away from his stereotyped parts and went into bigger, more important acting assignments. Although he was still technically a supporting actor, he was recognized as a top-notch performer in a long list of excellent productions.

It was in 1950 that Ward was launched to stardom when he played a leading role in *The Wagonmaster*. Directed by Ford and co-starring Ben Johnson, the film turned out to be one of the best Westerns ever made and it led to Bond's debut in television. Oddly enough, it was through TV that Ward was to receive his greatest fame. While still very active in motion pictures, he had been offered the leading part in a new television series called "Wagon Train" and was reluctant to accept because of the constant demands it would make on him. Finally, he decided to take the role, creating the part of Major Seth Adams in September, 1957. The show later became the No. 1 series on television.

On November 5, 1960, Bond's career came to an end at Dallas, Texas, when he died of a heart attack at the age of fifty-five. He had been divorced from Doris Sellers since 1944. Although he had given many fine performances on the screen, his most memorable films were *The Long Voyage Home, A Guy Named Joe, Tap Roots, The Wagonmaster* and *The Quiet Man*. He had been employed by every major studio in Hollywood.

FILMS: *Salute. Words and Music. Born Reckless. Hello Trouble. Justice of the Range. White Eagle. High Speed. It Happened One Night. Devil Dogs of the Air. Tall Timber. Born to the Wild. Dead End. Drums Along the Mohawk. The Long Voyage Home. Gone With the Wind. Hello Frisco Hello. Kit Carson. Swamp Water. Ten Gentlemen From West Point. Tobacco Road. Doctors Don't Tell. My Darling Clementine. The Sullivans. Gentleman Jim. Sergeant York. Santa Fe Trail. A Guy Named Joe. They Were Expendable. Dakota. Canyon Passage. Unconquered. The Fugitive. It's a Wonderful Life. Tall in the Saddle. Tap Roots. Operation Pacific. Joan of Arc. Only the Valiant. Fort Apache. She Wore a Yellow Ribbon. Singing Guns. Three Godfathers. The*

Wagonmaster. The Time of Your Life. Riding High. Hellgate. The Quiet Man. A Man Alone. The Long Gray Line. Great Missouri Raid. Kiss Tomorrow Goodbye. Dakota Incident. Hondo. Mr. Roberts. Blowing Wild. The Searchers. Pillars in the Sky. China Doll. Johnny Guitar. The Holliday Brand. Rio Bravo. The Wings of Eagles.

LON CHANEY, JR. (1915-)

This well-known screen player was born Creighton Chaney in Oklahoma City, Oklahoma on February 10, 1915, the son of Lon Chaney, the famous character actor. After attending Hollywood High and the Commercial Experts Training Institute, he worked at odd jobs before finally deciding on an acting career. With his famous father being one of the greatest stars of the silent screen, it was inevitable that he should enter motion pictures. In 1930, the year of his dad's death, he made his debut in movies under his real name, playing supporting roles. Two years later, he appeared in his first important part opposite Joel McCrea in *Bird of Paradise,* which led to leads in a series of Westerns.

Having established himself in pictures, he changed his name to Lon Chaney, Jr. and decided to try character acting. He began by playing villains in numerous serials and features for Republic, Universal and Paramount until he was more familiar to Western fans as a "heavy" than he had been as a hero. In 1939, he gave his finest performance when he portrayed the big, dim-witted Lennie in *Of Mice and Men,* a part that really showed what a fine actor he was. The following year, Universal Studios gave him the lead in a top-grade horror classic called *The Wolf Man,* which definitely made him a star.

During the years that followed, Lon made a long list of horror pictures and became known for his portrayals of grotesque characters. Following in the footsteps of his father, he lost his identity as an actor in Westerns and assumed a new one in films of terror. He was the only screen player to portray the four best-known movie monsters: "The Wolf man," "Frankenstein's Monster," "Dracula" and "The Mummy."

After years of terrifying audiences, Lon returned to less-fantastic villainy in another long list of Westerns. His big, brawny physique made him a tough opponent to overcome. In one particular film, *North of the Klondike,* he and fellow actor Brod Crawford staged one of the greatest movie brawls ever photographed. During more recent years, Lon has been playing milder, more likeable people on the screen. For awhile, he co-starred with John Hart in a TV series called "Hawkeye and the Last of the Mohicans," and then returned to feature films.

Having become a noted character actor, Lon has enjoyed three individual phases to his career: the first when he was popular in Westerns, the second as a top-notch villain, and the last as a movie monster. In private life, he has been married to the former Patsy Beck since 1937 and is the proud father of two sons.

FILMS: *Bird of Paradise. The Last Frontier. Son of the Border. Shadow of Silk Lenox. Heroes For Hire. The Life of Virgie Winters. Captain Hurricane. Accent on Youth. Wife, Doctor and Nurse. Overland Mail. Ace Drummond. Undersea Kingdom. Wild West Days. The Oregon Trail. Jesse James. Of Mice and Men. Union Pacific. Girl Crazy. One Million B.C. Northwest Mounted Police. The Wolf Man. Billy the Kid. The Daltons Ride Again. Screams in the Night. Eyes of the Underworld. Once a Thief. North of the Klondike. The Frozen Ghost. Man Made Monster. Ghost of Frankenstein. Son of Dracula. House of Frankenstein. The Mummy's Tomb. The Mummy's Ghost. Indestructible Man. Frontier Badmen. House of Dracula. The Mummy's Curse. Dead Man's Eyes. Riders of Death Valley. Pillow of Death. Sixteen Fathoms Deep. Abbott and Costello Meet Frankenstein. Captain China. Frankenstein Meets the Wolf Man. Too Many Blondes. Inside Straight. Only the Valiant. Behave Yourself. Flame of Araby. High Noon. Battles of Chief Pontiac. The Bushwackers. Tecumseh. The Black Sleep. Pardners. Bride of the Gorilla. The Big Chase. Black Pirates. Springfield Rifle. Not as a Stranger. A Lion Is in the Streets. The Defiant Ones. Boy From Oklahoma. Black Castle. Jivaro. Silver Star. I Died a Thousand Times. Manfish. Indian Fighter. Witchcraft. Stage to Thunder Rock. Night of the Beast. Johnny Reno.*

CHIEF THUNDERCLOUD (1899-1967)

Unknown to most movie fans, Chief Thundercloud's real name was Victor Daniels, a full-blooded Indian born at Muskogee, Oklahoma, in 1899. After working as a cowpuncher, miner, livestock foreman, professional boxer and rodeo performer, he made his entrance in motion pictures in 1928, doubling as a bit player and stuntman. As the need for real Indians became more acute due to increased production of Westerns, he took the name of Chief Thundercloud and made appearances in a number of features and serials for various studios.

His first important role came in 1937, when Republic Pictures made a chapter-play entitled *The Lone Ranger,* based on a popular radio and comic strip series. Cast as the Ranger's faithful Indian friend, Tonto, he gave a convincing performance in what became one of the best Western serials ever produced. Obviously pleased with its success, Republic quickly turned out a sequel called *The Lone Ranger Rides Again* which also featured Chief Thundercloud in the same role. This, too, proved to be good enough to re-issue as a full-length feature called *Hi-Yo Silver*. By then, Thundercloud had been thoroughly identified as the original "Tonto" by Western fans and the result was an escalation of his activities on the screen.

In 1940, Paramount Studios hired him to play the title role in a large-scale Western feature entitled *Geronimo,* which also starred first-rate performers like Preston Foster, Ralph Morgan and Andy Devine. This time, Thundercloud was cast as a cruel, bloodthirsty Apache and the part brought him further attention. His next assignments came when he joined cowboy veterans Hoot Gibson and Bob Steele in several features for the "Trail Blazers" series at Monogram. Among his other important screen work, he played a fierce South Sea island chieftain in *Typhoon* opposite Dorothy Lamour and was cast as one of the heroes in *Silver Stallion.* In 1950, he repeated his role as the Apache warrior in *I Killed Geronimo* and thereafter film audiences came to identify him with the part almost as readily as they had with the character of "Tonto" in earlier films.

Thundercloud's extensive career in motion pictures involved a variety of characterizations such as Indians, Eskimos and Polynesian natives. Although most of his work had been done for studios that were known for producing Westerns, Republic, Monogram and P.R.C., he did quite a few pictures for larger companies like Paramount, Universal, Columbia, Warner Bros. and 20th Century Fox. He died in Chicago, on January 31, 1967, at the age of sixty-eight, and was survived by his widow, two sons and four daughters.

FILMS: *The Big Trail. The Indians Are Coming. The Last Frontier. The Fighting Trooper. Custer's Last Stand. The Plainsman. Union Pacific. Young Buffalo Bill. The Lone Ranger. The Painted Stallion. The Lone Ranger Rides Again. Silver Stallion. The Great Adventures of Wild Bill Hickock. Typhoon. Geronimo. The Fighting Seabees. Buffalo Bill. Sonora Stagecoach. Romance of the West. The Senator Was Indiscreet. Broken Arrow. Ambush. A Ticket to Tomahawk. Colt '45. The Beautiful Blonde From Bashful Bend. The Dude Goes West. Santa Fe. I Killed Geronimo.*

DUNCAN RENALDO (1904-   )

This popular actor of motion pictures and television was born Renault Renaldo Duncan of French, Scotch and Spanish parentage in

225

1. *Ward Bond*
2. *Lon Chaney, Jr.*
3. *Duncan Renaldo*
4. *Chief Thundercloud with Hoot Gibson*
5. *James Stewart*
6. *Sunset Carson*

1. 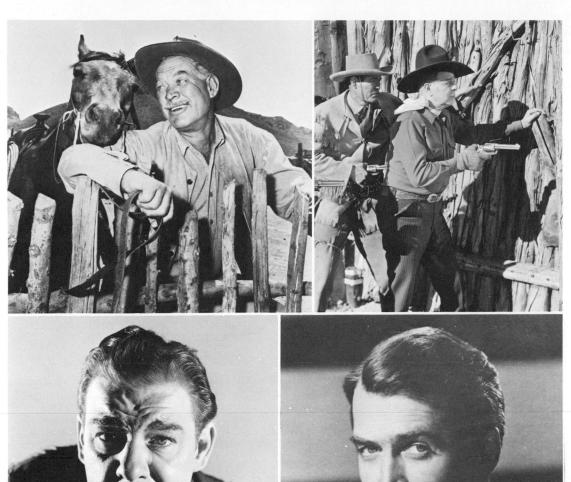 **4.**

5.

6.

Camden, New Jersey on April 23, 1904. He studied art and music in France, Spain and Argentina before making his first stage appearance in Europe as a musician and dancer. Returning to New York in 1921, he was hired as a stage designer for the Metropolitan Opera Company and later made his American debut in a play called "Bright Shawl."

During the following years, Duncan was an actor, writer and director for the Famous Lovers Film Productions at Long Island, New York, as well as a performer on the legitimate stage. His first important hit was a play entitled "My Son," which started him on his way to California. In 1927, he supported Edward Everett Horton in a stage presentation of "Her Cardboard Lover" and was spotted by a movie talent scout. Two years later, Duncan made his first motion picture appearance in *The Bridge of San Luis Rey* and was hailed as a bright newcomer.

It was not until he was featured with Harry Carey in M-G-M's classic of 1930, *Trader Horn,* that Duncan really made an impression on film audiences. The country was still undergoing the "Latin Lover" craze and he fit extremely well in that category, playing slick-haired romantic leads in dozens of features. The craze was soon over, however, and Duncan found himself cast in a series of minor supporting roles in a string of mediocre films.

In 1939, Republic Studios was in the process of reorganizing the popular "Three Mesquiteers" Westerns and the producers chose Duncan to play the part of "Chico" in a new series of features that also co-starred Bob Livingston and Ray Hatton. These pictures, although not quite as good as the previous series, were nevertheless well done and marked the beginning of Duncan's exclusive association with Westerns. After making seven features in the series, he appeared in many other films at Republic until 1945, when he joined Monogram Pictures to star in a group of "Cisco Kid" Westerns. As the fourth successive actor to play the part, Duncan continued to bring the famous caballero to the screen with as much vitality as his predecessors and, when Monogram ceased production on the series, he went to United Artists in 1949 to begin another. These were even better than the Monogram pictures because they also featured the veteran character actor Leo Carrillo as Cisco's sidekick, "Pancho." In 1950, "The Cisco Kid" became one of the earliest syndicated film series to appear on television with Duncan Renaldo and Leo Carrillo still playing their familiar roles. The show was very successful and remained active for several seasons. In fact, it is still being re-run in many parts of America and Europe.

Content with his long career in movies and TV, Duncan retired around 1962 to live a quiet, peaceful life at his beautiful home in Cali-

228

fornia, where he spends his time collecting antiques and writing an occasional story for the movies or TV.

FILMS: *The Bridge of San Luis Rey. Naughty Duchess. Trader Horn. The Devil's Skipper. Clothes Make the Woman. Marcheta. Romany Love. Rebellion. Pals of the Prairie. Trapped in Tia Juana. Rose of the Rio Grande. The Capture. Tiger Fangs. Two Minutes to Play. Jungle Flight. Kansas Terrors. Cowboys From Texas. Pioneers of the West. Heroes of the Saddle. Covered Wagon Days. Rocky Mountain Rangers. Oklahoma Renegades. Gaucho Serenade. Tiger Woman. For Whom the Bell Tolls. The Cisco Kid Returns. In Old Mexico. South of the Rio Grande. Valiant Hombre. Daring Caballero. Bells of San Fernando. Gay Amigo. Satan's Cradle. The Girl From San Lorenzo. The Lady and the Bandit.*

JAMES STEWART (1908-)

Despite the fact that James Stewart has been known as one of filmdom's finest dramatic actors, he appeared in so many excellent Western roles that it is only fitting he should be included among the cowboy stars in this book. He was born James Maitland Stewart in Indiana, Pennsylvania on May 20, 1908, the son of Elizabeth and Alexander Stewart, and graduated from Mercersburg Academy in 1928. He then entered the University of Princeton to study architecture, but the desire to act became stronger when he took part in several college theatricals. Joining a stock company at Cape Cod, Massachusetts, he spent a couple of years on the legitimate stage in plays like "Goodbye Again," "Springtime in Autumn," "Yellow Jack" and "Journey at Night."

In 1935, Stewart played his first part in a motion picture as a supporting actor in *We Love Again,* which was followed with a few other minor roles. His first noticeable acting assignment came a year later when he appeared with Nelson Eddy and Jeanette MacDonald in *Rose Marie.* Realizing that they had a potential star on their hands, the studio heads at M-G-M placed Jim under a long-term contract and proceeded to give him the star build-up through a series of choice roles.

The next few years saw Jim publicized as "the boy-next-door" type, cast as a leading man in a number of features which gradually worked him towards the top. In 1939, he received his first nomination for an Academy Award as best actor for his magnificent performance in *Mr. Smith Goes to Washington* and, although he didn't win that year, he did take the Oscar in 1940 for his part in *The Philadelphia Story.* In March, 1941, Jim became one of the first big movie stars to enter the Armed

229

Forces in World War II. Enlisting as a private in the Air Corps, he was later given a commission as a lieutenant, saw action over Germany and was discharged from active duty as a Colonel in 1945. His membership in the Air Force Reserve later earned him the rank of Brigadier General in 1959.

In 1946, Jim staged his comeback to the screen with a marvelous film called *It's a Wonderful Life* and quickly retained his place among the ten biggest money-making stars in the movies. He made pictures for M-G-M, R-K-O, Columbia, Warners, Fox and Paramount until 1950, when he starred in several action Westerns for Universal-International. Having long since outgrown his shy, countryboy parts, Jim emerged as a versatile super-star, particularly in his new rugged portrayals of frontier life. He had previously made a favorable impression in a Universal Western back in 1939, when he appeared with Marlene Dietrich in *Destry Rides Again,* but that had been the sum total of his work in cowboy roles. In 1950, Jim went after two-fisted parts with a vengeance when he scored heavily in hits like *Bend of the River, Broken Arrow* and *Winchester '73.* Since then, he has been constantly active in first-class Westerns that ranked high on the popularity polls.

In 1952, Jim set a new precedent in Hollywood by announcing that he would work in pictures on a free-lance basis without salary. Instead, he would accept a percentage of the gross profits of each film. In doing so, he was gambling on his ability to draw at the box-office, something which was then unheard of in the industry. In other words, if one of his pictures turned out to be a flop, he had lost his contribution of talent and time, but on the other hand, if the movie was a hit, he stood to reap quite a sum. At first, there were few producers willing to accept such a deal but, after due consideration, they came to realize that a picture would have to be a success before they had to pay Stewart a cent. As it turned out, the transaction proved immensely profitable to both Stewart and his producers. Shortly afterward, the same kind of proposition was adopted by a few other stars who lacked any doubts that their films could make money (such as Gary Cooper, Alan Ladd and John Wayne). It is interesting to note that these actors were all popular for making Westerns.

In recent years, James Stewart has been increasingly active in first-rate Westerns directed by John Ford. Having made so many films about the frontier, his fans have come to recognize him as a major part of that type of picture.

After forty years as a bachelor, Jim married Gloria McLean in 1949 and was the proud father of twins in 1951. Now the dad of four children, he is still among the most popular screen celebrities of the movie world.

FILMS: *We Love Again. Murder Man. The Barrier. Rose Marie. Small Town Girl. Wife Versus Secretary. After the Thin Man. The Gorgeous Hussey. The Next Time We Love. Born to Dance. Speed. Navy Blue and Gold. Seventh Heaven. The Last Gangster. Vivacious Lady. Shopworn Angel. Of Human Hearts. You Can't Take It With You. Ice Follies of 1939. Made For Each Other. It's a Wonderful World. Shop Around the Corner. The Mortal Storm. Mr. Smith Goes to Washington. Come Live With Me. Ziegfeld Girl. The Philadelphia Story. Pot o' Gold. Destry Rides Again. It's a Wonderful Life. No Time For Comedy. Rope. On Our Merry Way. Magic Town. Call Northside 777. Vertigo. You Gotta Stay Happy. The Stratton Story. Carbine Williams. Malaya. Winchester '73. Broken Arrow. Naked Spur. Bend of the River. Harvey. Jackpot. Thunder Bay. No Highway in the Sky. The Glenn Miller Story. The Greatest Show on Earth. The Far Country. Strategic Air Command. Rear Window. The Man From Laramie. The Man Who Knew Too Much. Night Passage. Battle of Apache Pass. F.B.I. Story. Spirit of St. Louis. Bell, Book and Candle. Mountain Road. Two Rode Together. The Man Who Shot Liberty Valance. Mr. Hobbs Takes a Vacation. How the West Was Won. Take Her She's Mine. Shenandoah. Cheyenne Autumn. Dear Brigitte. The Rare Breed. Flight of the Phoenix.*

THE SIDEKICKS

Except for a very few cowboy stars such as Hoot Gibson, Buck Jones and George O'Brien, who often chose to make themselves the object of ridicule in their films, the great majority of sagebrush heroes insisted on the presence of a sidekick, a saddle partner who could provide fleeting moments of comedy. In fact, even the above named trio often made use of a comedian-friend whenever they saw fit. Usually, actors who had been chosen to bring these bits of laughter into what was otherwise an action film were former professional comics. Some had their own particular gimmicks, such as Roscoe Ates, Fuzzy Knight and Syd Saylor. All three used a stuttering dialect, but Knight included some musical vocalizing while Saylor added a little extra something by being able to bob his Adam's apple up and down, thus distinguishing themselves apart. Each had some sort of identifying specialty.

Max Terhune was a skilled ventriloquist whose dummy, "Elmer," never failed to delight the younger fans. Al "Fuzzy" St. John and Andy Clyde were masters at slapstick comedy, while Andy Devine used his tremendous size and tricky voice to great advantage. Gabby Hayes made a fortune from playing the bewhiskered old sourdough whose tall tales rivaled those of the master story-tellers. For the most part, these players received second billing to the hero and were intended to be the means of providing a break in what otherwise was a steady diet of excitement and thrills.

It was not until 1940 that the individual Western comic really came into his own. That year, the talented Smiley Burnette was chosen to ninth place on the list of top ten money-making cowboy stars. Having risen to popularity alongside his pal, Gene Autry, Burnette became the first of the sidekicks to be selected to the exclusive Big Ten roster as an individual. In 1943, he even climbed as high as third place. Among the other sidekicks who made the first ten list were Gabby Hayes, who once reached second place in 1945; Max Terhune, Raymond Hatton, Rufe Davis and Jimmy Dodd, who, at one time or another, made the list while being members of the popular "Three Mesquiteers" trio; Fuzzy Knight and Andy Devine. To further illustrate the degree of popularity which these players attained, three of the top ten names selected in 1946 were Western sidekicks.

In the early silent picture era, some of the players in Western comedy had once been stars in their own right—Buddy Roosevelt, Bill Patton, "Big Boy" Williams, "Pee Wee" Holmes and Shorty Hamilton. Others were original comics, such as Hank Mann, Oliver Hardy, Frank Rice, Monty Collins and Slim Summerville. When the talkies arrived, the sidekicks found they had an even wider range to work in, adding their voices and sound effects to their mimicry. Performers like Leo Carrillo, Raymond Hatton and Gabby Hayes soon became inveterate scene-stealers, causing audiences to focus the attention on their antics rather than on the hero.

The list of well-known sidekicks is too long to fit here, but the following were among the most consistently active.

Frank Yaconelli—usually seen as a Mexican opposite Ken Maynard or Tom Keene.

Harry Harvey—saddle pal to Fred Scott.

Buck Connors—The white-haired gent riding with Bob Steele or Wally Wales.

Richard Martin— seen as "Chito Rafferty" alongside Tim Holt.

Si Jenks—the whiskered old codger in dozens of hoss-operas.

Hank Worden—the tall, thin, baldheaded comic who appeared with Bob Baker and in some John Wayne specials.

232

Ben Corbett—who played in the "Bud and Ben" series with Jack Perrin.

Horace Murphy—the short, cherub-faced sidekick of Tex Ritter whose voice was also familiar to radio fans.

Lee "Lasses" White—who portrayed Jimmy Wakely's pal.

Cliff Edwards—the original "Ukelele Ike" of vaudeville who rode alongside Tim Holt.

Pat Buttram—who succeeded Smiley Burnette as Gene Autry's sidekick at Columbia Pictures and in TV.

Pat Brady—one of the Sons of the Pioneers who later became Roy Rogers' favorite foil.

Guy Wilkerson—the tall, thin character actor who was a member of the "Texas Rangers" trio with Tex Ritter and Dave O'Brien.

Bud Buster—a veteran of dozens of Westerns who alternated between comedy and villainy.

Chris-Pin Martin—the Mexican with a crooked eye who furnished the Cisco Kid series with many chuckles.

Sterling Holloway—the original country bumpkin whose voice was also widely heard in Walt Disney features.

Eddy Waller—sidekick to Allan "Rocky" Lane.

Wally Vernon—a former vaudeville dancer whose hawk-nose made him a natural comic foil for Roy Rogers and Don Barry.

Gordon Jones—the big, beefy athlete who specialized in roles as a dimwit opposite Roy Rogers.

Emmett Lynn—the old, cantankerous sourdough in many Western features.

Slim Andrews—tall, bearded foil to Tex Ritter.

Dub "Cannonball" Taylor—whose thick, molasses drawl was heard in films starring Jimmy Wakely, Tex Ritter or Charles Starrett.

Slim Pickens—a tall, husky veteran of rodeos with an authentic Western accent and a flair for character roles.

Paul Hurst—an old-timer in the movies whose career saw him play equally convincing villains.

Eddie Acuff—another veteran comedian of Westerns and serials.

These and others too numerous to mention were the actors who played the Sidekicks to our favorite Western heroes. Some were extremely adept at their jobs while others were mediocre, allowing their comedy to overshadow the essential ingredient of Westerns—action. Rather than criticize, let us go on with the thought that the vast majority of them deserve our applause for a performance well done.

ANDY DEVINE (1905-)

Andy Devine was born Jeremiah Schwartz in Flagstaff, Arizona, on October 7, 1905. He received his education at St. Mary and St. Benedict's College, the Arizona State Teacher's College and at Santa Clara University, where he won recognition as a star football athlete. When he was sixteen, Andy's father died, leaving him to care for his mother and a younger brother. After months of hardship and poverty he became thoroughly discouraged and attempted to take his life by gas asphyxiation. Fate intervened when it turned out that the gas company had shut off the family's supply due to non-payment of bills. That was only one of the many tragic incidents that plagued Andy's early life. While still in his 'teens, he fell with a stick in his mouth and badly damaged the tissues of his palate and vocal chords. Having permanently injured his throat, the accident later proved to be a blessing in disguise when his high, raspy voice helped get him into motion pictures.

In 1926, Andy made his first attempt at entering the movies and succeeded in landing only a few minor roles in Paramount's *Collegiate Series*. Finding the going tough, he joined the U.S. Lighthouse Service and took an ocean voyage to the Bering Sea. On his return to California, he met a young actor named Richard Arlen who helped him get his first important break in a picture called *The Spirit of Notre Dame*. Then came a steady stream of films for studios like Paramount, First National and Universal until the coming of the talkies really gave Andy the chance for success. His peculiar voice lent itself well to the comic characterizations he took on the screen. Playing the big, soft-hearted but slow-witted clown, Andy soon wormed his way into the hearts of theatre audiences everywhere. With his huge physique and shy grin he specialized in playing the overgrown country-boy who never quite seemed to realize what went on around him. Despite his large size, Andy proved quite agile when it came to action scenes. He appeared in a series of Paramount adventure features with his old pal, Richard Arlen, after which he became associated with Universal Pictures for many years. To add to his popularity during the late 1930's, Andy was a featured guest on the Jack Benny Show on radio.

After having spent most of his career making films for Universal and Paramount, Andy was chosen to play Roy Rogers' sidekick in a chain of Republic Westerns during the mid-1940's. His particular skill at providing the comedy relief in that type of feature had previously been proven in films like *Geronimo* and *Stagecoach*. In 1948 and 1949, Andy was listed among the top ten cowboy stars and, when a new television series called "Wild Bill Hickock" began in 1950, he co-starred as the lovable "Jingles" with Guy Madison, who played Hickock. The series proved very successful through several seasons and the two stars recreated their TV roles on the large screen in a couple of full-length features.

Residing in Van Nuys, California, where he served as mayor for seventeen years, Andy has been married to the former Dorothy House since 1933, and has two grown sons. He is an actor who has been admired by his fellow workers as well as his fans and his place in the Western Hall of Fame is well deserved.

FILMS: *Collegiate Series. We Americans. Hot Stuff. Naughty Baby. Spirit of Notre Dame. Chinatown Squad. All American. Law and Order. Radio Patrol. Man Wanted. Never Say Die. Dr. Bull. Song of the Eagle. Escape From Hong Kong. Buck Benny Rides Again. Tropic Fury. Geronimo. Mutiny on the Blackhawk. Timber. Stagecoach. Men of the Timberland. Riders of Death Valley. The Road Back. Devil's Pipeline. Trail of the Vigilantes. Thunder Pass. Rhythm of the Islands. Danger in the Pacific. The Kid from Kansas. The Dangerous Game. Ali Baba and the Forty Thieves. Ghost Catchers. Follow the Boys. Sudan. Babes on Swing Street. Sin Town. Bowery to Broadway. The Michigan Kid. Frontier Gal. When the Daltons Rode. Canyon Passage. New Mexico. Slaughter Trail. On the Old Spanish Trail. Gay Ranchero. Springtime in the Sierras. Grand Canyon Trail. Montana Belle. Two Gun Teacher. Red Badge of Courage. Around the World in Eighty Days. The Adventures of Huckleberry Finn. Big Jim McLain. Island in the Sky. Pete Kelly's Blues. Two Rode Together. The Man Who Shot Liberty Valance. How the West Was Won.*

FUZZY KNIGHT (1901-)

John Forrest Knight was born in Fairmont, West Virginia on May 9, 1901. While studying law at the University of West Virginia, he decided to organize his own band, featuring himself on the drums, and discovered that requests for playing engagements came faster than he could handle them. Choosing show business as a career, he began in vaudeville and went from cabarets to musical stage revues before finally landing in the movies in 1928.

As the film industry restyled itself for making sound pictures, Knight was featured in a series of short musical subjects at Paramount and M-G-M, in which his peculiarly soft, mellow voice earned him the nickname of "Fuzzy." It was not until 1932 that he received his first important acting role when he played in a film called *Hell's Highway*. Having earned himself bigger and better parts, he was acclaimed for his acting opposite the inimitable Mae West in *She Done Him Wrong*, which established him as a capable supporting comedian. From that time on, Fuzzy made countless appearances on the screen for various major companies.

As a comedian in Westerns, Fuzzy provided laughs and an occasional song in dozens of features produced by Universal, Columbia and Monogram. His fresh, country-boy humor and singing talent enhanced many a picture, whether it was a class-B horse-opera or a big, expensive A-production. During the 1940's, he was featured with Johnny Mack Brown in at least twenty-five films and also played a saddle partner to Bob Baker, Russell Hayden and Tex Ritter in additional features. By 1946, Fuzzy was even included on the roster of top ten cowboy stars of the screen.

Besides movie work, Fuzzy has since extended into television. From 1955 to 1957, he appeared with Buster Crabbe in the "Capt. Gallant" TV series and has been semi-active in both mediums of entertainment. Married to the former Thelma de Long, he is an accomplished musician and composer and has had several of his songs published. Although he has been noted chiefly as a comic in Westerns, Fuzzy played an occasional straight dramatic role in which he proved himself equally capable. But to cowboy fans, his characterizations of an awkward, stuttering country hick stand out above all others.

FILMS: *Hell's Highway. She Done Him Wrong. Her Bodyguard. This Day and Age. To the Last Man. Moulin Rouge. Behold My Wife. George White's Scandals. Trail of the Lonesome Pine. The Plainsman. The Sea Spoilers. Horror Island. Apache Trail. Stagecoach Buckaroo. Silver Bullet. Boss of Hangtown Mesa. Deep in the Heart of Texas. Little Joe, the Wrangler. Corvette K225. Slick Chick. Frontier Gal. Pony Post. Ragtime Cowboy Joe. Son of Roaring Dan. Hills of Oklahoma. Hostile Country. Canyon Raiders. Bounty Killer.*

GEORGE "GABBY" HAYES (1885-1969)

George Hayes rose from the ranks of bit players to become one of the screen's most beloved actors by portraying a bewhiskered, toothless old codger with a weakness for telling tall tales. As a familiar figure in dozens of Westerns, he brought his original brand of humor (which appealed tremendously to his audiences) to motion pictures while earning a place for himself among the immortal performers of movie history.

He was born George Francis Hayes in Wellsville, New York, on May 7, 1885. While still in his youth, he ran away from home to join a traveling road show. After spending many years in vaudeville, he entered motion pictures around 1928, playing small parts in various features. The following year, he appeared in his first talkie, *The Rainbow Man*. During the early 1930's, he was an active performer in many films and was seen mostly as a villain until 1933, when he joined cowboy star John Wayne in making a long series of horse-operas for Lone Star Productions. Most of these features were "quickie Westerns" filmed on a tight budget and directed with little regard for technicalities, but the action was good and the fans enjoyed seeing Wayne go through his paces.

When veteran comedian Al St. John vacated his role in the "Hopalong Cassidy" series at Paramount, George stepped in to fill the gap in 1935, making a long string of features with William Boyd. It was in these popular films that he created his role as the lovable old rascal that so many fans came to admire. By 1940, he left Paramount to work with Roy Rogers at Republic Studios where he earned himself the nick-name "Gabby." Besides appearing in at least forty-seven films with Rogers, he found time to make additional features with Bob Steele, Bill Elliott and Don Barry. In 1943, he was listed with the top ten cowboy stars of the screen and remained there for twelve successive years.

When the series Westerns ceased to exist after 1954, Gabby left Republic to make appearances in major productions for various studios. An accomplished scene-stealer, he took his share of the honors when he played the sidekick to his old friend, John Wayne, and was featured alongside Randolph Scott in a number of class-A features. With a total of 225 pictures to his credit, Gabby retired from movies in 1956 to star in his own "Gabby Hayes Show" for ABC-TV. The series continued successfully for a few seasons, after which the famous performer undertook a nation-wide personal appearance tour. Since the early 1960's Gabby had been content living on his laurels while residing at his spacious ranch on the edge of the Nevada desert. His first marriage to Olive Ireland in 1914 only lasted a short time and ended in divorce. He then married Dorothy Earle with whom he enjoyed his retiring years. His death came on February 9, 1969, at the age of eighty-three.

FILMS: *The Rainbow Man. Haunted Gold. Desert Trail. Randy Rides Alone. Somewhere in Sonora. From Broadway to Cheyenne. Night Rider. Gallant Fool. Hidden Gold. The Plainsman. Mr. Deeds Goes to Town.*

1. *Andy Devine*

2. *Fuzzy Knight*

3. *Gabby Hayes*

4. *Rufe Davis (at right) and old-timer Emmett Lynn seem to have a problem in "Westward Ho"*

5. *Andy Clyde*

6. *Max Terhune (at right) with John King, "Snowflake" and Rex Lease*

1.

2.

3.

4.

5.

6.

Wild Horse Mesa. Riders of the Desert. Return of Casey Jones. Song of Arizona. Dragnet Patrol. Call of the Prairie. Three on the Trail. Heart of the West. Trail Dust. Hopalong Cassidy Rides Again. Borderland. Texas Trail. Klondike. Bar 20 Justice. Hopalong Cassidy of the Bar 20. The Phantom Broadcast. Young Buffalo Bill. Wall Street Cowboy. Young Bill Hickock. Dark Command. Sunset Serenade. Border Devils. Texas Buddies. Sunset on the Desert. Roll on Texas Moon. Silver Spurs. In Old Caliente. Sunset in Eldorado. Lights of Old Sante Fe. Utah. Bells of Rosarita. In Old Oklahoma. Bells of San Angelo. Along the Navajo Trail. Idaho. Carson City Kid. Jesse James at Bay. Dakota. Man from Cheyenne. Border Legion. Tall in the Saddle. Badman's Territory. Helldorado. Fighting Man of the Plains. Cariboo Trail. Man in the Saddle.

MAX TERHUNE (1891-)

Max Terhune was born in Franklin, Indiana on February 12, 1891. He made his first appearance in vaudeville in 1924, in a one-man show that won instant success with the public. An accomplished juggler, whistler, sleight-of-hand artist, card shark, impressionist, ventriloquist and imitator, he was an active performer throughout the 1920's and 1930's until he joined cowboy singer Gene Autry on the "National Barn Dance" radio program around 1933. When Autry struck it rich in movies, he helped Max make his debut in a film called *Ride Ranger Ride* in 1936 and, from then on, it was a steady climb upward to fame.

It was in 1936 that Republic Studios introduced a new series of Westerns featuring not one, but three principal characters called the "Three Mesquiteers." The first picture of the series had Bob Livingston, Ray Corrigan and Sid Saylor as the leading heroes but, after that, Saylor was replaced by Max Terhune. Together, the trio of cowboys rode to success in a meteoric rise to popularity and, almost overnight, became the greatest team of Western heroes the screen has ever known.

Before long, several other studios had sought to imitate the appeal of the "Mesquiteers" by introducing similar trios, but none could compare with Livingston, Corrigan and Terhune. As "Lullaby Joslin," Max provided the comedy for the series by showing off his skill as a ventriloquist with his dummy "Elmer." When he wasn't busy giving his moments of laughter, he took part in the action along with his two pals, Livingston and Corrigan, sharing the honor of being listed with the top ten Western movie stars.

After completing twenty-one features with the "Mesquiteers," Max left Republic in 1940 when contract difficulties forced him to vacate his role. A short while later, he was joined by his friend, Ray Corrigan, who also left Republic Studios to start a new series of trio Westerns for Monogram. There, they were co-starred with John King in the "Range Busters" series which enjoyed success until 1944. Max appeared in twenty-four of these features before Monogram ceased production. By 1945, Max had already completed eight years as a cowboy entertainer and had played a part in making two series of "trio Westerns" successful. When old-timer Ken Maynard starred in his last film, *White Stallion,* for Monogram in the latter part of 1945, Max joined him as a featured player. After that, Johnny Mack Brown was the next to have Max as a sidekick in another series of Monogram pictures which lasted for nearly two years. These films kept Terhune active until he went over to P.R.C. in 1949 to make a few more Westerns before his retirement in 1950. Since then, Max has appeared in television as a guest performer and has also shared the spotlight with his pal, Ray Corrigan, in a series of personal appearances. Happily married, Max has a son, Max, Jr. who is also active in Westerns as a stuntman and actor.

FILMS: *Ride Ranger Ride. Hit Parade of 1936. Ghost Town Gold. Roarin' Lead. Hit the Saddle. Riders of Whistling Skull. Gunsmoke Ranch. Come on Cowboys. Range Defenders. Heart of the Rockies. Trigger Trio. Wild Horse Rodeo. Purple Vigilantes. Call the Mesquiteers. Outlaws of Sonora. Riders of the Black Hills. Heroes of the Hills. Pals of the Saddle. Overland Stage Raiders. Santa Fe Stampede. Red River Range. Night Riders. Three Texas Steers. The Range Busters. Trail of the Silver Spurs. Arizona Stagecoach. Boothill Bandits. Fugitive Valley. The Kid's Last Ride. Rock River Renegades. Saddle Mountain Roundup. Texas Troubleshooters. Trailing Double Trouble. West of Pinto Basin. Tumbledown Ranch in Arizona. Underground Rustlers. Bullets and Saddles. Cowboy Commandos. Black Market Rustlers. Tonto Basin Outlaws. Texas to Bataan. Haunted Ranch. Two Fisted Justice. Trail Riders. White Stallion.*

RUFE DAVIS (1914-)

Rufe Davis was born in Oklahoma around 1914 and got his start in show business through vaudeville. An accomplished impersonator, he did a variety of imitations, sang folk songs, played the guitar and several home-made musical instruments until radio beckoned him in 1935. Shortly afterward, he appeared as a regular with the famous "National Barn Dance" radio program from Tulsa, where he entertained over the airwaves from coast to coast. By then, another graduate of the "National Barn Dance" show, Gene Autry, had struck it big in movies. Autry helped Davis get his chance in pictures by landing him a small part in *The Big Broadcast of 1937*. From then on Rufe was on his way. He made several appearances in Autry Westerns until 1940, when Republic Studios decided to use him for comedy relief in the popular "Three Mesquiteers" series.

By then, the studio heads had reorganized the "Mesquiteers" with Bob Livingston, Bob Steele and Davis cast in the roles of the famous trio. A year later, Tom Tyler succeeded Livingston while the series continued on, the "Mesquiteers" being consistent members of the top ten Western heroes. Having completed fourteen features, Davis stepped down to be replaced by Jimmy Dodd in 1942. He suffered a long absence from the screen until 1964, when he staged a comeback by landing a featured role in the popular "Petticoat Junction" television series where he has been active ever since.

FILMS: *Big Broadcast of 1937. Barnyard Follies. Under Texas Skies. Trail Blazers. Lone Star Raiders. Prairie Schooners. Pals of the Pecos. Saddlemates. Gangs of Sonora. Outlaws of Cherokee Trail. West of Cimarron. Gaucho of Eldorado. Code of the Outlaw. Raiders of the Range. Westward Ho. Phantom Plainsmen.*

ANDY CLYDE (1892-1967)

On May 18, 1967, Andy Clyde passed away in his sleep at his home in Hollywood. He was seventy-five years of age and had enjoyed a successful career in films for no less than forty years. One of the screen's funniest men, he had brought laughter to thousands of moviegoers all over the world by his appearances in over 150 pictures.

He was born in Blairgowrie, Scotland on March 25, 1892, the son of a theatrical producer-manager, and made his debut on the stage at an early age. He arrived in America where he continued his career in vaudeville and musical comedy until 1927, when he accepted an offer to appear in films for Mack Sennett. For several years, he made a long series of two-reel comedies for Sennett under the banner of Educational Pictures, a company devoted to making short films while utilizing the funniest comedians of that period. It was at this time that Andy became familiar to audiences as the typical henpecked husband who always encountered troublesome situations which invited the wrath of his domineering wife. In several of these comedies, Andy was teamed up with Harry Gribbon and, together, they constituted one of the most hilarious duos on the screen.

Besides his activities in two-reelers, Andy also appeared in full-length features, his first being in support of George O'Brien in *Blind-Fold* for the Fox Studio in 1929. In addition, he made a number of films for Paramount, Columbia and Universal in which he distinguished himself for his comical antics and as a serious character actor. He continued to star in short comedies until the early 1940's, after which he concentrated on his work in major productions for various companies. Around 1946, he became associated with the popular "Hopalong Cassidy" Westerns at Paramount, sharing the spotlight with William Boyd and becoming well-known for his role of "Windy Holliday." When the series ended in 1949, Andy went to Monogram where he appeared opposite Whip Wilson in another string of horse-operas. Two years later, William Boyd had resumed production on the "Hopalong Cassidy" films exclusively for television and Andy was back at his old post as "Hoppy's sidekick." As could be expected, he became a hit with TV fans while enjoying renewed success in the medium of television. After a few years, the Cassidy Westerns came to a close and Andy found his talents suitable for other popular TV series such as "The Real McCoys," "The Andy Griffith Show," "No Time for Sergeants" and "Lassie."

Undoubtedly, it was Andy's unique style of comedy which enabled him to remain active for so many years. A veteran of the early slapstick school, he was equally adept at more subtle humor and could provide a happy medium between the two that did not detract from the basic story content. In Westerns, he was an excellent comedy-relief making just the right amount of impression to offset the noble deeds of the hero without subtracting from his image.

When death overtook him in 1967, Andy joined the dozens of screen personalities who were immortalized in the minds of motion picture fans all over the world. He was survived by his wife, the former Elsie Maud Tarron, an ex-Mack Sennett bathing beauty, whom he had married in 1933.

FILMS: *Uppercut O'Brien. Blindfold. Clancy at the Bat. Ships of the Night. Midnight Daddies. Goodbye Legs, Hello Television. The Average Husband. Vacation Loves. McFadden's Flats. Yellow Dust. Speed. Taxi Troubles. Bad Lands. Shopping With Wifie. Annie Oakley. Abe Lincoln of Illinois. This Above All. Straight From the Shoulder. Devil's Playground. Fool's Gold. Hoppy's Holiday. The Marauders. Unexpected Guest. Silent Conflict. Dangerous Venture. Sinister Journey. The Dead Don't Dream. False Paradise. Strange Gamble. Borrowed Trouble. The Green Years. Texas Jamboree. Throw a Saddle on a Star. The Plainsman and the Lady. Crashing Thru. Abilene Trail. Range Land. Guns Roar at*

Rock Hill. Fence Riders. Cherokee Uprising. Gunslingers. Arizona Territory. Silver Spurs. Outlaws of Texas. Canyon Raiders. Nevada Badmen. Hired Guns. Rider of the Dusk. Shadows of the West. The Gunman.

TIM HOLT (1918-)

Tim was born John Charles Holt, Jr. in Beverly Hills, California on February 5, 1918, the son of Jack and Margaret Holt. At the early age of four, he appeared in his first movie with his famous father in Paramount's *Red River Valley* and, two years later, took part in another Jack Holt Western called *The Vanishing Pioneer*. Educated at the Culver Military Academy and the University of Southern California, Tim took up acting by joining a stock company and taking part in stage theatricals until he had enough experience to enter motion pictures. His first important screen role came in 1937 when he appeared with Barbara Stanwyck in *Stella Dallas,* which led to a long series of juvenile parts in various productions. The following year saw him featured in a couple of R-K-O Westerns that starred George O'Brien and another with Harry Carey that led the studio into giving him the leads in a few pictures of his own.

As a cowboy star, Tim was thoroughly capable of handling the rough-and-tumble type of features which constituted his series at R-K-O. He was tried out in a few major productions and, in 1941, turned in two of his best performances in *Swiss Family Robinson* and *The Magnificent Ambersons.* The studio promptly gave him another string of action features which skyrocketed him to the list of top ten cowboys in 1941, 1942 and 1943.

With World War II raging strong, Tim entered the U.S. Air Corps in 1943, serving until the end of the war came two years later. He returned to motion pictures around 1947 by resuming his work with R-K-O and was again voted one of the ten biggest money-making cowboy stars in 1948. It was in that same year that he succeeded in being nominated for an Academy Award as best supporting actor for his performance opposite Humphrey Bogart and Walter Huston in *Treasure of Sierra Madre.* Although Tim lost out to fellow actor Huston, his role was among the finest he had ever played on the screen.

Throughout the 1940's, Tim was a familiar figure in Westerns and was doing well following in his famous father's footsteps. Before the untimely death of his dad in 1951, he had been fortunate enough to have co-starred with him in *Arizona Ranger.* A constant favorite among the list of top ten cowboys, Tim made a large number of excellent features and remained active in Westerns until the very end of B-class horse-opera productions came in 1954.

Now retired, Tim runs a spacious ranch just outside Hurrah, Oklahoma where he spends his leisure hours.

FILMS: *Red River Valley. The Vanishing Pioneer. Stella Dallas. Laddie. History Is Made at Night. Gold Is Where You Find It. Renegade Ranger. The Fargo Kid. The Law West of Tombstone. Stagecoach. Rookie Cop. Spirit of Culver. Fifth Avenue Girl. Swiss Family Robinson. The Magnificent Ambersons. Along the Rio Grande. Bandit Trail. Come on Danger. My Darling Clementine. Cyclone on Horseback. Dude Cowboy. Thundering Hoofs. Land of the Open Range. Robbers of the Range. Riding the Wind. Six Gun Gold. Stagecoach Kid. Bandit Ranger. Red River Robin Hood. Avenging Rider. Pirates of the Prairie. Sagebrush Law. Fighting Frontier. Hitler's Children. Thundering Mountain. Under the Tonto Rim. Treasure of Sierra Madre. Guns of Hate. Guns Smugglers. His Kind of Woman. Arizona Ranger. Riders of the Range. Rustlers. Storm Over Wyoming. Brothers in the Saddle. Marked Raiders. Mysterious Desperado. Border Treasure. Dynamite Pass. Rider From Tucson. Rio Grande Patrol. Saddle Legion. Road Agent. Hot Lead. Gunplay. Desert Passage. Pistol Harvest. Law of the Badlands. Overland Telegraph. Law of the '45's. Trail Guide. Target.*

EDDIE DEAN (1910?-)

Edgar Dean Glosup was born near Posey, Texas around 1910. Having enjoyed music since he was very young, he bought himself a guitar and sang at social functions until he entered vaudeville as part of a singing cowboy quartet. In 1930, he made his initial performance on radio over station WLS in Tulsa, Oklahoma, where Gene Autry had first launched his career. As an entertainer, he appeared on the "National Barn Dance" program, eventually broadcasting on the major networks from Chicago. By 1944, Eddie was the featured male vocalist on the popular "Judy Canova Show" emanating from Hollywood. Next, he became a soloist on the "Western Varieties" program over station KTLA.

Despite the fact that he had made his debut in motion pictures back in 1936 as a bit player, Eddie did not reach stardom until 1945. That year, he was selected to play the lead in a series of musical Westerns for the Producers' Releasing Corporation and was named one of the top ten cowboy stars of 1946 and 1947. On completing three years with P.R.C., he started another series of features for Eagle-Lion Productions in 1948 that lasted for two years. Unfortunately, he achieved his star-

1. *Tim Holt*
2. *Eddie Dean*
3. *Clayton Moore*
4. *Jimmy Wakely*
5. *James Newill*
6. *Whip Wilson*

1.

4.

5.

6.

dom too late and his films lacked real production value. He had a good singing voice and he handled action fairly well, but that was not enough in a field that was already swamped with personalities.

By 1952, Eddie was making the personal appearance route touring with rodeos and circuses and playing minor roles in Western features and on television. However, as a singer, he has been active with radio and recordings in the area of Country and Western music and was also responsible for composing several cowboy ballads such as "Cry, Cry" and "One Has My Heart, the Other Has My Name."

FILMS: *Golden Trail. Song of Old Wyoming. Caravan Trail. Driftin' River. Romance of the West. Colorado Serenade. Wild West. Stars Over Texas. Prairie Outlaws. Hawk of Powder River. West to Glory. The Wild Country. Check Your Guns. Black Hills. The Tioga Kid. Law of the Pecos. Saddles and Guns. Outlaws of the Pecos.*

"WHIP" WILSON (1919-1964)

Born Charles Meyers in Pecos, Texas on June 16, 1919, "Whip" Wilson was a direct descendant of General George A. Custer. His dad took the family to live in Granite City, Illinois, where young Charles grew up and received his education. After leaving high school, he labored at odd jobs and eventually returned to Texas to work as a ranch-hand. Becoming an expert horseman, he followed the rodeo circuits, competing in various events until he had won trophies for bronc-riding, calf-roping and bulldogging. In 1939, he was voted the best "All Around Cowboy" at the West Texas Championship Rodeo.

When the U.S. entered World War II in 1941, Charles enlisted in the Marine Corps and underwent training at San Diego. He saw action at Guadalcanal and Tarawa in the Pacific where he was wounded and awarded the Purple Heart Medal. On his release from the service, he went back to participating in rodeos, acquired a skill with a bullwhip and gave exhibitions. A movie talent scout saw him perform and offered him a chance to get into pictures. In 1948, he made his screen debut in a Jimmy Wakely Western entitled *Silver Trails*.

Impressed with his skill, the producers at Monogram signed him for a series of cowboy features and gave him the name of Whip Wilson. Riding a white horse named "Silver Bullet" and aided by old-time comedian Andy Clyde, he starred in over forty features during his six-year association with Monogram-Allied Artists. At that time, Republic's Sunset Carson and P.R.C.'s Lash LaRue were also being spotlighted as whip-snapping cowboy heroes, but Wilson seemed to have the edge over them when it came to dealing out justice to outlaws.

By 1954, the B-Westerns produced as a series were things of the past. Studios were no longer keeping large rosters of players under contract for the purpose of starring in groups of fast, inexpensive horse-operas. Whip Wilson left the screen around 1952, retiring to his ranch with his wife, the former Monica Heberlie (whom he married in 1938), and their two daughters. He kept active with appearances in rodeos, circuses and TV until he died of a heart attack in Hollywood on October 23, 1964.

FILMS: *Silver Trails. Crashing Thru. Guns Roar at Rock Hill. Range Land. Fence Riders. Cherokee Uprising. Arizona Territory. Gunslingers. Outlaws of Texas. Silver Spurs. Abilene Trail. Canyon Raiders. Nevada Badmen. Hired Guns. Riders of the Dusk. Shadows of the West. The Gunman. Stagecoach Driver.*

JIM NEWILL (1911-)

James Newill was born in Pittsburgh, Pennsylvania on August 12, 1911. He became a student at the University of Southern California where he studied music and excelled in college sports. Possessing a good singing voice, he entered show business by way of vaudeville and then made a series of appearances on the musical stage and on radio. He was spotted by a movie talent scout and was given his first screen role in 1937, when he appeared in *Something to Sing About*. From there, it was a steady climb upwards as he alternated between motion pictures and musical stage productions.

In 1941, he accepted an offer to star in a series of Canadian Mounted Police features for Monogram which was based on a popular radio show called "Renfrew of the Mounted." With Jim in the title role and actor Dave O'Brien as his sidekick, these action films continued with success for two years. Then came another string of Westerns for P.R.C. popularly known as the "Texas Rangers" series. In these films, the team of Newill and O'Brien was expanded to include Guy Wilkerson, who provided the comedy relief, thus adding to the growing number of "trio Westerns" that were flooding the field of horse-operas.

Jim made many of these action features for P.R.C., appearing as the singing cowboy of the group. He collaborated with Dave O'Brien in writing some of the screenplays and songs that were used for the series and remained a part of the "Texas Rangers" until he retired in 1945. Unfortunately, Westerns that featured three principal heroes were on their way out when Jim came on the scene. Republic had made a fortune with its "Three Mesquiteers," while Monogram had done the same with "The Range Busters" and "The Rough Riders." When Jim foresaw that it was only a short time before the "trio Westerns" would disappear from the screen, he left the movies and returned to the musical stage.

FILMS: *Something to Sing About. Renfrew of the Mounted. Yukon Flight. Renfrew and the Stolen Treasure. Sky Bandits. Danger Ahead. Murder in the Yukon. On the Great White Trail. The Great American Broadcast. The Falcon's Brother. The Texas Rangers. The Rangers Take Over. Crashin' Through. Fighting Valley. Border Buckaroo. Boss of Rawhide. Outlaw Roundup. Spook Town. Pinto Bandit. Brand of the Devil. Gunsmoke Mesa. Badmen of Thunder Gap.*

JIMMY WAKELY (1914-)

This well-known performer in the field of Country and Western music was already famous through radio and recordings before he entered movies. Born in Mineola, Arkansas, on February 16, 1914, Jimmy Wakely was brought up in Oklahoma where he attended school and sang at barn dances. In 1937, he teamed up with Johnny Bond and Scotty Harrel to form a singing cowboy group that performed regularly over radio stations in Oklahoma City. From there, the trio was signed to appear on the popular "National Barn Dance" program on station WLS in Tulsa.

Having won nation-wide recognition as a top cowboy vocalist, Wakely entered the field of recordings by signing with the Decca Recording Company in 1938. In the meantime, he appeared with cowboy star Gene Autry on the "Melody Ranch" radio show which eventually led him into motion pictures. In 1939, he made his screen debut in a Western called *Saga of Death Valley* for Republic, where he was also featured in a few Gene Autry films. His first opportunity to star in his own pictures came during the early 1940's when Columbia Studios hired him for a series of horse-operas. By 1944, he had left that company to join Monogram for another series of musical Westerns which lasted for five years.

Although his pictures were popular enough, Wakely made the mistake of permitting himself to be patterned too much in the style of Gene Autry, even to the point of wearing identical cowboy costumes. He had the talent and personality to form his own individual style but, as a result of imitating Autry, he never quite reached major status as a Western star. After finishing at Monogram, he made a few features for Universal and Paramount, then returned to Columbia where he made his last regular series. During the early 1950's, Jimmy went into the field of production by making several films of his own, but this venture only lasted a short time. Since then, he has been seen in supporting roles in feature movies and TV as a source of musical relief.

With motion pictures as a secondary interest, Wakely went into semi-retirement during the 1960's, making only occasional screen appearances. In recent years, he has channeled his attention towards managing his own music publishing company, making recordings and doing guest shots on TV and radio. An accomplished composer, he was responsible for many hit tunes, including "Six Lessons From Madame La Zonga," "Too Late" and "I'll Never Let You Go." Since 1935, he has been married to the former Inez Miser and is the father of four children.

FILMS: *Saga of Death Valley. I'm From Kansas. Song of the Range. Moon Over Montana. West of the Alamo. Song of the Saddle. Strictly in the Groove. Cheyenne Roundup. Lone Star Trail. Springtime in Texas. Robin Hood of the Pampas. Cowboy in the Clouds. Sundown Valley. Song of the Sierras. Swing in the Saddle. Cowboy From Lonesome River. Sagebrush Heroes. Song of the Wasteland. Song of the Drifter. Cyclone Prairie Rangers. Cowboy Canteen. Oklahoma Buckaroo. Melody of the Plains. Gun Law. Trail to Mexico. Silver Trails. Oklahoma Blues. Courtin' Trouble. Brand of Fear. The Marshal's Daughter. Arrow in the Dust.*

CLAYTON MOORE (1918-)

Born in Chicago in 1918, Clayton Moore gained his greatest fame by portraying the fabulous "Lone Ranger" on television and in feature films. He became so totally connected with the role that the contract he had with his producers strictly forbade him to make any personal appearances that were associated with the "Lone Ranger" without wearing a mask. To real Western fans, however, Clayton is a familiar figure in the field of horse-operas and serials. A former trapeze aerialist, he performed with a circus throughout the U.S.A. before making his motion picture debut in 1938. Beginning as a bit player he participated in many features and serials which also made use of his talents as a stuntman before gaining stardom in 1942. That year, he was chosen for the male lead in a Republic chapter-play called *The Perils of Nyoka,* in which he shared top billing with Kay Aldridge.

In the years that followed, Clayton was to become well-known for his two-fisted action portrayals in serials for studios like Republic and

Columbia. Working under the direction of Yakima Canutt, he performed some of the most hair-raising stunts ever devised for the movies and, on occasions, doubled for stars like Don Barry, Roy Rogers and Gene Autry.

Unfortunately, the studios seemed to overlook Clayton when it came to giving him a regular series of feature Westerns. He was so busy with stunting and serials that all he had time for was to make appearances as a villain. Nevertheless, he did manage to turn out some good chapter-plays that had a Western theme, *The Adventures of Frank and Jesse James, Jesse James Rides Again, Ghost of Zorro* and *Son of Geronimo.*

Having earned his reputation for being a top-notch action star, Clayton was chosen to portray "The Lone Ranger" on TV in a new syndicated series that began in 1950. After successfully being presented on radio, comic strips and motion pictures, it was only natural that the famed masked rider be brought to television and it was a role that Clayton Moore was ideally suited for. With the exception of a very brief interval when an actor named John Hart played the part, Clayton remained the star of the popular series throughout its existence on TV. Riding his white horse "Silver," and aided by his faithful Indian friend "Tonto," the Lone Ranger raced across the television screen in one glorious adventure after another.

The series was so popular on TV that, in 1956, Warner Brothers decided to film a full-length color feature entitled *The Lone Ranger* with Clayton Moore in his usual role and Jay Silverheels repeating his part as "Tonto." The picture was such a hit that United Artists took no time in deciding to follow up with an equally successful film called *The Lone Ranger and the Lost City of Gold.* Released in 1958, it also had the team of Moore and Silverheels in their original roles.

When television production ceased on "The Lone Ranger" series around the early 1960's, Clayton retired from the screen to live a peaceful life at his home in Tarzana, California with his wife, the former Sally Allen.

FILMS: *Dick Tracy Returns. Daredevils of the Red Circle. Kit Carson. Son of Monte Cristo. Montana. Sons of New Mexico. Perils of Nyoka. Jesse James Rides Again. Adventures of Frank and Jesse James. Ghost of Zorro. G-Men Never Forget. The Return of Frank James. The Crimson Ghost. Son of Geronimo. Buffalo Bill. Black Dakotas. Hawk of Wild River. Night Stage to Galveston. Montana Territory. Barbed Wire. Buffalo Bill in Tomahawk Territory. The Lone Ranger. The Lone Ranger and the Lost City of Gold.*

JAY SILVERHEELS (1922-)

Jay Silverheels is a full-blooded Mohawk Indian who first reached national fame on television as "Tonto," the faithful friend of "The Lone Ranger." Having made his screen debut in 1938 as a bit player, he did not achieve any notice until he was given his first important role as an Aztec warrior opposite Tyrone Power in *Captain From Castile*. Released in 1947 by 20th Century Fox, the picture was a costume epic that had a cast headed by big-name performers like Tyrone Power, Cesar Romero and Lee J. Cobb. In spite of all this stiff competition, Jay was able to distinguish himself in several key scenes that started his career on the upswing.

Born at the Six Nations Indian Reservation near Ontario, Canada around 1922, Jay made a name for himself as a champion lacrosse player before entering motion pictures as an extra. He spent almost nine years trying to reach stardom but only managed to receive small insignificant parts in Westerns which insisted on showing Indians as villains. For over thirty years it had been the custom of film producers to give only the white man's viewpoint in Western pictures and it was a rare event when the Redman was shown as a good character. Finally, things changed with the release of productions like *Broken Arrow, Apache* and *Buffalo Bill*. Before long, the plight of thc Indians became more favorable on the screen when movie audiences started to realize that the white men had done little to improve their co-existence in the Old West.

Being tall, muscular and handsome, Jay Silverheels was the ideal figure for portraying the "good Indian" in movies. He played a large part in reversing the public's opinion of his race when he took more likeable roles. Since 1933, "The Lone Ranger and Tonto" had been favorite characters of Western fans all over the world. Through the media of radio and newspaper comic strips, the masked rider and his Indian friend had captured the imagination of audiences who wanted to share in their adventures of the Old West. Republic Pictures had been the first to bring the popular duo to the screen by producing two hit chapter-plays and a full-length feature during the late 1930's. In 1949, the characters were revived for television in a weekly syndicated series with Clayton Moore as the Lone Ranger and Jay Silverheels as Tonto. Their success was so complete that major film companies like Warner Bros. and United Artists decided to cash in on their popularity by each producing a full-length color feature during the late 1950's.

Having stepped into a role originally created on the screen by veteran actor Chief Thundercloud, Jay Silverheels was able to portray the part of Tonto with a bit more fervor and expression. When he and Clayton Moore undertook a series of personal appearance tours to further promote their activities on the screen, the audiences demanded to see him as well as the famous masked man. After years of exposure on TV, the series petered out but the reruns may still be seen on many home screens. Meanwhile, Jay is still very active in feature pictures for various studios.

FILMS: *The Prairie. Fury at Furnace Creek. Singing Spurs. Yellow Sky. Captain From Castile. Laramie. Lust For Gold. Sand. Trail of the Yukon. The Cowboy and the Indians. Broken Arrow. Red Mountain. Battle of Apache Pass. Brave Warrior. The Pathfinder. The Nebraskan. Jack McCall, Desperado. War Arrow. Saskatchewan. Drums Across the River. Four Guns to the Border. The Black Dakotas. Masterson of Kansas. The Vanishing American. The Lone Ranger. Walk the Proud Land. The Lone Ranger and the City of Gold. Return to Warbow. Alias Jesse James. War Paint.*

"LASH" LARUE (1921-)

Alfred LaRue was born in Gretna, Louisiana on June 14, 1921. After attending the College of the Pacific in California, he worked as a real estate salesman before finally deciding he wanted to become an actor. He took part in stage theatricals, picking up enough experience to allow him to try the movies, and after some difficulty, managed to get a screen test at Warner Brothers Studios. He was turned down because he looked too much like Humphrey Bogart, one of Warners' biggest stars.

For the next couple of years, Al found the going real tough. Playing minor roles in an occasional B-class picture, he almost starved to death for lack of work. Finally, his luck changed in 1945 when he was given the chance to appear with Milburn Stone in a Universal serial called *The Master Key*. That proved to be the turning point of his career. The following year, he was selected to play a dashing outlaw character known as the "Cheyenne Kid" in one of Eddie Dean's Westerns for P.R.C. The producers were suddenly swamped with fan mail asking who the new cowboy was in *Caravan Trail*.

Al was launched into a new series of features of his own. Aided by veteran screen comic Al "Fuzzy" St. John, he made a whole list of "Cheyenne Kid" Westerns which kept him active for a couple of years. In these films he went contrary to an old standard of horse-operas by choosing to wear a completely black costume and riding a black horse called "Rush." Very few cowboys stars had been able to get away with breaking the unwritten rule that black clothes and horses usually belonged to the villains. Armed with two guns and a bullwhip, Al rode through at least two dozen pictures for the P.R.C. organization. When the "Cheyenne" series ended, he made another group of features for Eagle-Lion and a third for Screen Guild. In these Westerns, Al used the nickname of "Lash" which stuck to him throughout the remainder of his career.

Unfortunately, most of LaRue's films were "quickie" features that were made on low budgets. The B-class Westerns were approaching the end of their existence by 1950 and were lacking the drawing power at the theatre box-office. Oddly enough, they found an even greater audience after they were issued to television. With his career at an end, Al turned to character roles for a short time until he accepted an offer to tour with a circus. For awhile, he hosted a TV show called "Lash of the West" which re-ran his old movies for home viewers. He then retired to a quiet life with his wife, Paddy, and their son.

FILMS: *The Master Key. Caravan Trail. Song of Old Wyoming. The Cheyenne Kid. The Return of Cheyenne. Cheyenne Takes Over. Cheyenne Rides Again. Border Feud. Fighting Vigilantes. The Lash. Law of the Lash. King of the Bullwhip. Return of the Lash. Lash of the West. Dead Man's Gold. Frontier Revenge. Ghost Town Renegades.*

ALAN LADD (1913-1964)

Alan Ladd was one of those rare super-stars whose pictures had appeal for men, women and children alike. His tremendous popularity lasted for twenty-two years, a period in which he earned a fortune for himself and his studio.

Alan was born at Hot Springs, Arkansas, on September 3, 1913, the son of Ina and Alan Ladd. After his father died in 1917, his mother took him to live in Oklahoma City where she opened a boarding house. In 1921, she married a man named James Beavers, who took the family to Los Angeles, California. When he was not attending school, young Alan worked as a newsboy and race track attendant in order to help the family income. Being a sickly youth, he decided to take up sports to build himself up and, thus, developed into a star athlete. While he was a student at North Hollywood High, he was elected class president and excelled at swimming, diving and track. In 1932, he won the West Coast Diving championship but, because his family needed money, Alan turned down an athletic scholarship to USC and went to work instead.

After a series of odd jobs, Alan managed to become an acting student at the Universal Studio School of Drama. Having had little experience, he was dismissed a few months later. He then worked as a reporter for the *San Fernando Sun-Record* before deciding that journalism was not his field either. Uncertain as to what he wanted to do, Alan wandered through a variety of jobs such as salesman, store clerk and short-order cook before he chose to register at the Ben Bard School of Acting. A short time later, he managed to get a few acting parts in radio and motion pictures until the turning point of his career came when he met and married Sue Carol in 1942. A former actress who had turned agent for film players, Miss Carol had first heard Alan on the radio and was impressed with his voice. After their marriage, she concentrated on getting him a good part and succeeded in convincing director Frank Tuttle at Paramount to give Alan a break. This resulted in Alan's winning the coveted role of the cold-blooded killer "Raven" in *This Gun For Hire*. Released in 1942, the picture was a smash hit and Alan Ladd was an overnight sensation. Paramount quickly signed him to a contract and gave him the choicest roles in a series of films that were all very successful.

Having catapulated to fame, Alan became one of the ten biggest money-making stars in the movies. He was such a hit that other studios where he had previously worked promptly re-released all the old films in which he had played minor parts, making certain to call attention to the fact that Alan Ladd was in the cast. It took very little time for Paramount to realize that the name of their new star on a theatre marquee was enough to insure a big profit at the box-office.

With the Second World War at its peak, Alan's career was temporarily interrupted while he served as a machine-gunner with the U.S. Air Force. After he was discharged as a sergeant, he returned to his studio to start where he had left off. Fortunately, movie fans had not forgotten him and he quickly resumed his position as a leading motion picture idol. He remained with Paramount until 1952, then became a free-lance player, appearing in films for Warners, Universal, Columbia, M-G-M and 20th Century Fox. In later years, Alan organized his own Jaguar Productions and was one of the few screen personalities who chose to appear in a picture for a percentage of the gross profits rather than take a flat salary.

Although he was known primarily as a tough, two-fisted he-man in all sorts of adventure films, Alan began to lean more towards Westerns after starring in his first "sagebrush thriller" in 1948. It was then that he had made a picture called *Whispering Smith,* which allowed him to display his talents as a cowboy. His genuine love for horses and the outdoor life became evident as he brought more exciting Westerns to the screen. In 1953, his memorable performance of *Shane* brought him the praise of critics and audiences alike and the picture became an all-time classic.

Alan was in the process of completing plans to star in a sequel to his last picture, *The Carpetbaggers,* when he died of cerebral edema at his Palm Springs, California home on January 28, 1964. He was survived by his wife, Sue, their children Alana and David, a step-daughter, Carol, and a son, Alan, Jr. by a previous marriage. Buried at Forest Lawn Memorial Park, Alan was a veteran of over 100 pictures.

FILMS: *Pigskin Parade. Last Train From Madrid. The Howards of Virginia. Citizen Kane. Beasts of Berlin. Rulers of the Sea. Light of the Western Stars. In Old Missouri. Meet the Missus. Captain Caution. Her First Romance. Those Were the Days. Petticoat Politics. The Black Cat. Paper Bullets. Joan of Paris. This Gun For Hire. Lucky Jordan. The Glass Key. Star Spangled Rhythm. China. And Now Tomorrow. Duffy's Tavern. Salty O'Rourke. The Blue Dahlia. O.S.S. Two Years Before the Mast. Calcutta. Variety Girl. Wild Harvest. Saigon. Beyond Glory. Whispering Smith. The Great Gatsby. Chicago Deadline. Captain Carey U.S.A. Appointment With Danger. Branded. Red Mountain. The Iron Mistress. Thunder in the East. Shane. Botany Bay. Desert Legion. Paratrooper. Hell Below Zero. Saskatchewan. The Black Knight. Drum Beat. The McConnell Story. Hell on Frisco Bay. Santiago. The Big Land. Boy on a Dolphin. The Deep Six. The Proud Rebel. The Badlanders. Man in the Net. Guns of the Timberland. All the Young Men. One Foot in Hell. 13 West Street. The Carpetbaggers.*

GEORGE MONTGOMERY (1916-)

George Montgomery Letz was born in Brady, Montana on August 26, 1916. He attended the University of Montana, then sought an acting career by working his way to Hollywood and trying to get into movies. Unsuccessful at first, he took a job as a photographer's model until given the opportunity to become a stuntman. In 1937, he made his debut in a Republic serial called *The Lone Ranger* which brought him to the attention of producers at 20th Century Fox. Beginning as a featured player, George appeared with Cesar Romero in *The Cisco Kid and the Lady* and was signed to a Fox contract in 1938. He made a few more pictures, gradually rising to leading roles and scored his first big hit in *Ten Gentlemen From West Point* in 1942. His studio then decided to

257

1. *Lash La Rue*
2. *George Montgomery*
3. *Monte Hale*
4. *Alan Ladd*
5. *Jay Silverheels*
6. *Kirby Grant*

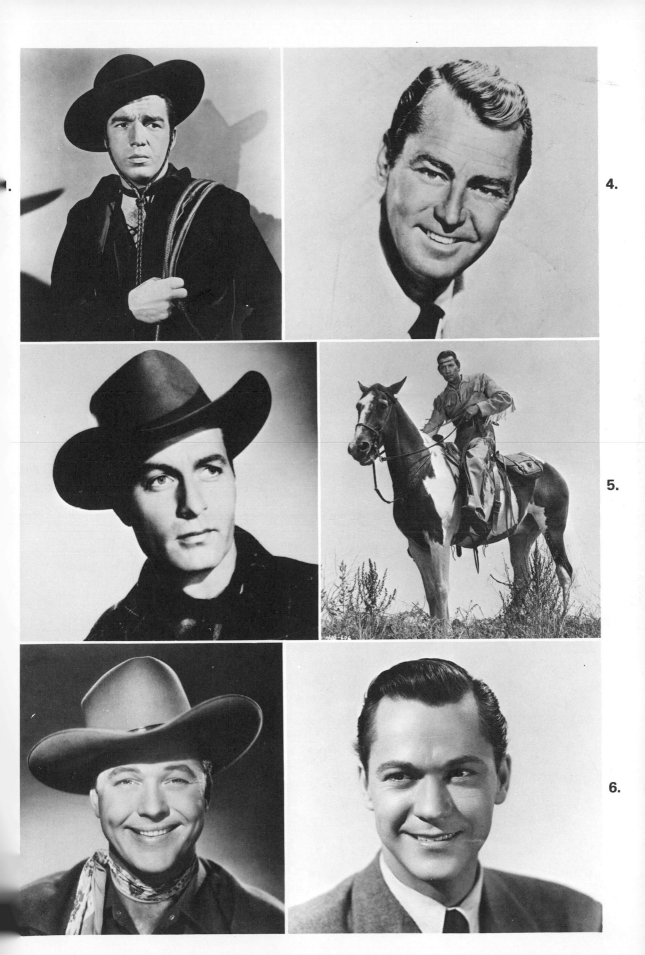

4.

5.

6.

star him in a series of Westerns based on the novels written by Zane Grey.

With the Second World War raging at its peak, George entered the U.S. Army and postponed his film career temporarily. While on leave in 1943, he married singer Dinah Shore, whom he had met a few years before and when the war ended, he returned to his wife and a promising career. His old studio gave him the chance to play leads opposite some of the most important feminine stars in movies—Betty Grable, Maureen O'Hara, Linda Darnell and Carole Landis. Unfortunately, George was dissatisfied with the way his career was turning. After having contract difficulties, he left Fox and went to work for several other companies under a free-lance basis. Columbia, Warner Brothers and Allied Artists were the biggest studios making use of his talents, casting him mostly in Westerns which seemed to fit George better than any other type of film. He even produced a few pictures of his own in which he proved himself a very capable action star.

Besides appearing in feature films, George branched off into television during the mid-1950's by starring in a weekly hour-long series called *Cimarron City*. It lasted for a couple of seasons after which he concentrated more on acting and producing movies. As a sideline, George opened a profitable furniture manufacturing business that also occupied plenty of his time. In 1962, the divorce that separated him from his wife shocked the movie colony because their marriage had been considered among the most stable and had resulted in two wonderful children.

Ever since then, George Montgomery has spent his attention on making more films and supervising his furniture company. Although he seems to have abandoned cowboy roles, the majority of his pictures have been top-notch Westerns.

FILMS: *The Lone Ranger. The Cisco Kid and the Lady. Stardust. Young People. Jennie. The Cowboy and the Blonde. Last of the Duanes. Riders of the Purple Sage. Cadet Girl. Bomber's Moon. Accent on Love. Charter Pilot. China Girl. Ten Gentlemen From West Point. Roxie Hart. Coney Island. Orchestra Wives. The Brasher Doubloon. Three Little Girls in Blue. Belle Starr's Daughter. Girl From Manhattan. Lulu Belle. Dakota Lil. Davy Crockett, Indian Scout. Huk. Iroquois Trail. Sword of Monte Cristo. The Texas Rangers. Indian Agent. Indian Uprising. Cripple Creek. Fort Ti. Gunbelt. War Cry. Jack McCall, Desperado. The Pathfinder. The Lone Gun. Battle of Rogue River. Seminole Uprising. Last of the Badmen. Street of Sinners. Canyon River. Pawnee. Badman's Country. Bat Masterson of Kansas. Too Many Crooks. Stallion Trail. Samar. The Steel Claw. Watusi. Battle of the Bulge.*

MONTE HALE (1921-)

Monte Hale was born in San Angelo, Texas, on June 8, 1921 and educated in schools in Houston. While still in his youth, he earned himself enough money to buy a guitar and appeared at barn dances and rodeos as a singing cowboy. A short time later, he made his entrance in vaudeville and radio, then went on a tour for the U.S.O. entertaining the armed forces in camp shows. That was how he was spotted for the movies by a man named Phil Isley, the father of actress Jennifer Jones.

After making his screen debut in a film entitled *Steppin' in Society* in 1944, Monte received a contract from Republic Studios to star as a new singing cowboy in a series of musical Westerns. Having already lost Gene Autry to the Air Corps, the company had replaced him with Roy Rogers. When the producers began to fear the loss of Rogers, they started giving the buildup treatment to Monte Hale and another newcomer named Rex Allen. As it turned out, Rogers remained in the top spot and Monte had to be content with his position. Nevertheless, he did make a long series of pictures which showed off his capabilities as a singer and an action star.

Unfortunately, Monte got his start a bit too late in Westerns. The era of the singing cowboys was drawing to a close and the studios noted for horse-operas were getting away from producing any more B-class sagebrush features. In 1951, Monte made his last series of Westerns and then retired from the screen. The companies like Republic, Columbia and Universal were no longer interested in making these pictures in series which required them to hire a cowboy star for at least seven features. Instead, each film would be made on an individual basis and, after 1954, the old type of cowboy series would be a thing of the past.

Having left the movies, Monte went on tour with a singing cowboy group headed by Ray Whitley, which appeared with rodeos all over the country. Since then he has performed on television and made other tours with circuses and rodeos. An accomplished composer of Western ballads, Monte wrote several popular tunes, his most famous being a patriotic song called "That Statue in the Bay." Many of his recordings are well-known to lovers of cowboy music.

One of Monte Hale's pet hobbies is collecting Western mementoes and among his most prized possessions are a pair of hand-tooled, silver-inlaid boots, a Brahma bull trophy which he won at a rodeo, and a deputy sheriff's badge which once belonged to cowboy star Buck Jones.

FILMS: *Steppin' in Society. California Gold Rush. Sun Valley Cyclone.*

261

Out California Way. Yukon Vengeance. Trail of Robin Hood. Along the Oregon Trail. California Firebrand. Law of the Golden West. Pioneer Marshal. Prince of the Plains. Ranger of Cherokee Strip. San Antone Ambush. South of Rio. The Vanishing Westerner. The Old Frontier. The Missourians.

KIRBY GRANT (1911-)

Kirby Grant Hoon was born in Butte, Montana on November 24, 1911. At the age of ten, he started taking violin lessons and two years later gave his initial concert with the Seattle Symphony Orchestra. After winning a musical scholarship to the University of Washington, he followed his training in music, furthering his education by attending Whitman University, the Chicago Institute of Art and the American Conservatory of Music. By the time he left school, he was an accomplished violinist, pianist, artist and sculptor.

When he had completed two years on the concert stage, Kirby became convinced that the field of classical music had little to offer him in the way of success. He proceeded to organize his own dance band and toured the country performing one-night stands in cabarets and ballrooms until 1937, when he accepted the chance to appear on radio. Two years later, he won first place on the popular "Gateway to Hollywood" program, a show dedicated to discovering new talent, and was awarded a six-month contract with R-K-O Studios.

After a short period of training, Kirby made his initial debut in motion pictures under the name of Robert Stanton, playing small parts in several George O'Brien Westerns. In 1941, R-K-O saw fit to give him the leads in a series of musical horse-operas, billing him as a new singing cowboy hero. Unfortunately, these pictures failed to gather any attention because of their lack of real production value. Besides that, the field of Westerns was overrun by singing cowboys. Having obtained his release from R-K-O, Kirby decided to tour Europe and North Africa on missions of entertaining Allied troops during World War II. In 1944, he made his return to motion pictures by appearing in leads for Universal musicals. These features, although not exactly first-class productions, were nevertheless entertaining and made good use of Kirby's singing voice.

After four years of musical comedies for Universal, Kirby was signed by independent producer Robert L. Lippert to star in a series of Canadian Mounted Police features. When these were completed, he made another string of similar pictures for Monogram in which he appeared with the dog star, Chinook. By 1952, Allied Artists was presenting them in still another series which lasted until the end of B-type feature productions in 1954. With his stereotyped roles as a "Mountie" exhausted, Kirby left Hollywood for a long-overdue vacation.

Having been absent from the screen for almost two years, he returned to acting by accepting the leading role in a new television series called "Sky King" in 1956. The show consisted of a string of half-hour films that were syndicated to the networks and shown weekly to home audiences. As "Sky King," Kirby introduced a somewhat different type of Western hero who made use of an airplane more often than he used a horse in order to capture the outlaws. Adding this modern touch to the standard horse-opera theme, the series enjoyed several successful seasons on the air. When production ceased, Kirby retired from acting to take a job as a director of TV films for the Wilding Motion Picture Company in Chicago. Since then, he has been active in the supervisory end of film-making and, when not busy turning out movies, he enjoys the relaxation of a quiet life at home with his wife, Caroline, and their two children.

FILMS: *Bullet Code. Lawless Valley. Red River Range. Code of the Lawless. Three Sons. Hi Good Lookin'. In Society. Ghost Catchers. The Lawmen. Babes on Swing Street. I'll Remember April. Penthouse Rhythm. Easy to Look At. Comin' 'Round the Mountain. The Spider Woman Strikes Back. Badmen of the Border. Gun Town. Indian Territory. Chinook. Chinook of the North. Snow Dog. Northwest Territory. Call of the Klondike. Yukon Gold. Northern Patrol. Fangs of the Arctic. Rustler's Roundup. Gunman's Code. Western Honor. Rhythm Inn. Blazing Guns. Yukon Vengeance. Yukon Manhunt.*

ROD CAMERON (1912-)

This star of motion pictures and television was born Roderick Cox in Calgary, Canada on December 7, 1912 and educated at schools in Canada and New York. He worked as a truck driver, skin diver, salesman, file clerk, fruit picker and construction laborer before he finally landed in the movies as a bit player in 1939. While his climb to stardom was slow and tedious, he appeared in several major productions, playing in minor roles that gradually grew bigger and more important as he went along. For years, Rod could be seen in the background in features for Paramount, Universal and Columbia Studios.

In 1945, producer Walter Wanger gave Rod his first leading role in an all-star Technicolor feature called *Salome, Where She Danced.*

With a cast that included Yvonne deCarlo, David Bruce, Albert Dekker and Walter Slezak, the picture had a Western theme and was loaded with action. It brought Rod Cameron to the attention of movie fans and led to his stardom in a series of Westerns for Universal and Monogram. It was that same year that he was listed among the top ten cowboy favorites of the screen.

With success finally achieved, Rod went over to Republic Pictures and made a number of serials and horse-operas. After he had finished there, he returned to Monogram to star in another series of Westerns, then resumed his career with his home studio, Universal. During the years that followed, Rod was active in a variety of adventure stories. But no matter what kind of screenplay he starred in, it was sure to have plenty of two-fisted action. Standing six feet, four inches tall, he was one of the biggest heroes on the screen and cowboy roles were well suited to his particular talents. He had spent some time as a stuntman and was very capable of handling any rough stuff that might come his way. When the B-class Westerns ceased to exist after 1954, Rod remained well-occupied in outdoor features of a higher grade for companies like Columbia, Allied Artists, Warners and United Artists.

Not content with motion pictures alone, Rod branched out into television in 1958 by playing the lead in a series called "City Detective." When that had run out, he started another called "State Trooper," which was, in turn, succeeded by a third series entitled "Coronado 9." His activities in movies and TV have served to keep him busy throughout the years and he can still be seen in an occasional film.

In private life, Rod had three unsuccessful marriages end up in divorce courts and, about 1963, had all the Hollywood gossip columnists buzzing when he married his former mother-in-law, Angela Alves Lico.

FILMS: *The Old Maid. Northwest Mounted Police. Henry Aldrich For President. Christmas in July. Wake Island. Forest Rangers. The Monster and the Girl. Gung Ho. The Secret Service in Darkest Africa. Salome, Where She Danced. G-Men vs. the Black Dragon. Frontier Gal. Beyond the Pecos. Stampede. Strike It Rich. Renegades of the Rio Grande. Riders of Santa Fe. The Old Texas Trail. Boss of Boomtown. Trigger Trail. The Plunderers. Brimstone. Dakota Lil. Cavalry Scout. The Sea Hornet. Oh Susannah. Ride the Man Down. Woman of the North Country. Steel Lady. San Antone. Santa Fe Passage. Hell's Outpost. Headline Hunters. Double Jeopardy. Fighting Chance. Spoilers of the Forest. Short Grass. River Lady. Wagons West. Stage to Tucson. Yaqui Drums. Pirates of Monterey. Gun Hawk. Fort Osage. Bounty Killer. Requiem For a Gunfighter.*

DICK JONES (1927-)

Richard Jones was born in Snyder, Texas on February 25, 1927. By the time he had reached the age of five, he could ride a horse and twirl a lasso with the experts. In 1933, cowboy star Hoot Gibson saw Dick giving some riding and roping exhibitions with a rodeo and immediately hired the youngster to perform with his circus. Billed as the "youngest trick rider and roper in the world," he was a sensation while touring the U.S.A. and Canada. A year later, Dick was signed up for motion pictures, making his debut in an all-star film called *Wonder Bar*.

As a child actor, he was featured in many productions opposite some of the biggest names in the industry. Whether his roles called for trick riding or heavy emotional dramatics, Dick came through like a real trouper and was among the most active juvenile performers of the 1930's. In Westerns, his work was particularly noticeable as he appeared with almost all the top sagebrush heroes of the period such as Hoot Gibson, Buck Jones, Ken Maynard, Tim McCoy and countless others.

Among the dozens of screen assignments Dick received in movies, one of the most unique was in 1940 when Walt Disney selected him to provide the voice characterization for the leading part of "Pinocchio" in the full-length cartoon feature of the same title. By 1942, Dick was heard from coast-to-coast as the star of the popular radio series, "Henry Aldrich," which was among the most successful comedy programs of its day. Having already completed twelve years in motion pictures and radio, he entered the U.S. Army in 1944, serving in Alaska until his release from active service in December, 1946.

On his return to Hollywood, Dick was no longer classified as a juvenile actor, for he was a matured young man and an experienced screen performer. For awhile, he found it difficult getting started in films but, with his skill as a rider, he soon rose to prominence again in Westerns that starred Alan Ladd, Errol Flynn and Randolph Scott. It was not until 1948, however, that Dick received his biggest break since the beginning of his career. That year, he renewed his association with Gene Autry, who was busy making pictures at Columbia Studios. During the mid-1930's, Dick had appeared with Autry in several Westerns for Republic and the two of them were well-acquainted. After being featured in a few Columbia releases with the famous singing cowboy star, Dick was offered a chance to play opposite Jock Mahoney in a new "Range Rider" television series produced by Autry. Accepting the job, he portrayed the role of "Dick West" in what later became one of the greatest

265

action-series that TV has ever known. The daredevil stunts that he performed with Mahoney rank among the most dangerous ever staged for the sake of movies. Scorning the use of "doubles" for their fight scenes, the pair never failed to bring continuous excitement and suspense to the home-audience while true Western fans delighted in seeing them in action.

When "The Range Rider" series ended after a few successful seasons, Gene Autry's "Flying A Productions" brought Dick back again with another weekly show called "Buffalo Bill Jr." Although not quite as good as his series with Jock Mahoney, Dick managed to do fairly well in this new television program until it ceased to exist in 1960. Since then, except for an occasional guest appearance, Dick has been content with living quietly with his wife and former childhood sweetheart, Betty (Bacon) Jones. In all, Dick performed in some 200 films.

FILMS: *Wonder Bar. Moonlight on the Prairie. Daniel Boone. The Black Legion. Westward Ho. Don't Pull Your Punches. Love Is on the Air. Stella Dallas. The Frontiersman. The Cowboy and the Kid. Hollywood Roundup. Woman Doctor. Kid Galahad. Young Mr. Lincoln. I Am Not Afraid. The Kid Comes Back. Mr. Smith Goes to Washington. A Man to Remember. Destry Rides Again. Renfew of the Mounted. Sky Patrol. Dodge City. Heaven Can Wait. Virginia City. Tumblin' Tumbleweeds. Singing Dude. Brigham Young. Little Men. The Old West. Sands of Iwo Jima. Fort Worth. Rocky Mountain. Montana. Requiem For a Gunfighter.*

JOCK MAHONEY (1919-)

"Jock" was born Jacques O'Mahoney in Chicago on February 7, 1919, of French and Irish parents which accounts for his unusual name. While still a young lad, his family took him to live in Davenport, Iowa, where he attended school and earned himself an athletic scholarship to the University of Iowa. An all-around athlete, he distinguished himself in football, baseball, track and boxing.

Jock had gone through two years of pre-medical school before he decided to accept an offer to be a swimming coach at a California college. At the outbreak of World War II, he joined the U.S. Marines, serving as a swimming instructor and teaching Leatherneck pilots in the art of survival at sea. After his discharge from the Corps, he made the rounds of the movie studios hoping to get a chance to act but, instead, landed a job as a stuntman doubling for stars like Errol Flynn and Gregory Peck. By 1946, he was among the most active stuntmen in Hollywood, earning as much as $20,000 in one year for risking his neck.

It was about that time that Jock was called upon to perform some dangerous tricks in a couple of Charles Starrett Westerns at Columbia. Recognizing his ability to handle action, Starrett helped Jock to get his first acting part in a film called *Fighting Frontiersman* which resulted in a contract to do more Westerns with Starrett, Gene Autry, Bill Elliott and a few other Columbia stars. At first, Jock was cast as a "heavy," but he quickly rose to featured parts and wound up starring in several action-packed serials.

In 1949, Gene Autry became the first cowboy star to enter the field of television when he started producing a series exclusively for TV. Among his many enterprises, he decided to begin a new show called "The Range Rider" which consisted of a series of half-hour programs for television. Instead of playing the lead himself, he chose Jock Mahoney for the title role and gave the secondary part of "Dick West" to the young veteran actor Dick Jones. The "Range Rider" series turned out to be one of the earliest hits in TV and the team of Mahoney and Jones provided some of the most spectacular stunts ever filmed. While performing all their own tricks, these two were unbeatable when it came to rough riding and knock-down drag-out fights. During the 1950's, when their TV show was at the height of its popularity, the duo also found time to give personal exhibitions while touring with the Gene Autry Rodeo. It was in one of these performances that Jock broke a leg and a collar-bone, forcing him to take time to recuperate. As a stuntman, he was used to broken bones and it was only a short time before he was appearing in front of the cameras again.

Despite the fact that he was a recognized cowboy star, Jock completely surprised movie directors and fans when he displayed a real talent for straight dramatics in TV productions like "The Loretta Young Show." Having convinced the movie-makers that he was also capable of other things besides action features, he made a number of light comedies and melodramas for Columbia and Universal-International. When the "Range Rider" series ended, he starred in another TV show called "Yancy Derringer" which also met with success.

In 1960, Jock played the "heavy" opposite Gordon Scott in Paramount's *Tarzan the Magnificent* and two years later, he was portraying the famous jungle king himself. The thirteenth consecutive actor to play the part of Tarzan, he appeared in a couple of exciting features which permitted him to display his athletic ability at its best. Since then, Jock has been seen regularly in movies and TV.

In private life, he is a good-health addict and teaches physical culture. Married to actress Margaret Field since 1951, he is the father of three children, one of them an aspiring young actress known as Sally Field.

1. *Dale Robertson*
2. *Dick Jones*
3. *Audie Murphy*
4. *Rex Allen*
5. *Jock Mahoney*
6. *Rod Cameron*

1.

4.

Hi Pal
Dick Jones
"Buffalo Bill Jr"

5.

6.

FILMS: *Fighting Frontiersman. Smoky Canyon. South of the Chisholm Trail. Stranger From Ponca City. Blazing Across the Pecos. The Doolins of Oklahoma. Horsemen of the Sierras. Bandits of El Dorado. Renegades of the Sage. Frontier Outpost. Junction City. The Kid From Broken Gun. Santa Fe. Rim of the Canyon. Kangaroo Kid. Overland Pacific. Gunfighters of the Northwest. Away All Boats. Roar of the Iron Horse. Cody of the Pony Express. Slim Carter. Joe Dakota. Land Unknown. Tarzan the Magnificent. Battle Hymn. A Time to Love and a Time to Die. Day of Fury. Showdown at Abilene. Tarzan Goes to India. Tarzan's Three Challenges. I've Lived Before. Walls of Hell. Money, Women and Guns. Last of the Fast Guns.*

DALE ROBERTSON (1923-)

Dale LaMoine Robertson was born in Oklahoma City, Oklahoma on July 14, 1923. He studied law at the Oklahoma City College, where he also gained a reputation for being a top athlete, winning no less than twenty-eight letters in athletic events. Leaving school, he worked as a shipping clerk, construction laborer and cowpuncher before becoming a professional boxer. In September, 1942, Dale entered the U.S. Army, received a commission as a second-lieutenant and served with General Patton's Third Army in Europe. He was wounded by shrapnel and sent back home where he was honorably discharged as a first-lieutenant in June, 1945.

During the years that followed, Dale made nine unsuccessful attempts to get into motion pictures, traveling back and forth from Oklahoma to Hollywood. He was finally given a chance on his tenth try in 1949, when producer Nat Holt gave him a part in a Randolph Scott Western called *Fighting Man of the Plains*. This was followed by a featured role in another Randolph Scott film, *Cariboo Trail,* which caused audiences to react favorably to the handsome new actor.

Dale signed a contract with 20th Century Fox where he was given a build-up as a romantic leading man opposite such stars as Betty Grable, Jeanne Crain and Mitzi Gaynor. By 1951, he was voted one of the "Stars of Tomorrow" and was well on his way to becoming a big star at the Fox studio. With success within his grasp and a promising career ahead of him, he appeared in a number of first-grade Westerns which served to disengage him from the romantic-type roles he had been playing. A sudden fit of temperament led to squabbles over contracts and a choice of films, until Dale parted company with his studio around 1957.

For awhile, he starred in a few Westerns for other companies, then accepted an offer to appear in a TV series called "Tales of Wells Fargo." His fame spread rapidly as the new series caught on and lasted for several successful seasons. Having established himself in cowboy roles, he became a favorite among action stars in both television and feature films. Since his return to picture-making, Dale has appeared in movies on a free-lance basis, preferring to associate himself with various producers instead of signing with one individual studio. In recent years, he has also produced a few films of his own.

When he is not busy making pictures or appearing on TV, Dale concentrates his efforts towards his Oklahoma ranch where he breeds and trains horses. Divorced from actresses Jacqueline Wilson and Mary Murphy, he is married to Lulu Mae Harding and is the father of a daughter.

FILMS: *Fighting Man of the Plains. Cariboo Trail. Two Flags West. Call Me Mister. Golden Girl. Take Care of My Little Girl. The Farmer Takes a Wife. Lydia Bailey. Return of the Texan. Devil's Canyon. Sitting Bull. Gambler From Natchez. Full House. Outcasts of Poker Flat. City of Badmen. The Silver Whip. Dakota Incident. Day of Fury. Top of the World. Son of Sinbad. Hell Canyon Outlaws. Gun For a Town. Blood on the Arrow. One Eyed Soldiers.*

REX ALLEN (1922-)

Rex Allen was born in Wilcox, Arizona on December 31, 1922. After graduating from Wilcox High School in 1939, he won a state-wide talent contest by giving a guitar solo which landed him a job on the radio. A year later, he became a featured vocalist over station WTTM in New Jersey, singing and playing Country and Western music. He followed in the footsteps of other noted cowboy singers such as Gene Autry and joined "The National Barn Dance," radio show around 1946, broadcasting from Tulsa, Oklahoma and later, from Chicago. For the next four years, Rex was a headliner with the popular radio program and also branched off into recordings.

In 1949, Republic Studios gave Rex a chance to appear in motion pictures when he was offered the lead in *Arizona Cowboy*. As a new singing cowboy hero, he became an overnight sensation and was catapulted to fame. By 1951, he was among the top five Western stars in movies and remained so for four years. Having lost Gene Autry to Columbia Studios a few years earlier, Republic took no chances in having the same thing happen to their current No. 1 star, Roy Rogers, and studio heads decided it wise to develop a possible replacement. As a result, Rex Allen and another shining newcomer named Monte Hale were given the big build-up.

Riding a handsome chestnut pony called "Ko-Ko," Rex appeared in over thirty-five Western adventures for Republic. In most of them, he shared the spotlight with his sidekick, Slim Pickens, and earned a large following of admirers. His films were well above average in production value, while his excellent singing voice and likeable personality made him an ideal subject for the type of career he had chosen. Unfortunately, he arrived on the scene a bit too late in order to gain full advantage from movies. By 1954, the three studios that had been actively producing groups of horse-operas, namely, Republic, Universal and Columbia, all ceased to make any more B-Westerns in series. In spite of this, Rex had turned out a sufficient amount of films to allow him to be prominently identified with the Western genre.

Like many other film players, Rex directed his attention towards the new medium of television. Within a short time, he appeared as the star of a weekly TV series called "Frontier Doctor" which endured several successful seasons during the late 1950's. Following that, he undertook a number of personal appearance tours with rodeos, circuses and television guest shots. In addition, he became quite active with radio and recordings until he found a new career as a singing commentator for Walt Disney and other studios. During the New York World's Fair of 1965-66, Rex's pleasing voice could be heard in the fabulous General Electric and Sylvania displays and a few other attractions as well.

In private life, Rex is married to the former Bonnie Linder and is the proud father of two sons. When he is not busy with film features and TV, he maintains a beautiful ranch just outside Hollywood.

FILMS: *The Arizona Cowboy. Hills of Oklahoma. Redwood Forest Trail. Under Mexicali Stars. Trail of Robin Hood. Thunder in God's Country. Colorado Sundown. Border Saddlemates. The Rodeo King and the Senorita. Silver City Bonanza. South Pacific Trail. Phantom Stallion. Utah Wagon Trail. Old Oklahoma Plains. Iron Mountain Trail. Down Laredo Way. Old Overland Trail. Shadows of Tombstone. Red River Shore. For the Love of Mike. The Tomboy and the Champ.*

AUDIE MURPHY (1924-)

Audie Murphy's life story is one of a boy who rose from the depths of poverty to become his country's most decorated hero of World War II. He was born Audie Leon Murphy near Kingston, Texas on June 20, 1924, one of eleven children brought into the world by Emmett and

Josephine Kilian Murphy, poor sharecroppers on a cotton farm. In 1939, the despondent father left home and, two years later, Audie's mother died, thus leaving the children to support themselves. In an effort to stay together, the older members went to work and Audie took a job as a $14-a-week grocery clerk. By 1941, his big brother had decided to take a wife, followed shortly by the marriages of his two older sisters. As the younger children were then taken to a county orphanage, Audie enlisted in the U.S. Army in June, 1942, lying about his age and getting his sister Corinne to sign his enlistment papers. He received his training at Camp Wolters, Texas and Fort Meade, Maryland before shipping overseas with the 3rd Infantry Division in February, 1943.

After taking part in the campaigns in Sicily and Italy, Audie won himself a commission as a lieutenant and saw further action in France and Austria. Wounded four times, he was sent back home in June, 1945 and honorably discharged the following September as America's most decorated soldier of World War II. He had been awarded no less than fourteen principal decorations that included the Distinguished Service Cross, the Legion of Honor Medal, two Silver Stars, the Bronze Star, four Purple Hearts, a Good Conduct Medal, the Distinguished Unit Badge, Combat Infantryman's Badge, the Expert Infantryman's Badge and, last but not least, America's highest award, the Congressional Medal of Honor.

Audie had intended to enter West Point Academy but the sudden death of his sponsor, General Alex. Patch, shattered his dream. In 1948, he made his debut in motion pictures after an airline stewardess submitted his photograph to film producer William Cagney. His first movie was *Beyond Glory,* in which he appeared with Alan Ladd, followed by the leading role in *Bad Boy* in 1949. Placed under contract to Universal-International, Audie starred in a series of first-class Westerns and was selected as one of the "Stars of Tomorrow" in 1952. He quickly established himself as a box-office attraction through a number of pictures for Universal, United Artists, 20th Century Fox, Columbia and Allied Artists, emerging as a top-rate actor.

After being married to actress Wanda Hendrix for a year, Audie was divorced in 1950 and wed Pamela Archer, the former airline stewardess who had first sent his picture to Hollywood back in 1948. In recent years, they have separated after becoming the parents of two sons.

Meanwhile, the end of the B-Westerns became a reality in 1954 and only a few known cowboy stars were left to make horse-operas. Among those that continued to appear in a steady flow of Westerns, the most active were Audie Murphy and Randolph Scott. By 1962, Scott had retired, leaving Audie to singularly uphold the traditions of

273

the old sagebrush on the large theatre screens. Although TV had more or less taken over the horse-opera and introduced a whole new parade of cowboy stars, Audie remained extremely active in feature films and, by 1965, was the only recognizable Western hero left in the movies.

FILMS: *Beyond Glory. Bad Boy. Texas, Brooklyn and Heaven. The Kid From Texas. Kansas Raiders. Cimarron Kid. Sierra. Duel at Silver Creek. Red Badge of Courage. Gunsmoke. Column South. Destry. Tumbleweed. Joe Butterfly. Ride Clear of Diablo. To Hell and Back. Night Passage. The Quiet American. Ride a Crooked Trail. The Wild and the Innocent. The Unforgiven. Battle at Bloody Beach. Six Black Horses. Drums Across the River. Guns at Fort Petticoats. Cast a Long Shadow. Apache Rifles. Bullet For a Badman. The World in My Corner. Walk the Proud Land. No Name on the Bullet. Gun Runner. Hell Bent For Leather. Seven Ways From Sundown. Posse From Hell. Gunpoint. Trunk to Cairo.*

HARRY CAREY, Jr. (1921-)

With his father being one of the all-time greats among Western stars, it was only natural that Harry Carey, Jr. should pursue a career in motion pictures. He was born in Saugus, California on May 16, 1921, the son of actress Olive Golden and Harry Carey, both brilliant personalities of the screen, and attended the Black Fox Military Academy. His first job was to work as a page-boy for the National Broadcasting Company Studios in Hollywood and in New York, followed by a tour in summer stock with his father. Taking part in stage theatricals, he earned himself a chance at bigger and better parts until his career was temporarily interrupted in 1941 when he entered the U.S. Navy.

Discharged from the service in 1946, Harry returned to acting and made his debut on the screen in *Rolling Home* opposite Russ Hayden. At the time of his dad's death in 1947, he was regarded as a rising young newcomer to motion pictures with the road to stardom directly in his path. Having had his start as a film director with Harry Carey, Sr. back in the early 1920's, John Ford decided to make a super-Western in 1949 called *Three Godfathers*. His selection for the three leading roles involved John Wayne, Pedro Armendariz and Harry Carey, Jr. whom the famous director had taken under his wing as a protegee. The film was a big success and was dedicated to the memory of Harry's dad.

Under the guidance of Ford, Harry was featured in several fine productions, among them a series of top-notch action Westerns which permitted the young actor to show audiences what he could really do. When the director made his thrilling epics of the U.S. Cavalry, such as *She Wore a Yellow Ribbon* and *Rio Grande,* he gave Harry the opportunity to appear with stuntman Ben Johnson as a team of rough-riding troopers whose fancy horsemanship added a finishing touch to the action. Another excellent Ford picture that had Harry teamed with Johnson was *The Wagonmaster,* which ranks among the best outdoor adventures of the screen.

Besides making these films with John Ford, Harry did some other good features for various studios. Although he has never quite reached the status that his father had, he has proven himself quite capable as an actor. In recent years, his work has spread into television and fans have seen him active in many feature pictures. As for his private life. Harry was married to Marilyn Fix in 1944 and is the proud father of two children.

FILMS: *Rolling Home. Pursued. Red River. Three Godfathers. She Wore a Yellow Ribbon. Rio Grande. Moonrise. Copper Canyon. Silver Lode. The Wagonmaster. The Outcast. Beneath the Twelve Mile Reef. Warpath. San Antone. Island in the Sky. The Wild Blue Yonder. Gentlemen Prefer Blondes. Monkey Business. The Long Gray Line. From Hell to Texas. Escort West. Mister Roberts. House of Bamboo. The Raiders. Taggart. The Great Locomotive Chase. Cheyenne Autumn.*

BEN JOHNSON (1920-)

Ben Johnson is one movie cowboy who has never had to fake an action scene or employ the use of a double to perform his stunts in pictures. Having experienced more than his share of danger while he was a rodeo performer and stuntman, he was quite capable of handling his own rough-and-tumble sequences.

Ben was born in Pawhuska, Oklahoma on June 13, 1920 and was a student at Bartlesville High before taking a job as a cowpuncher. Entering the rodeo circuit as a contestant, he soon accumulated a batch of trophies and cash prizes for trick-riding, calf-roping, bulldogging and bronco-busting. He established a new world's record of 13 4/5 seconds in the calf-roping event and became one of America's foremost rodeo performers.

By 1940, Ben had landed in California where he was hired as a horse-wrangler by producer Howard Hughes during the filming of *The Outlaw.* An expert rider, he started out as a movie stuntman, specializing in taking hazardous falls from a galloping horse. In 1949, he was

1. *Ken Curtis*
2. *Ben Johnson*
3. *Dennis Moore*
4. *Harry Carey, Jr.*
5. *Wayne Morris*
6. *Jim Bannon*

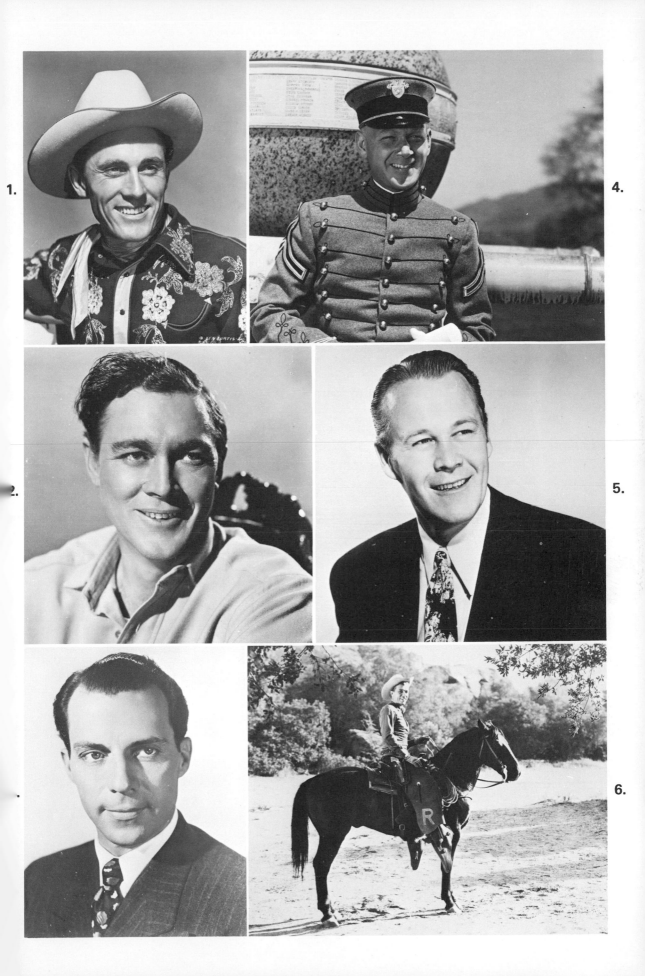

1.

2.

4.

5.

6.

finally given a chance to act when he was chosen for the male lead in *Mighty Joe Young* which brought him to the attention of director John Ford. Immediately recognizing Ben's amazing skill with horses, Ford gave him an important part as "Sergeant Tyree" opposite John Wayne in two successive features dealing with the frontier adventures of the U.S. Cavalry entitled *She Wore a Yellow Ribbon* and *Rio Grande*. In these large-scale Westerns, Ben revealed his excellent riding ability and special knack for cowboy roles. The result was the leading part in Ford's next epic of the West, *The Wagonmaster,* in which Ben appeared with film veteran Ward Bond.

Ben made a series of action features for R-K-O, Allied Artists, Columbia and Warners, each one loaded with thrills and excitement. In spite of his busy schedule in movies, he had not given up being a contestant in rodeos and in 1953, once again became the world's champion calf roper. He somehow managed to distribute his time in acting, stunt work and rodeos. Although he played a heavy, he gave two of his finest performances in *Shane* and *One Eyed Jacks* which added prestige to his growing popularity.

Married to Carol Jones since 1940, Ben supervises a profitable ranch in the San Fernando Valley when he is away from his regular duties, and has become a noted horse-breeder and trainer.

FILMS: *Mighty Joe Young. She Wore a Yellow Ribbon. Rio Grande. The Wagonmaster. Three Godfathers. Wild Stallion. Fort Defiance. War Party. Shane. The Tomboy and the Champ. One Eyed Jacks. Fort Bowie. Cheyenne Autumn. Major Dundee. Rebel in Town.*

JIM BANNON (1918?-)

James Bannon was born in Kansas City, Missouri around 1918 and attended the Rockhurst University where he was a star athlete in baseball and football. He eventually landed a job as a sportscast announcer in Kansas City and, after a year, graduated to the major networks in St. Louis. By 1938, he was in California working as a radio actor and sports announcer for NBC and CBS, while also appearing in bit parts in movies.

In 1940, Jim started out as a stuntman and character player in a wide variety of films and serials. When Columbia Studios decided to make a series of detective features based on a popular radio show called "I Love a Mystery," Jim was selected to take the leading roles. He met with only temporary success as the series lasted for a short time. His first encounter with Westerns came when his studio offered him a chance to

278

star in a few action features. Unfortunately, it was the cycle of the singing cowboys and Jim could barely keep up with the competiton. With his series completed at Columbia, he returned to radio and character parts.

By 1948, Republic Studios had abandoned their popular "Red Ryder" Western series after successively featuring no less than three capable performers in the role. Don Barry had been the first to portray the famous comic-strip character on the screen until "Wild Bill" Elliott had succeeded him during the early 1940's. When Elliott vacated the part to make his own features, Allan Lane had stepped in to fill the void. When Republic Studios ceased production on the series, Eagle-Lion Productions took over with an entirely new string of Westerns in 1949 giving the role of "Red Ryder" to Jim Bannon. These fast-action films finally gave Jim the chance to establish himself on the screen in the type of pictures he enjoyed and, during his association with the cowboy character, he made personal appearance tours throughout the country. His success as "Red Ryder" continued until 1951, after which he resumed his career as a stuntman and character player. For awhile, Jim was cast as a Western villain until 1954 when the B-grade horse operas became a thing of the past. Entering the field of television, he appeared in a soap-opera series called "Hawkins Falls" and has been active in radio and TV ever since. He was divorced from actress Bea Bernaderet.

FILMS: *I Love a Mystery. Soul of a Monster. The Missing Juror. Riders of the Deadline. The Devil's Mark. Sergeant Mike. The Gay Senorita. Jack Slade. Redheaded Cowboy. Ride Ryder Ride. The Cowboy and the Redhead. Roll Thunder Roll. The Cowboy and the Prizefighter. Dangers of the Canadian Mounted. The Fighting Redhead. The Great Missouri Raid.*

DENNIS MOORE (1914-1964)

Born Dennis Meadows at Fort Worth, Texas, in 1914, this familiar figure in Western films first worked as a commercial pilot and then became a physical education director before being bitten by the acting bug. He accepted the chance to appear on the stage with a Texas stock company around 1932. This eventually brought him to California. After a difficult period, he managed to land a few parts that drew him to the attention of a movie talent scout for Columbia Studios. Making his screen debut in 1936, he took the name of Dennis Moore and played in a string of straight dramatic roles which did little to enhance his career.

Around 1938, he went to Republic Pictures where he found work as a stuntman and bit-player in Westerns and serials. Two years later, he was being featured as an outlaw opposite stars like Roy Rogers, Gene Autry and Bob Livingston. He finally received his first leading role in a 1940 Western feature called *The Man From Tascosa,* a picture filmed in a new process that became known as Cinecolor. Having finally broken away from villainous parts, Moore became familiar to cowboy fans through dozens of sagebrush sagas for companies like Republic, Columbia and Monogram.

In 1943, he took over one of the leading roles in several films for the "Range Busters" series co-starring Ray Corrigan and Max Terhune and proved himself capable of playing heroes as well as badmen. Throughout the 1940's, he was engaged in many features and serials, his most noted being *The Purple Monster Strikes,* in which he co-starred with heroine Linda Stirling. With his athletic ability, he was a natural for two-fisted roles that called upon him to perform some dangerous stunts. Another part that boosted his popularity was when he took the lead in a chapter-play entitled *Perils of the Wilderness* for Columbia. He seemed particularly well-equipped to handle the rough-and-tumble action that serials demanded and it was in this type of film that he was at his best. Ironically, his best-remembered part came in 1956 when he starred in *Blazing the Overland Trail,* which was also the last serial ever produced. Following that, he reverted back to playing villains opposite Allan Lane, Gene Autry, Jimmy Wakely and Bill Elliott.

Unfortunately, Moore's career on the screen was spent playing minor secondary roles. Although he was not exactly good-looking for a Western hero, there were others who were not as handsome. He could act as well as his competitors, but somehow, lacked the special personality which appealed to movie fans.

After completing almost thirty years in motion pictures, Dennis passed away on March 1, 1964. His face had been well-known to thousands of people but his name was practically non-existing.

FILMS: *Down the Stretch. China Clipper. Here Comes Carter. Mutiny in the Big House. I'm From Missouri. Bachelor Mother. Arizona Territory. The Man From Tascosa. Wells Fargo Days. Springtime in Texas. The Man From Sonora. Blazing Bullets. The Purple Monster Strikes. Fort Defiance. Canyon Ambush. Perils of the Wilderness. The Old Frontier. Timber Trail. Brand of Fear. Saddle Outlaws. The Outlaw Brand. Blazing the Overland Trail.*

KEN CURTIS (1916-)

To TV audiences, Ken Curtis is more popularly known as "Festus," the ragged, cantankerous old side-winder of the "Gunsmoke" series. Having originally created the role for guest appearances, he became a regular performer on the long-running Western show which seems destined to go on forever.

Born Curtis Gates in Lamar, Colorado on July 12, 1916, he attended Colorado College, where he first became engrossed in writing music, a profession which later landed him a job on the staff of the National Broadcasting Company. A short while later, Tommy Dorsey hired him as the male vocalist with his band, which also led to a recording contract for RCA. Then came a job as a singer with the Shep Fields orchestra, doing radio and one-night stands throughout the country. It was during the early 1940's that Ken stepped in to fill a vacancy in the ranks of the popular cowboy singing group, "The Sons of the Pioneers." Featured exclusively in Republic's Roy Rogers Westerns, the troupe made some personal appearance tours, recordings and radio guest shots before Ken left to star in pictures on his own.

It was in 1945 that Columbia Studios decided to make a series of musical Westerns with Ken. Although the competition was keen due to an overdose of singing cowboy heroes, he managed to score well in some above-average films. By the late 1950's, he had strayed away more and more from his music until he found himself playing in only straight-dramatic supporting roles. Although most of these were in top ranking productions such as the classic Westerns put out by producer-director John Ford, Ken looked for greener pastures.

His chance came when he made a hit as "Festus" on the popular "Gunsmoke" television series. As the whiskered sidekick to Marshal Matt Dillon, he added just the right touch of comedy to the role and became a regular fixture on the show. In private life, Ken is married to the former Torrie Connelly and has two stepchildren. Besides his acting in television and movies, he still manages to find enough time to make an occasional recording, much to the surprise of his younger fans who have forgotten that he was once a favorite singing cowboy of not too long ago.

FILMS: *Apache Rose, Rhythm Roundup. Song of the Prairie. Singin' on the Trail. Cowboy Blues. That Texas Jamboree. Throw a Saddle on a Star. Lone Star Moonlight. Call of the Forest. My Dog Buddy. Rio Grande. The Searchers. Two Rode Together. How the West Was Won. The Horse Soldiers.*

281

WAYNE MORRIS (1914-1959)

Bertram DeWayne Morris was born in Los Angeles on February 17, 1914. He attended L.A. Junior College and made his first motion picture appearance in 1936, playing a small role in *China Clipper*. He was signed to a long-term contract with Warner Brothers Studios but did not reach stardom until after he had caused a minor sensation in the title role of *Kid Galahad*. Almost overnight, he zoomed to the top of the list of bright newcomers on the screen, emerging as one of Warners' favorite leading men. In the years that followed, he was given some of the choicest acting parts and scored with a number of hits, such as *Brother Rat, Badmen From Missouri* and *Valley of the Giants*.

In 1943, Wayne answered the call to arms when he entered the U.S. Navy and was commissioned a Lieutenant (Junior Grade) with the Naval Air Force. During the war, he saw action while serving aboard the aircraft carrier, *U.S.S. Bon Homme Richard,* becoming an air ace with fifty-seven combat missions to his credit. On his return to motion pictures, Wayne made his comeback by appearing in *Voice of the Turtle* in 1947. By then, he no longer had the zestful appeal to audiences he had possessed earlier and, after a few mediocre films, ended his association with Warner Brothers to star in a series of Westerns for Allied Artists. Being big and brawny, he proved himself easily capable of handling the tough assignments that cowboy roles required and went on to make a series of features for Monogram, Lippert, Columbia and then back to Allied Artists. In 1954, it was Wayne Morris who starred in the last of what was commonly called the "B" Westerns, entitled *Two Guns and a Badge*. By then only a handful of actors known basically as Western stars were left on the scene.

During the years that followed, Wayne played character parts until he finally went to England where he starred in some features released in 1955-1956. Returning to America, he continued to play supporting roles in better-than-average pictures until 1959, when he died of a heart attack on September 14, while visiting his wartime squadron leader aboard the *U.S.S. Bon Homme Richard*. Survived by his widow, Patricia, two daughters and a son from a previous marriage, he was buried at Forest Lawn Memorial Park in Glendale, California.

FILMS: *China Clipper. Submarine D1. Kid Galahad. Love, Honor and Behave. Men Are Such Fools. Gambling on the High Seas. The Kid From Kokomo. The Return of Dr. X. Brother Rat. Brother Rat and the Baby. Angel From Texas. Double Alibi. The Quarterback. I*

Wanted Wings. Badmen of Missouri. The Smiling Ghost. Three Sons O' Guns. Valley of the Giants. The Kid Comes Back. Ladies Must Love. Deep Valley. Voice of the Turtle. The Time of Your Life. The Younger Brothers. Johnny One Eye. Stage to Tucson. John Loves Mary. Sierra Passage. The Tougher They Come. Yellow Fin. The Big Gusher. The Bushwackers. Desert Pursuit. Arctic Flight. Port of Hell. Riding Shotgun. Lord of the Jungle. A Kiss in the Dark. The Desperado. Task Force. The Dynamiters. Plunder Road. Star of Texas. Crooked Sky. The Big Punch. Master Plan. The Green Buddha. Cross Channel. Fighting Lawman. Lonesome Trail. Fighting Plainsman. Texas Badman. The Marksman. Paths of Glory. Buffalo Gun. Two Guns and a Badge.

HONORABLE MENTION

Along with the impressive roster of noted personalities already mentioned in this book, let us not exclude an additional group of performers who at least deserve Honorable Mention in this catalogue of Western stars. Their contribution to the genre was equally important, although their careers were comparatively short in length.

DICK HATTON: Cowboy star and director of Westerns during the early 1920's, he was active in independent productions for Arrow and Rayart. His most notable films were *Riders Up, Whirlwind Ranger, Come on Cowboys, Rip Snorter* and *Roaring Bill Atwood.*

ROY HUGHES: Star of the silent picture era, he enjoyed his greatest period of activity between 1915 and 1925.

AL HOXIE: Full name, Alton Hoxie, brother of Jack Hoxie—although not as popular as his brother, Al made a series of features for Anchor Distribution Company in 1926-27, after completing a few years at Rayart. He starred in twenty-four Westerns before retiring in the 1930's.

MONTE BLUE: An important star during the 1920's, he took part in many Westerns until talking pictures forced him into character roles.

RICHARD ARLEN: One of Paramount's biggest names during the 1930's, he made a number of impressive Westerns besides starring in numerous other types of screen adventures. He is best remembered for his roles in *Wings* (1927) and *The Virginian* (1929).

GUY MADISON: Better-known as "Wild Bill Hickock" in the television series of that title, he was active in cowboy features during the 1950's and starred in the first Western filmed in 3-Dimension process, *The Charge at Feather River.*

MONROE SALISBURY: A silent film player, he was popular for his Indian roles.

CHARLES HUTCHISON: Star of silent serials, he entered pictures in 1914 and became one of the most popular action stars of that era. Noted for his daring stunts, he made a number of exciting films for Pathe and Vitagraph, many of which were Westerns. His best roles came in *Hurricane Hutch* and *Hidden Aces*.

REED HADLEY: An excellent narrator for films like *House on 92nd Street* and *Guadalcanal Diary,* he made a few good Western appearances, his best being in the 1939 serial, *Zorro's Fighting Legion.*

TEX FLETCHER: A singing cowboy on radio, he made only one picture of a tentative series which never reached completion.

GEORGE LEWIS: Mexican-born, he was a featured player since 1929 and made a number of features and serials at Republic, sometimes playing the lead but usually involved in secondary roles.

TEX HARDING: A tall, rangy cowboy, he played in a few Paramount Westerns then supported Charles Starrett at Columbia.

SAMMY BAUGH: An All-Star football great, he made a few appearances as a cowboy hero during the 1940's but lasted only a short time.

JOHN KIMBROUGH: Another famous gridiron star, he entered Westerns but lasted even a shorter period than Sammy Baugh.

EDDIE DEW: He appeared with Smiley Burnette in several Republic Westerns, but never quite made the grade to stardom during the early 1940's.

JOHN CARPENTER: He produced, directed and starred in his own horse-operas during the 1950's, but never reached any important status.

JAMES WARREN: A tall, curly-haired actor who played in several Westerns for R-K-O and Paramount, principally in Zane Grey stories.

BILL WILLIAMS: An athletic star who first reached fame as "Kit Carson" on television and made a number of good Western features.

JOHN KING: He made a string of horse-operas during the 1920's with his horse "Cactus," and a dog called "Kazan" (not to be confused with John "Dusty" King).

JACK BEUTEL: The actor who starred as "Billy the Kid" in the much-publicized feature *The Outlaw,* he made a few other films before vanishing from the screen.

JOHN CARROLL: A tall, dark actor known as a devil-take-care rogue in many features, he appeared in several good Western roles, among which the serial *Zorro Rides Again* (1937) stands out as the best.

JACK MOWER: A popular leading man of the silent picture era, he was particularly well-known for his adventurous roles in serials.

JACK PADGEON: Another popular cowboy star of the 1920's, he made a string of films for the independent producers but never achieved much stature as a star.

FRANKIE DARRO: An excellent, but under-rated juvenile star who appeared in a number of Westerns with Tom Tyler, Rex Bell and Wally Wales. More recently, he has been active on the "Red Skelton" TV show.

THE VILLAINS WE LOVED TO HATE

Without a doubt, the largest single category of actors on the screen was that of the Western villains. Due to their countless number, these familiar character players became well-known to movie audiences all over the world in a manner that defied listing. Although the cowboy heroes that are recorded within the pages of this book are numerous enough, the roster of Western Outlaws far outweighs them. Basically, the heroes could never have achieved their fame without "the bad guys" since they were judged by their ability to overcome the evil intent of the villains. The greater the evil, the better a hero seemed to be. Thus, it is only fitting that we should dedicate a chapter to those unsung players of Westerns—"The Villains We Loved to Hate."

Down through the years, dozens of film actors have started their careers by playing badmen in horse-operas. On the other hand, many more found that outlaw roles were a sign of fading popularity and ending careers. For the most part, the villains began in pictures by portraying unlikeable characters and went on to develop a real talent for this type of part until they were in demand. Almost unanimously, the choice for the best all-around movie villain of all time would be Noah Beery, Sr. An excellent actor, he stood head and shoulders above all others when it came to providing the screen with thoroughly despicable characters. His performances were spread throughout a variety of pictures ranging from costume dramas to comedies.

Next in line would be Fred Kohler, Sr., a big, burly roughneck who perfected the evil sneer until it became his trademark in pictures. As a villain·in Westerns, he was at his best. To the audience, there were times

1. *Fred Kohler, Sr.*
2. *Bud Osborne*
3. *Tom London*
4. *Noah Beery, Sr.*
5. *Walter Miller*
6. *George Chesebro with Tim McCoy*

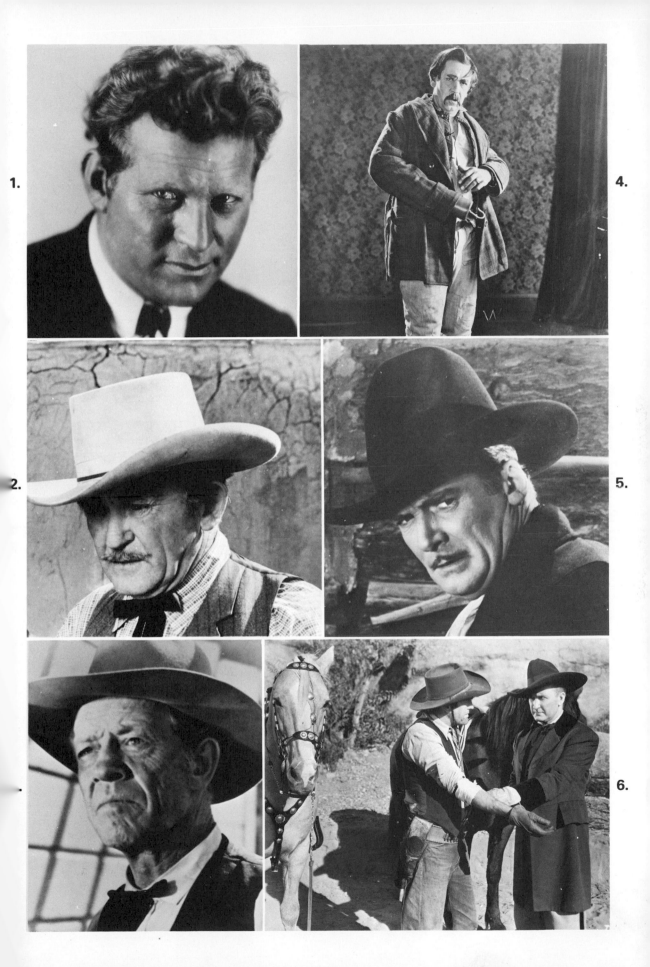

1.

2.

4.

5.

6.

when he seemed to be Satan himself. Following close behind Beery and Kohler, Walter Miller was one of the most convincing outlaws in Westerns. He was also capable of playing in a variety of pictures, but horse-operas were his specialty. Having outlived a period where he had been a popular serial hero, he went on to fame as a movie badman in dozens of films.

Oddly enough, the great majority of faces we saw as Western bandits appeared to be nameless to most of us. In spite of the fact that they were seen almost weekly in different pictures, the audience was content to let these consistent performers remain anonymous. Except for an excellent book entitled *The Bad Guys,* recently authored by William K. Everson, the cowboy villains have practically escaped notice. For the sake of casting a little more light on this category of players, let us concentrate on a list of the most prominent performers among them.

During the silent picture era, the first real identifiable villain of the movies was Tom Santschi, who performed opposite William Farnum in the first filmed version of *The Spoilers* (1914). Following close behind were Paul Panzer, Frank Farrington, Devore Palmer, Redfield Clarke, Eddie Hearn, Nipo Strongheart, Sam de Grasse, Jack Tomek, Pat Christman, Harry Spingler, M. Lee Glowner, Bill Gettinger, Fred Dana, Walter Spencer, Chief Standing Bear (who was probably the first Indian actor), Alfred Hollingsworth, James Mason, Frank Rice, C. E. Anderson, Frank Campeau and Otto Bibber.

As the movies entered the 1920's, actors were readily associated with certain types of roles. By then, the roster of villains had really grown to include such notable performers as J. P. McGowan (a former star who was also producing, writing, directing and acting in many Westerns), Francis MacDonald, John War Eagle, Frank Lackteen (the skull-faced badman best remembered as the treacherous "Hawk" in *Hawk of the Wilderness* (1927), Al Ferguson (the heavy in many "Tarzan" films), Russell F. Bradley, Bryant Washburn, Floyd Ames, Joe Ryan, Vester Pegg, Charles Walter Beyer, Wade Boteler, Robert Frazier, Robert McKim, Alan Bridge, Les Bates, Robert Chandler, James Bradbury, Jr., Edmund Breese, Joe Bennett, Tom Brooker, Fred Burns, Lynn Anderson, Jim Corey, George Chesebro, Lew Meehan, Walter Long, Tom Wilson, Chief Yowlachie and Iron Eyes Cody.

It was during the 1930's that the screen really introduced an array of Western Outlaws that defied comparison. Most of these became the old familiar standbys who had started back in the '20's and remained through the end of the '40's, but their greatest activity rested between 1930 and 1949. Among the better-known were Wheeler Oakman, Stanley Blystone, Ted Adams, Jack Rockwell, Harry Woods (a real master of villainy), Yakima Canutt (a former star and stuntman), Walter Miller (one of the best of the badmen), Cliff Lyons, Fred Grahame, Dale van Sickle, Bud Osborne and Tom Steele (all ace-stuntmen), Robert Kortman (probably the ugliest villain of them all), Earl Dwire, Glen Strange, Ethan Laidlow and John Merton (all first-class masters of deceit), Kenneth MacDonald, Leroy Mason, Roger Williams, Willard Robertson, John Miljan, Douglas Dumbrille, C. Henry Gordon, Tristram Coffin, Walt McGrail and Stanley Andrews (a group of smooth connivers who could really make things tough for any hero), Jack Kirk, Herb Holcombe, John "Blackie" Whiteford, Hooper Atchley, Steve Clark, Francis Ford, Tom Chatterton, Jack Ponder, Paul Hurst, Jack Wise, Harry McCabe, and Grant Withers (a former hero turned badman). Three of the most active badmen in Westerns throughout the 1930's were Charles King, Charles Middleton and Jack Ingram. The output of films this trio made could fill a book since they menaced almost every cowboy hero on the screen at that time. King was the better-known of the group and he played a convincing part in countless pictures. He was equally at home as an outlaw leader, or as a bandit henchman. Middleton was a sour-faced actor who is best remembered as "Ming the Merciless" in the popular Flash Gordon serials of the '30's. He was always crafty, evil, and could devise some wicked schemes just for the sake of villainy. Jack Ingram came upon the scene a bit later than the other two but he was capable of equally unlikeable characters.

Charles "Slim" Whittaker was another well-known heavy in Westerns. Big, beefy and mustached, he could always convince an audience that he was up to no good. Following in the same vein as Whittaker was Richard Alexander, a giant brute who was more than a match for the huskiest of heroes. Monte Montague, Jim Thorpe (the famous Indian athlete who took part in films as a warlike savage), Reed Howes, Forrest Taylor, Bud Geary, Ben Corbett, Bob Reeves, Ed Cassidy, Stanley Price, Harry Todd, Edwin Maxwell, Bob Terry, Harry Cording, Norman Willis, Harry Worth, Noble Johnson, Walter Woolf King, Carl "Cherokee" Matthews, Fred Kohler, Jr., Morris Ankrum, Art Mix, Ernie Adams, Kenne Duncan, Wally West, Ed Cobb, Charlie Stevens (reported to have been a direct descendant from the Apache war chief, Geronimo), Chief Big Tree, Karl Hackett, Richard Cramer, Lane Bradford, Dick Curtis, Anthony Warde, George Lewis, Joe Sawyer and Dennis Moore were all proficient in the field of Westerns.

By the time the 1940's rolled around, Roy Barcroft had established himself as the leading cowboy villain. Big and husky, he was a formidable foe for any hero and could be seen threatening the entire stable of stars at Republic Studios, not to mention a few at Columbia

1. *Dennis Moore with Bud Buster, Glenn Strange, Ted Adams and Gang*

2. *Bob Kortman*

3. *Earl Dwire*

4. *Al Ferguson*

5. *Charles Middleton (as "Ming the Merciless" in "Flash Gordon")*

6. *Wheeler Oakman*

1.

2.

4.

5.

6.

and Universal. Later, his crown passed on to another burly brute named Bob Wilke, a former lifeguard. Among the more recent performers were Jack Elam, tall, thin and treacherous; Barton McLane, cruel and sadistic; Jim Davis, Henry Brandon, Ray Teal, Myron Healy, Paul Fix, Cy Kendall, Jack O'Shea, Terry Frost, Denver Pyle, Claude Akins, Ted de Corsia, Forrest Tucker (better known for his TV role in "F Troop"), Leo Gordon, William Bishop, John Dehner, David Brian, Doug Fowley, Frank de Kova, Rudolfo Acosta, Lyle Bettger, Nestor Paiva, Neville Brand, Mike Muzurki, Lee van Cleef, Sheb Wooley, Emile Meyer, Michael Pate, Trevor Bardette, Robert Barrat, Roy Roberts, Lyle Talbot, Richard Jaeckel and Skip Homeier (two Western juvenile delinquents), Ian MacDonald, Jack Lambert, Dick Reeves, Harry Lauter, Red Morgan, Carleton Young, Leon Ames, Michael Ansara, Harry Shannon, I. Stanford Jolley, John Doucette, Marshall Reed and Doug Kennedy.

Last but not least, the Western villains included a group of fine actors who were known as first-rate performers in various types of films. Their versatility had either given them stardom or near-stardom because of unusual talents. The impressive list was headed by Brian Donlevy, Albert Dekker, Victor Jory, Charles Bickford, John Ireland, Lon Chaney, Jr., Ernest Borgnine, Lee Marvin, Richard Boone, Lee J. Cobb, Warner Oland (a veteran performer since silent days and better known as the screen's first "Charlie Chan"), Warren William (a smooth, polished actor who was also more familiar as the lead in "The Lone Wolf" detective series), Bruce Cabot (a former leading man best remembered as the hero who saved Fay Wray from the clutches of "King Kong"), Anthony Quinn (an Oscar-winning star who used to play bloodthirsty Indians), Steve McNally, Joseph Calleia, Edgar Buchanan, Lloyd Bridges, Steve Cochrane, J. Carrol Naish (an excellent character actor usually seen as an Italian or a Mexican), John Carradine (also known for his roles in horror pictures), Broderick Crawford (a big, husky brute who once took an Oscar as best actor of 1949), and Dan Duryea (a specialist at playing hateful characters).

These and several others were the bulk of players who comprised the category of Western villains. To the movie audience, it seemed bad enough that a hero should have to confront any one of them singly, but when an occasion came up for the star to remain victorious over three or four of them, the odds seemed insurmountable. The bad guys were all skilled at skulduggery. Some were openly defiant of all that was honest and proper, while others were sly, underhanded and shifty. The more hateful they seemed to be, the better they were at their performance. When cowboy stars like Tom Tyler, Bob Steele, Kermit Maynard, Bob

Livingston, Tom Keene and "Big Boy" Williams undertook to play villains, their reputations as heroes had been too firmly established for them to be thoroughly convincing. For one outstanding example, veteran star Buck Jones had taken the occasion of playing the heavy opposite Chester Morris in Republic's *Wagons Westward* (1940) and he caused his fans to literally swamp him with letters of protest that ended his taking any other similar roles. Even at that, he had merely taken the part of a crooked sheriff and, unlike most villains who were usually beaten at the end by the hero, had met his demise by tumbling off a cliff with his horse while a posse was in hot pursuit.

Randolph Scott was another fine actor who was too well-liked to be convincing as a badman. In *Western Union,* he was a member of a gang of rustlers. In *The Spoilers* (1942), he played the part of McNamara with skill but was equally as popular as co-star John Wayne. In *Ride the High Country,* he was a badman-turned-good opposite Joel McCrea's upstanding hero. In all of these, he was looked upon by the audience as a good guy who had merely stepped out of line.

As a group, the Western villains were all specialists in their field. Their reward was to be hated by the audience while they appeared on the screen and there was no doubt that they achieved their purpose. According to experts, an actor's work is judged on how convincing he can be in a part. Although the majority of Western villains never reached stardom, it can never be said that they were not convincing.

NOAH BEERY, Sr. (1884-1946)

If the movie industry ever decided to give out a special award to the best screen villain of all time, Noah Beery would undoubtedly be the recipient by unanimous choice. This famous actor portrayed so many despicable characters with equal skill that it is extremely difficult to pick out one particular role as his best. Among those that should certainly be considered would be in film masterpieces as *Beau Geste* (the silent 1926 version), *The Sea Wolf, The Mark of Zorro* (with Doug Fairbanks), *The Dove* and especially in the Zane Grey Westerns.

Noah was born in Smithville, Missouri on January 17, 1884 and started his theatrical career at the age of sixteen as a singer in vaudeville. He later appeared with the headline teams of Cohan and Harris, and Klaw and Erlanger, before beginning an association with H. B. Harris who helped him become a stage success. In 1918, Noah entered motion pictures, making his debut in *His Robe of Honor*. Shortly afterwards, he was hailed for his performance opposite Wallace Reid in *Believe Me*

Xantippe, which led to a series of pictures for companies like Paralta, Artcraft and Metro. By 1919, he had become part of the Lasky Film Corporation where he directed as well as acted in many silent features. Later, when the Lasky organization developed into Paramount Studios, Noah was among the company's most popular featured players.

Although versatile enough to act in any sort of part, Noah was a specialist in playing black-hearted villains and he seemed particularly capable in Western films. When Paramount started the first series of features based on the popular Zane Grey novels, he was constantly on hand to threaten hero Jack Holt by being the leader of the outlaws. Usually, his chief henchman was none other than that equally evil Fred Kohler, another fine example of movie villains. In spite of his menacing roles, Noah rose to full-fledged stardom and became known as the "villain's villain." Probably no other actor on the screen ever committed as many wrong-doings for the sake of playing the badman.

When talkies arrived, he hurdled the transition period without any difficulty for he possessed a deep resonant voice that suited him perfectly in movies. Among the many studios vying for his talents were First National, Warners, R-K-O, M-G-M, and, of course, Paramount. During the early 1930's, the latter company decided to revive the Zane Grey Westerns by making a new series of talking versions starring such stalwarts as Randolph Scott and Richard Dix. To add to this, R-K-O joined in with a few features that had Tom Keene and Buster Crabbe alternating as heroes. Meanwhile, Noah was welcomed back into the fold playing the same roles he had done in the silent series and continuing his foul deeds with even greater zest.

By the time 1940 rolled around, he was involved as the villain in a number of serials for Republic and Universal. He gradually relinquished his title of "King of the Movie Villains" to the smoother but less-appealing badmen the Second World War films brought on.

In 1945, Noah took an excursion to the Broadway stage to appear in a comedy hit called "Up in Central Park" which proved to be his last important work before he died in 1946. A soft-spoken gentleman off-screen, Noah was greatly admired by his co-workers as well as his fans. He was divorced from Margaret Lindsay and Mary Abbott. A son, Noah, Jr. and a brother, Wallace, were also well-known on the screen.

FILMS: *His Robe of Honor. White Man's Law. Believe Me Xantippe. Whispering Chorus. The Source. The Mormon Maid. Johnny Get Your Gun. Under the Top. The Squaw Man. The Coming of Amos. Red Lantern. Passion Song. Linda. Careers. Paradise. Crown of Lies. Padlocked. Beau Geste. The Sea Wolf. The Devil Horse. Four Feathers.*

The Godless Girl. Enchanted Hill. Wanderer of the Wasteland. In the Days of the Thundering Herd. North of '36. Heritage of the Desert. The Mark of Zorro. Father and Son. Love in the Desert. Sage Brusher. Go and Get It Dinty. Bob Hampton of Placer. Bits of Life. Penrod. The Dove. Quicksands. Ebb Tide. Wild Honey. I Am the Law. The Show of Shows. Noah's Ark. Crossroads of New York. Flesh and Blood. Good Men and True. Omar the Tentmaker. Isle of Lost Ships. Out of Singapore. The Spoilers. Man of the Forest. Riders of the Purple Sage. Heritage of the Desert. The Thundering Herd. To the Last Man. The Vanishing American. The Drifter. Wanderer of the Wasteland. Big Stampede. Sunset Pass. Pioneers of the West. Badman of Brimstone. Barbary Coast Gent. Zorro Rides Again. Riders of Death Valley. Sweet Adeline. The Tulsa Kid.

TOM LONDON (1882-1963)

A magazine article once reported that Tom London had appeared in more motion pictures than any other screen player living at that time. Whether the article was accurate or not, you may be certain that Tom was one of the most consistent performers in the years between 1917 and 1963. Having begun his acting career in the early silent picture days, he appeared in an endless list of features, first as a star and then as a character actor, until his face became as familiar to movie fans as those of the matinee idols. Probably not one cowboy star exists who was not ably supported by Tom in at least one feature.

He was born Leonard Clapham in Louisville, Kentucky, in 1882. As soon as he was old enough to hold down a job, he worked as a salesman in New York and Chicago and then introduced himself to the motion picture industry by laboring as a prop man for the old Selig Company of Chicago. When Col. William Selig became the first film producer to take advantage of the California sunshine by moving his company out west, young Leonard followed. It was there that he made his acting debut in one-reel pictures for Selig and for G. M. (Broncho Billy) Anderson, who had traced Selig's steps to the West Coast. In 1917, with the help of film star J. W. Kerrigan, who hailed from his home town, Leonard gained a chance to appear in featured roles for Universal Studios. Still using his real name, he became a star when he played leads in action features during the period between 1919 and 1923. The following year, he changed his name to Tom London and continued his career as a character actor portraying mostly villains or sheriffs. It was this alternating between roles that kept him active in films and, in 1928,

295

1. *Fred Kohler, Jr.*
2. *Jack Ingram and John Merton are caught red-handed by heroine in "The Mysterious Rider"*
3. *LeRoy Mason*
4. *Charles King listens attentively to Gladys George*
5. *Roy Barcroft*
6. *Harry Woods (at left in black hat) with Buck Jones*

1.

4.

5.

6.

he made his first talking pictures when Pathe Studios starred him in three of their earliest sound features. Although the arrival of the talkies caused a decline in film production, Tom kept busy by appearing in independent releases.

Because of his occasional roles as a good guy, Tom was never completely branded as a Western outlaw. Even though the majority of his screen assignments was portraying badmen, he managed to keep in the good graces of Western fans. During the rest of his career, he free-lanced by working at various studios and appearing in support of practically every cowboy star of the 1930's. At one time he seemed to be employed exclusively by Republic Pictures where Tom provided the opposition to such stalwart heroes as Gene Autry, Roy Rogers, Don Barry, Bill Elliott, Allan Lane and a host of others.

After what seemed to be an endless career, Tom London died on December 5, 1963. For the last ten years of his life, he had been playing more favorable characters in motion pictures and television.

FILMS: *The Lion Man. Nan of the North. Under Northern Lights. Forest Runners. When the Devil Laughed. Timber Wolf. Mystery Rider. Snowed in. Return of the Riddle Rider. Yellow Cameo. Bronc Stomper. Border Wildcat. King of Kings. Call of the Canyon. Top of the World. The Cowboy and the Lady. Arizona Terror. Untamed Justice. Harvest of Hate. Toll of the Desert. Firebrand Jordan. Woman Racket. River's End. The Secret Six. Hell Divers. The Men in Her Life. Without Honors. Spell of the Circus. Freaks. Dr. Jekyll and Mr. Hyde. Sunset Pass. One Year Later. Burn 'Em Up Barnes. Lawless '90's. Lure of the Wasteland. Arizona Bound. Westbound Stage. Pals of the Pecos. Down Texas Way. West of the Law. Red River Robin Hood. Courage of the North. Out California Way. High Noon. Saga of Hemp Brown.*

BUD OSBORNE (1888-1964)

It would take quite a few pages indeed just to list all the movies that Bud Osborne appeared in since he entered motion pictures. Having started when films were still in their infancy, Bud was one of those cowboy actors who enjoyed a few years as a star then gained even greater popularity as a western villain. Taking part in a countless number of features and serials until his face was as familiar to movie fans as some of the heroes, he played the bad guy opposite every major cowboy star in the business. He was born Miles Osborne in Knox County, Texas on July 20, 1888, and grew up on a ranch where he learned to ride horses at an early age. Working as a cowhand, he was employed by various

298

ranchers throughout Texas and the Oklahoma Territory until he became an assistant arena director for the famous Miller 101 Ranch at Fort Bliss, Texas. In 1912, he joined Buffalo Bill Cody's Wild West Show, touring with the organization throughout the U.S.A., Canada and Europe until his entrance in motion pictures in 1915. Beginning as a bit-player and stuntman, Bud graduated to leading roles the following year when he starred in Westerns for the Ince-Nestor Company. He took part in the first five-reel feature ever made and by 1918 had reached the peak of his career as a cowboy star. Four years later, he was portraying villains as well as heroes in a number of Westerns.

Among his outstanding accomplishments, Bud Osborne had a special talent for driving a stagecoach or a team of horses over unbroken ground at a breakneck speed. Movie directors were constantly calling for his services as a stunt driver and he became known as the best in that particular field. In addition to stunt work, Bud managed to add a touch of villainy to the dozens of pictures he participated in during the silent movie era. When talking pictures arrived, he found no difficulty in remaining constantly in demand and continued playing outlaws on an even greater scale. In many cases, Bud found himself working hand-in-hand with other noted Western villains such as Charles King, Harry Woods, Walter Miller or Roy Barcroft and it seemed a wonder that any single-handed hero could possibly overcome such menacing characters. By the time the 1950's rolled around, Bud had surpassed his fame as a badman and mended his ways by portraying more likeable roles such as sheriffs or stagecoach drivers. He died on February 2, 1964 after a long, active career. His endless screen credits are a monument to his memory.

FILMS: *The Moon Riders. The Prairie Mystery. Lariat Kid. White Eagle. Smiling Terror. Way of a Man. Fighting Ranger. Below the Border. Stormy Trails. Fighting With Buffalo Bill. Man From Wyoming. Hidden Loot. Huntin' Trouble. The Demon Rider. Stolen Ranch. Trail Rider. Double Dealing. Man in the Saddle. Dude Cowboy. Law Rustlers. The Sunset Trail. Rodeo Mixup. The Set Up. Saddle Cyclone. Rawhide. Rainbow Trail. No Man's Gold. Mystery Rider. Desperate Game. The Vanishing Rider. The Indians Are Coming. Saddle Aces. Sunset Pass. Border Justice. The Painted Stallion. Roll Along Cowboy. The Plainsman. The Vigilantes Are Coming. Flaming Bullets. Guns of the Law. The Cheyenne Kid. Border Feud. Return of the Lash. Lawless Town. Border Buckaroo. Boss of Rawhide. Return of the Rangers. Fighting Valley. Outlaw Roundup. Western Cyclone. Valley of Vengeance. Caravan Trail. Colorado Serenade. Black Hills. Son of Geronimo.*

WALTER MILLER (1892-1946?)

Not many actors have ever been capable of creating equal success on the screen in two different types of roles. Among the few who were able to do this was a man named Walter Miller. Throughout the 1920's he won the admiration of moviegoers by portraying clean-spirited, two-fisted heroes in a number of silent thrillers, particularly in Pathe serials. By the mid-1930's, he had outlasted his years as a "good guy" and was enjoying equal popularity from playing villains. In fact, some critics were of the opinion that Miller made an even better outlaw than he had a hero.

Walter Miller was born in Dayton, Ohio, on March 3, 1892, the son of Isabella Corwin and George E. Miller. Shortly after he was born, the family moved to Atlanta, Georgia, where Walter received his elementary education. Later, he attended the Manual Training High School in Brooklyn, New York and then took up acting by joining the Roe and Stanley Stock Company. During the years that followed he acquired a vast amount of experience in acting with the Hall Stock Company of Jersey City, the Lyceum Company of Troy and Brooklyn and performed in five different vaudeville acts throughout the East. As a juvenile lead, he majored in light comedies which eventually drew him to the attention of film director D. W. Griffith in 1912.

Hired by Griffith, Miller became a member of the original Biograph Film Company in New York, making his screen debut in *The Informer*. He developed into one of the silent screen's favorite leading men, starring in pictures for Reliance, Fox, Metro, Vitagraph and Universal. By 1919 his name had appeared alongside such superstars as Lillian Gish, Corinne Griffith and Nita Naldi.

The year 1925 brought the arrival of a new team on the screen, one that achieved greater popularity with each successive film. It all began when Pathe Studios matched a young heroine named Allene Ray with Walter Miller in a chapter-play called *Sunken Silver*. An instant hit, the team was quickly shoved into one serial after another until they had completed no less than ten. After Miss Ray retired, Miller continued making cliff-hangers for Pathe, Artclass and Mascot, starring in the first serial produced in both silent and sound versions, *King of the Kongo*.

With talking pictures firmly established by 1930, Miller found himself in greater demand as a character actor rather than a hero. He was able to make the transition almost unnoticed since his change from good guy to villain was so smoothly and gradually done. The 1930's saw him playing crooked politicians, corrupt detectives, gangsters and Western badman until he had earned himself a reputation as one of the screen's most admired heels. As usual, Westerns made up the largest portion of his success as they had done during the silent era. Miller was at home when he opposed such cowboy heroes as Buck Jones, Ken Maynard, Gene Autry and The Three Mesquiteers. In 1939, he was still involved with serials as he portrayed the heavy in Republic's *Dick Tracy's G-Men*.

Having completed a film career that lasted over thirty years, Walter Miller died during the mid-1940's. He had been married to dancer Eileen Schofield.

FILMS: *The Informer. Musketeers of Pig Alley. The Marble Heart. Woman in White. The Mothering Heart. A Mother's Ordeal. The Slacker. Miss Robinson Crusoe. Draft 258. A Girl at Bay. The Stealers. Sunken Silver. Play Ball. The Green Archer. The Unfair Sex. Snowed in. House Without a Key. Melting Millions. Hawk of the Hills. Man Without a Face. The Terrible People. The Black Book. The Fighting Marine. Police Reporter. King of the Kongo. Mysterious Airman. Rough Waters. Smoking Guns. Wild Horse Rodeo. Lawless Valley. Dick Tracey's G-Men.*

GEORGE CHESEBRO (1888- ?)

Few screen players have lasted as long as George Chesebro in motion pictures. He enjoyed many years as a leading man before becoming equally successful as a Western villain. To list his screen credits would fill an entire volume because he was in the select company of that distinctive minority that remained in constant demand.

George was born in Minneapolis, Minnesota on July 29, 1888 and endured only a few years of schooling before giving it all up to seek a career on the stage. In 1907, he joined a stock company of actors, working at various jobs and traveling all over the country until 1911, when he made a tour of the Orient. After two years, he returned to San Francisco where he completed eight more years of vaudeville, stock and repertoire before answering a call to enter motion pictures. Having made his first film back in 1915, he was given his chance at a real important role in Universal's *Money to Burn*.

George decided that movies were easier than the stage and accepted a few minor parts in some two-reelers for various companies. In 1917, he joined the Triangle Studios, starring in a group of fast-paced Westerns that brought him to the attention of film fans. A year later, he made a hit as Ruth Roland's leading man in a Pathe serial called *Hands Up,* which brought him closer to stardom. Unfortunately, World War I interrupted his career as he entered the U.S. Army and served with the American Expeditionary Forces in France. On his release from military service in 1920, George made a successful comeback in films by appearing opposite Juanita Hansen in another smashing serial entitled *The Lost City* for Warners.

During the early 1920's, George found himself well established among the leading players in Western features and serials. He made a number of pictures for Universal, Pathe, F. B. O., Paramount and several independents. Just before the arrival of talkies, the avalanche of new cowboy stars caused him to lose ground at the box-office until he finally decided to change to character roles. Luckily, he had already made an impression as an outstanding movie badman when sound took over the film industry in 1928 and he found his career continuing without too much difficulty. From that time on, George made it his specialty to play heavies and he did it so well that his services were always in demand. During the 1930's and '40's, he menaced every popular cowboy star on the screen from Ken Maynard and Bob Steele to Gene Autry and Tex Ritter. Being at home on horseback, he was equally convincing as the chief villain or as the leading henchman who did the dirty work. It became a fact that no Western star after 1928 was able to continue his adventures on the screen without at least once being challenged by the foul plans of George Chesebro.

When the B-class Westerns vanished after 1954, George seemed to disappear with them. In the productions of today, the lack of good cowboy villains makes his absence even more noticeable for he was able to add a special something which few newcomers can do. His presence is sadly missed as many of us remember him as a grand performer.

FILMS: *Money to Burn. Blind Circumstances. Unconquered Bandit. Hands Up. The Lost City. Diamond Queen. The Hope Diamond Mystery. Danger Ahead. The Return of Jimmy Valentine. Caryl of the Mounted. Speed Reporter. Block Signal. Roamin' Wild. Trail Dust. Tumblin' Tumbleweeds. The Old Corral. Toll of the Desert. Fighting Champ. White Eagle. Gorilla Ship. Lucky Larrigan. Tex Takes a Holiday. County Fair. Confidential. Mark of the Spur. Gallant Defender. Lawless Valley. Caravan Trail. Arizona Ranger. The Man From Guntown. Arizona Cowboy.*

FRED KOHLER, SR. (1888-1938))

Down through the years, the movies have introduced dozens of extremely talented actors who could portray villains to such a fine degree of excellence that audiences developed a particular fondness for them. The more he was scorned, the better a performer seemed to be for it meant that he had done his job well. Only a few of these villains shared the affection of an understanding audience. In the field of Westerns, the list of villains was endless. Critics and experts seemed unanimous in their choice of Noah Beery, Sr. as the Best-All-Around Bad Man, but in the category of horse-operas, Fred Kohler, Sr. gave Beery his stiffest competition. A born scene-stealer, this big, burly brute developed an evil sneer that became his trademark on the screen while his wicked deeds made him the personification of black-hearted villainy.

Fred was born in Kansas City, Missouri on April 20, 1888 and ran away from home at the age of fourteen to seek a fortune on the stage. After two years of meager existence in vaudeville, he had all but decided to return home when he met an actor named William Carleton, who helped him become a member of a traveling troupe of performers. For the next four years, Fred took part in various stage theatricals until he had a chance to make his debut in silent films in 1916. Working for the Selig Studio, he played a small role in his first picture, *Code of Honor*.

By 1920, Fred was a featured actor under contract to Paramount and was considered one of the high-ranking character players on the screen. Within a short time he had established the reputation for villainy which earned him a fortune and made him one of Hollywood's most sought-after players. When Paramount made the first series of Westerns based on the popular Zane Grey novels, Fred was constantly seen as the chief badman and his performances were enough to make any lesser hero than Jack Holt cringe in his boots. When director John Ford made the memorable classic *The Iron Horse* in 1924, he had leading man George O'Brien contending with Fred's evil opposition in what became one of the best Westerns ever made. As a result of all this, Fred Kohler rose to full-fledged stardom in a long series of films for Paramount, Fox, Universal and First National.

A highly versatile actor, Fred sometimes directed his pictures and he often took excursions into a variety of roles. For the most part, producers were too impressed with his ability to portray villains and he was destined to make his mark as a notorious badman. When talkies arrived, Fred proved to be an even better performer since his gruff voice made him a valuable asset. When Paramount decided to film remakes of the old Zane Grey Westerns in sound during the early 1930's, he was often seen in the same parts he had made popular earlier, recreating his original roles. Some of these pictures even called on him to play the chief henchman to Noah Beery and, when these two masters of villainy got together, the odds against any hero were practically insurmountable.

In 1938, Fred Kohler's brilliant career came to an end when he died at the age of fifty. His last films had been made for R-K-O, Universal, Republic and United Artists and for more than twenty years, he had chalked up an impressive list of features and serials that made him one of filmdom's most familiar figures. Off the screen, he was noted as a kind, soft-spoken gentleman, happily married and the devoted father of a son, Fred, Jr., who also became well-known as a movie villain.

FILMS: *Code of Honor. The Tiger's Trail. Old Ironsides. The Way of All Flesh. The Thundering Herd. Wild Horse Mesa. City Gone Wild. Shootin' Irons. Three Bad Men. The Leatherneck. The Iron Horse. The Quitter. Underworld. The Case of Lena Smith. Broadway Babies. The Dummy. River of Romance. Hell's Heroes. Roadhouse Nights. Stairs of Sand. Thunderbolt. Under a Texas Moon. Wanderer of the Wasteland. Dragnet. Winds of Chance. Forbidden Valley. The Country Beyond. Crashing Timbers. The Rough Riders. Honor of the Range. Open Range. The Showdown. The Fourth Horseman. The Deluge. Carnival Boat. The Painted Desert. Call of the Savage. Desert Gold. Blood Ship. The Buccaneer. Barbary Coast. Trail's End. The Frisco Kid. Fighting Caravans. Men of Action. The Pecos Kid. Hard Rock Harrigan. Heritage of the Desert. The Lawless Valley. The Plainsman. The Vigilantes Are Coming.*

ALPHABETICAL INDEX OF WESTERN STARS